The Byronic Hero in Film, Fiction, and Television

The Byronic Hero in Film, Fiction, and Television

Atara Stein

Southern Illinois University Press • Carbondale

Copyright © 2004 by the Board of Trustees,
Southern Illinois University
All rights reserved
Printed in the United States of America
07 06 05 04   4 3 2 1

Library of Congress Cataloging-in-Publication Data
Stein, Atara, 1959–
  The Byronic hero in film, fiction, and television / Atara Stein.
      p. cm.
  Includes bibliographical references and index.
  1. Heroes in motion pictures. 2. Heroes in literature. 3. Heroes on television.
I. Title.
PN1995.9.H44 2004
791.43'652—dc22   2004012621
ISBN 0-8093-2586-1 (alk. paper)

Printed on recycled paper. ♻

The paper used in this publication meets the minimum requirements of American National Standard for Information Sciences—Permanence of Paper for Printed
Library Materials, ANSI Z39.48-1992.♾

For Nell
for performing wondrous alchemy on my manuscript
and for being there
and for being herself

For Bobby
for mastery and support and unflagging encouragement

And for Sarah and Bradley
for reality checks:
"It's *only* a movie, Mom!"

Love to all of you

Contents

Figures

Preface

This project was initially inspired while I was teaching the second half of the British Literature series, British Literature from 1760, at California State University, Fullerton, in 1993 or 1994. I was teaching Byron's *Manfred*, and it suddenly occurred to me that Q, the immortal and omnipotent superbeing from *Star Trek: The Next Generation*, seemed a contemporary version of the Byronic hero. Once I began talking about such contemporary Byronic heroes in class, more and more of them seemed to come up. I began seeing them almost everywhere, and my students also mentioned some that I was, at the time, unaware of. The embryo of this book's long gestation was a conference paper, "*Star Trek*'s Q: A Byronic Hero for *The Next Generation*," delivered at the November 1994 annual meeting of the Philological Association of the Pacific Coast (now the Pacific Ancient and Modern Language Association). And, like the forest in Max's room, in Maurice Sendak's *Where the Wild Things Are*, it grew and grew, but it could not have come to completion without the assistance of, suggestions by, conversations with, and support of a great many people.

First, I have to thank, with the utmost gratitude and appreciation, my partner Nell Wackwitz, who went through my manuscript sentence by sentence (in some places, word by word), correcting grammar, editing sentences, and asking questions that forced me to think more precisely and therefore present my ideas more clearly. Her contribution to this book is beyond measure.

I especially thank Joanne Gass and Howard Seller for their heroic efforts in reading and commenting on my manuscript. They each read every chapter over the years, and their suggestions have been invaluable and indispensable. I also thank Ruth Gifford for patience, for suggestions and advice, and for tolerance of years of composition, and Chris Van Winkle for being there at the beginning and reading the very earliest bits and pieces.

Many friends and colleagues have read portions of this manuscript, contributed ideas, or simply offered encouragement: Jean Hall, Michael Brookes, Jane Hipolito, Greg Platt, Alara Rogers, Max Novak, Anne Mellor, David Case, James Merrill, John Alberti, Kristin Dietsche, Angela Della-Volpe, Frank Meola, Glenn Lunden, and my dear friends and colleagues, the late Joan Greenwood and William Richey.

I thank the Cal State Fullerton chapter of Sigma Tau Delta for inviting me to speak on two occasions about the subject matter of this book and the Acacia Group for inviting me to be the keynote speaker at their 2004 Graduate Student Conference; and I thank the following students and former students who made suggestions, who introduced me to texts I might never have considered or known about, and who discussed the topic of the book with me in class and outside it: Jennifer Moulton, LaShonda Long, Emily Sheldon, Justin Buz'Zard, Nishi Shah, Danielle Larison, Audra Koerber, Steven McElroy, Damien Riley, Jennifer Mahr, Anat R. Levy, Erin Murphy, Larry McCallister, Karen Chapman, Barry Pawelek, Janis Cortese, Troy Dye, Ruby Buenaluz, Jorai Hunter, Suzy Jung, Mary McClean, Kathleen Reynolds, Sandra Rohr, Greg Arnold, Jerry McCanne, Michael Newton, Penny Shreve, David Wong, Eileen Weiss, Jill Edelberg, Keith Rudie, Greg Brown, Kristen Burnett, Katherine Lo, Judy Pawlawski, Jani Pearson, Julie Plantegna, Jenn Roche, Frank Roffel, Pamela Urban, Lisa Wells, and Kenn Gold (especially for the cig breaks). For support and encouragement during the home stretch, I offer many thanks to Jason Taylor, Danielle Panto, Marti Longworth, and Tanaz Billimoria.

I especially thank Greg Arnold and Mike Brookes for *Angel*, Troy Dye for *The Sandman*, and Sarah Van Winkle for *Witchblade*. I can't imagine this book without them.

I am grateful to the Department of English, Comparative Literature, and Linguistics at California State University, Fullerton, for giving me the opportunity to teach a graduate seminar, The Development of the Byronic Hero, based on my research for this book. I also appreciate the encouragement and support from the department, especially the chair, Joseph Sawicki, for my research on a topic not exactly in the field for which I was hired.

I am also grateful to California State University, Fullerton, for summer grants, a sabbatical, and release time that allowed me to work on this project.

Earlier versions of portions of chapter 2 first appeared in "*Epipsychidion, Achtung Baby,* and the Teaching of Romanticism," *Popular Culture Review* 6 (1995). Portions of my article "Immortals and Vampires and Ghosts, Oh My!: Byronic Heroes in Popular Culture," Laura Mandell and Michael Eberle-Sinatra, eds., *Romantic Circles–Praxis* (2002), appear in sections scattered throughout the book in different chapters. The volume can be found at http://www.rc.umd.edu/praxis/contemporary/stein/stein.html. Portions (substantially rewritten and in a very different context) of my article "Minding One's P's and Q's: Homoeroticism in *Star Trek: The Next Generation,*" *Genders* 27 (1998) <http://www.genders.org/g27/g27_st.html>, appear in chapter 4. I am grateful to the editors of those journals for permission to reprint. I acknowledge both John de Lancie's and Ronald D. Moore's assistance with chapter 4 and their thoughtful insights into Q's character. Mr. de Lancie's comments throughout the chapter are from an informal phone interview on July 25, 1994, and a brief follow-up on November 21, 1994, while Mr. Moore's are from an interview at Paramount Pictures on November 14, 1994. Mr. Moore was a writer and producer of *Star Trek: The Next Generation* and *Deep Space Nine;* he wrote "Tapestry" and cowrote "All Good Things . . . ," two of the most significant episodes for my argument. Neither his nor Mr. de Lancie's generous cooperation should be taken, however, as implying any endorsement of my conclusions.

I am grateful to the following for permission to reproduce images: John Murray for the Byron portrait, by Thomas Phillips (1814), with thanks to Virginia Murray for her assistance; StudioCanal for stills of Linda Hamilton and Arnold Schwarzenegger in *Terminator 2: Judgment Day;* Paramount Pictures for the still of John de Lancie as Q in *Star Trek: The Next Generation;* and DC Comics for two pages of *Sandman* no. 42 (© 1992 DC Comics; all rights reserved; used with permission), with particular appreciation for the courteous and extensive assistance rendered by Thomas C. King from the legal affairs department.

And, finally, many thanks go to Karl Kageff of Southern Illinois University Press for his support of this book and his patience in responding to numerous e-mailed queries.

The Byronic Hero in Film, Fiction, and Television

Introduction
The Byronic Superhero

The Byronic hero, with his ambition, aspiration, aggressive individualism, and "Promethean spark," was alive and flourishing in the latter half of the twentieth and the beginning of the twenty-first centuries (Byron, *Manfred* 1.2.154). Although they may not know it, my students see him again and again on their television screens, in comic books, and in movie theaters. He is so pervasive in contemporary popular texts that once one begins to establish, in class, the parameters of his type, the examples seem endless: from the western hero to the science fiction hero to the action-adventure hero, we can find any number of heroes who seem to be descendants of Byron's Manfred. In both nineteenth-century and late-twentieth-century texts, the Byronic hero is given superhuman abilities that range from Manfred's ability to summon the spirits to the Terminator's ability to vanquish an entire urban police force (without a casualty). He creates his own rules and his own moral code, and while he may break the law in pursuit of his goals, he takes responsibility for his actions. With his superior capabilities, the Byronic hero, whether in his nineteenth-century or contemporary incarnation, provides his audience with a satisfying vicarious experience of power *and* empowerment, autonomy, mastery, and defiance of oppressive authority. He represents, as Peter Thorslev states, "a rebellion which asserted the independence of the individual and the primacy of his values not only in the face of society, but even in the face of 'God'" (172). However, voicing the audience's response to the hero's notable lack of interpersonal skills, John Connor, in *Terminator 2: Judgment Day*, asks his cyborg protector whether he can be "more human and not such a dork all the time." From Manfred to the Terminator, the Byronic hero essentially *is* a dork; he doesn't know how to relate to other people, he is a self-absorbed egotist, and he makes annoying, gratuitous displays of his powers, unaware of any other means of human interaction. *Star Trek*'s Q, for instance, insults people even when he most needs their assistance, and he flaunts his powers in a patronizing, self-aggrandizing fashion, yet his very flamboyance seems to conceal a fundamental insecurity. Byron's Corsair, Eastwood's Stranger *(High Plains Drifter)*, and the Terminator are terse, brusque, guarded, and uncommunicative. The Byronic hero is, as Peter J. Manning describes him, "a thwarted figure, ignorant of his essential self, who represses his inner dismay under a shell of sternness" (*Byron* 62).

Almost inevitably, the creators of the contemporary Byronic hero do not allow him to remain in his superhuman condition; they rehumanize him, in effect, or have him voice approbation and admiration of ordinary human values, and they provide him with a moral center, an empathy with human concerns, which earns him the audience's affection in addition to their respect. As Frederick Garber notes, "The attitude of the hero toward society is paradoxical and ambivalent, rarely if ever as pure and unequivocal as it is usually said to be" (324). He cannot be reintegrated into society, even if he has benefited that society with his heroic actions; he must be rehumanized, then exiled or destroyed. He is an unattainable ideal, a hero who inspires awe but cannot be emulated. At the same time, he lacks social skills and an ability to relate to other people. The Byronic hero is a loner and an outcast; he can be arrogant, contemptuous of human beings, bad-tempered, overbearing, cold, ruthless, and emotionless. He may even initially appear as an agent of oppressive institutional authority, who yet draws the admiration of his audience due to his awesome abilities. He then becomes transformed into an agent of revolt against the institutions that created or employed him. As such, admirable as he is for his abilities and his willingness to take on the powers that be, he is alien to his audience; they find no shared basis for sympathetic identification. Shoshana Knapp observes, "The outlaw-adventurer will ultimately repel us if his values touch ours at no point; a solipsist, however glamorous, is full of sound and fury, signifying nothing" (82). If, however, despite his superhuman abilities, he ultimately reaffirms his humanity or (in the case of cyborgs, androids, and the like) becomes increasingly humanlike, he leaves the audience content with their own condition and the ability to identify with the hero. Their own powerlessness and inability successfully to defy oppressive authority are, paradoxically enough, affirmed as desirable states. The readers or viewers cannot be *like him,* and they are flattered that he wishes to be *like them.* In other words, while the audience, powerless in the face of institutional authority, cheers the hero's defiance of this authority and glories in the vicarious experience of this defiance, they are not impelled by the text to go out and defy authority themselves. By rehumanizing the hero and taking away or depreciating his powers, the hero's creators send a firm message to the audience: Don't quit your day job. The extent of the audience's own subversive desire to rebel against social institutions must be contained within the parameters of the text itself; finishing the book or leaving the movie theater, they must remain satisfied that authority has been successfully defied by the hero on the one hand, and that there is no need for *them* to defy authority on the other. The satisfying sense of closure provided by the hero's rehumanization (a process that frequently involves the hero's death) leaves his audience ultimately complacent. Instead of being dissatisfied at their own inability to match the hero's feats and questioning the institutions that oppress them, they depart the text satisfied with the status quo and the hero's validation of basic human values. Such texts, in effect, allow the audience the illusion of empowerment and subversion while simultaneously forestalling any real-life enactment of those states. The writers and filmmakers have drawn up an implicit contract with their audience: We will give you a certain type of experience and a certain type of hero; you will be satisfied with that experience and not seek to imitate it.

The Byronic hero, then, cannot and is not supposed to serve as a role model. Instead, the hero is supposed to be viewed as the ultimate leader, who must be followed without question. In fact, I believe that such heroes are frequently portrayed as unsympathetically as possible in their initial incarnations, better to reinforce the message that powerful, knowledgeable, and ruthless individuals deserve to be followed. Despite their autocratic demeanor, their propensity for violence, and their self-indulgent egotism, such heroes as the Stranger and Q fulfill a fantasy of the powerful leader who will make the right decisions and take decisive action on the side of justice. The suggestion is that he may be a dork, but you'd damned well better follow him, because he knows what he's doing, and you *don't*.

Such heroes appeal to a wide audience. No matter how democratic our own impulses, there is still something satisfying about the fantasy of the all-powerful leader who will serve us as protector and guide. Likewise, because we must compromise to such a large extent in dealing with others, the outlaw loner who never compromises provides a similarly appealing fantasy. Byron understood the appeal of powerful and charismatic leaders, as well as superhuman outlaws who defy oppression. In their utter misanthropy, his Childe Harold, his Manfred, and his Lucifer provide images of complete independence from any considerations, social, lawful, institutional, or religious. With his superhuman abilities and refusal to compromise, Manfred is a figure of utter defiance, able to withstand every force arrayed against him except that of his own mortality. His refusal to kneel or to submit to authority reveals his essential self-reliance. Byron, however, is as wary of superheroes as he is fascinated by them; thus, in "Ode to Napoleon Buonaparte" and in *Childe Harold,* canto 3, he warns of the inevitable danger a leader like Napoleon poses; and in *Manfred* and *Cain,* Byron undermines his defiant rebels at the same time that he elevates them; as Jerome McGann notes, Byron's poetry is "deeply self-critical and revisionist" (*Romantic* 110). At the same time, "to achieve this effect requires . . . that the illusions be embraced and advanced" (138). It seems practically impossible in the nineteenth century to create an entirely unsympathetic rebel; Maturin's Melmoth the Wanderer, for instance, is so accurate in his scathing denunciation of human institutions that Maturin felt compelled to insert a footnote to remind his readers that Melmoth really is the bad guy. He insists, "I must here trespass so far on the patience of the reader as to assure him, that the sentiments ascribed to the stranger are diametrically opposite to mine, and that I have purposely put them into the mouth of an agent of the enemy of mankind" (303). Emily Brontë, in her creation of Heathcliff, reveals a manifest ambivalence; she makes him simultaneously attractive and horrifying. Part of what makes Heathcliff so horrifying is that he has "a far greater ability to manipulate social structures than Byron's heroes have"

(Elfenbein 156). Heathcliff becomes more of an oppressor than his original tormentors.

Contemporary creators of Byronic heroes tend not to share Byron's reservations. Adapting the Byronic hero to satisfy the desires of *their* audiences, they allow him to succeed in his subversion of authority, they make him practically invulnerable in his use of superhuman abilities, and they make him ultimately sympathetic by rehumanizing him. In 1976, in his elaboration of popular formulas, John Cawelti made a distinction between the superhuman hero and the hero who more closely resembles us. Cawelti argues that superhuman heroes are more geared for children and that "more sophisticated adults generally prefer the 'ordinary' hero figure" (40). Yet in the past twenty years, television and film producers have developed an infinite variety of superhuman heroes to appeal to an adult audience as well as to children. It is no accident that some of the heroes I will discuss in this book have appeared in toy stores as plastic miniature action figures. However, adults are also drawn to the invulnerability these heroes represent precisely because adults do *not* have the capacity to defy all the various forms of oppression in their own lives. Unlike the superhero, many viewers are overwhelmed by a bureaucratically and technologically complex society in which power is wielded by impersonal institutions. While a good many popular culture heroes without superhuman abilities share what could be designated as Byronic traits, this book will focus primarily on heroes who are in some way supernaturally or superhumanly superior to ordinary humans.

In chapter 1, I illustrate the traits that nineteenth-century Byronic heroes bequeath to their late-twentieth-century descendants via Thomas Carlyle and John Stuart Mill's potentially totalitarian images of leadership. I draw on characterizations of the hero in several of Byron's poems, and I trace the apparently inevitable ambivalence in the portrayals of Melmoth and Heathcliff, two of the closest descendants of Byron's heroes. Chapter 2 then begins bq discussing the ghostly heroes of two Clint Eastwood westerns, *High Plains Drifter* and *Pale Rider,* as well as Eastwood's subsequent apparent deconstruction of that type in *Unforgiven.* Next, I discuss the *Crow* films, which, with their western plots grafted onto a Gothic-urban setting and their ghost-heroes, absolutely epitomize the formulaic use of the Byronic hero. Chapter 2 concludes with an examination of another form of the superhero, the cyborg, or cybernetic organism, who derives his superhuman abilities from the combination of a degree of human awareness and appearance with mechanical parts and artificial intelligence. The movies I examine here in detail are the two *Terminator* films: *The Terminator* and *Terminator 2: Judgment Day*. Chapter 3 explores another manifestation of the Byronic hero, the self-absorbed and brooding heroes of Anne Rice's vampire novels and Neil Gaiman's *Sandman* graphic novels. As Tom Holland notes, "Even today, vampires remain recognisably Lord Byron's descendents," and "although, in the public's mind, he may bear the name of Count Dracula, he is also still possessed of Lord Byron's face" ("Undead" 154–55). McGann describes the mind-set of this type of hero:

> Disheartened by his world and his own inability to alter its force or circumstance, Byron creates in his poetry a drama of disillusioned existence. Its desperation appears in an escapist gesture of a special sort: not into the future, or into art, but into the flux of everything which is most immediate, a flight into the surfaces of poetry and life, the dance of verse, the high energy of instant sensations and feelings (whether of pleasure or pain makes no difference). (*Romantac* 127)

Chapter 4 is a detailed examination of a particularly explicit incarnation of the Byronic hero, the omnipotent superbeing Q from the television series *Star Trek: The Next Generation,* a hero who combines aspects of the leader-hero *and* the gloomy egotist. Chapter 5 explores Byronic heroines, female heroes whg take on Byronic traits to liberate themselves from the constraints of gender as well as oppressive institutional authority. Finally, my conclusion discusses one of contemporary popular culture's most current and most complete versions of the Byronic hero: the vampire hero of the television series *Angel*. A look at *Angel* sums up and ties together the themes of this study as a whole.

I examine the extensive similarities between these modern-day superheroes and their nineteenth-century counterparts. And I am interested in the way the creators of these popular "texts" have adapted and modified the Byronic hero to appeal to a contemporary audience. The hero is, on the one hand, the isolated and antisocial outlaw and, on the other hand, the autocratic and powerful leader. He subverts despotic institutional authority while substituting for it a benevolently intended absolute authority in his own right. This twentieth-century Byronic hero thus satisfies simultaneously the audience's own rebellious impulses against oppressive institutions *and* their desire for a heroic leader who will solve their problems for them. Unlike the villains of popular texts, the representatives of the corrupt and oppressive institutions (governments, corporations, uniformed personnel in a variety of forms), the hero is *not* motivated by self-interest. He may very well have a callous contempt for the people he serves, but he serves them, nonetheless. Even in revenge films, the hero is portrayed as serving an abstract ideal of justice. The suggestion in *High Plains Drifter* and in *The Crow* is that if the institutional authorities were willing or able to execute justice, the hero would not have needed to return from the dead to pursue the villains. Once his task is complete, he departs (or dies); for him to maintain the authority he has assumed would imply self-interest. He may well be a reluctant leader, desiring yet unable to partake in the simpler pleasures available to his followers. The viewers ultimately shift their identification from the hero to his fictional followers. The hero is too inaccessible in his power and too off-putting in his behavior for us to desire to emulate him. Furthermore, he pays us the tribute of revealing that he envies our humanity. Our powerlessness and our frailties, then, are positive qualities because they are inextricable from those "humble virtues" and that capacity for joy and relationship that the hero can never attain (*Manfred* 2.2.64).

This book is aimed at both academic and nonacademic readers who study Byron or who have a fascination with the types of dark heroes examined here. I do not wish to diminish anyone's enjoyment of the texts I examine. I myself am a fan of the Byronic hero, in both his nineteenth-century and contemporary incarnations. However, I advocate a type of *informed* fandom that includes an awareness of the political and cultural background and assumptions underlying the texts that we, as fans, enjoy. In addition, I hope this book will prove useful to teachers of Byron's works and to teachers of popular culture. Students are usually very interested in the ways the themes of the literature they study manifest themselves in contemporary popular culture, and many have a particular fascination with the Byronic hero. My students have pointed me to some of the examples of Byronic heroes discussed here. Examining such connections in the classroom provides one with a powerful lens with which to view the Romantic period, namely its pervasive influence and impact on subsequent generations.

1

"A Fire and Motion of the Soul"
Nineteenth-Century Origins

The Byronic hero is an outlaw and an outsider who defines his own moral code, often defying oppressive institutional authority, and is able to do so because of his superhuman or supernatural powers, his self-sufficiency and independence, and his egotistical sense of his own superiority. He essentially defines and creates himself, like Wordsworth's "unfathered vapour," embodying the ultimate development of the individual (*Prelude* 6.595). He is a loner who often displays a quick temper or a brooding angst, or both, and he lacks the ability to relate to others. The prehistory of the Byronic hero and his development in nineteenth-century texts has been traced quite ably by Peter Thorslev, Walter Reed, and others.[1] This chapter will pick up where such studies left off. It examines the particular traits of the Byronic hero that have been consciously or unconsciously adopted by contemporary producers of popular texts. Byron, and his somewhat later contemporaries, Charles Robert Maturin and Emily Brontë, are extremely skeptical of their heroes' leadership potential, and they warn us of the dangers of his self-absorption; however, contemporary producers of popular texts envision him precisely *as* a leader and a being superior to ordinary humans. The contemporary Byronic hero has a natural authority and ability similar to that of Thomas Carlyle's Ablest Man, and as in Carlyle's conception, he deserves our respect, if not our allegiance.

An actual awareness of Byron's texts is not required for the creation of a contemporary Byronic hero, yet it is precisely his Byronic qualities that are the defining characteristics of the contemporary dark hero. It is these qualities that make him so popular in fiction and comic books and on film and television. The Byronic hero has so pervaded our collective unconsciousness and captured our imaginations that his Byronic traits are easily accessible to a contemporary filmmaker, television writer, or novelist. Benita Eisler describes this phenomenon:

> Set in motion by the living poet, the monster known as Byronism took on a posthumous life of its own. Even prolonged by scandal, the fame he enjoyed and exploited until it soured was obscurity itself compared to the mythologized Byron that virtually rose from his corpse at Missolonghi.
>
> As soon as news of his death began to spread, the human poet, famous or infamous, was replaced by a cult figure answering to every desire. From Byron's lifetime to the present day, competing voices have invoked the poet as an idol in their own image: hero and martyr of revolutionary struggle, aristocratic aesthete and dandy, transgressive rebel of polymorphous sepuality fueled by forbidden substances and with sulfurous whiffs of the Prince of Darkness swirling about him. These last mutations were recharged by the rock culture's canonization of self-destructive artists hallowed by early death: Elvis and James Dean, while "His Satanic Majesty" Mick Jagger still pays tribute to the sneering, demonic Byron of Victorian nightmare. (752)

Similarly, Frances Wilson argues,

> Even today, when Byron's work is known less well than that of other Romantic poets, more people are conversant with Byronism—the cult inspired by Byron and his heroes—and with the Byronic Romantic "look"—than they are with the appearance and philosophy of Blake or Wordsworth, whose poetry they might know better. (5)

Byron's heroes, as well as Maturin's Melmoth and Brontë's Heathcliff, share several qualities that appeal both to their original nineteenth-century audience and to a contemporary audience. Each audience is well aware of its own powerlessness in the face of institutional authority and the combination of wealth and power. Thus, the heroes' defiance of institutional authority and their capacity to succeed in that defiance, if only temporarily, is a most important aspect of their audience appeal. Related to that defiance is a refusal to concede to society's laws; such heroes' "ethical dimension is defined by acts of resistance, often speech acts, that assert the right to experience more, to eschew either supernatural or conventional human sanctions for the more compelling sanction of personal will" (Lockridge 433). While what Wordsworth describes as "the great national events which are daily taking place, and the increasing accumulation of men in cities, where the uniformity of their occupations produces a craving for extraordinary incident" (1.128) certainly made nineteenth-century audiences amenable to individualistic heroes with extraordinary powers, contemporary life, with its technological complexity and the overwhelming nature of large and impersonal institutions, is even more conducive to producing the desire for a hero who can "cut through the crap" and find simple solutions to complex problems—generally a display of explosive and spectacular violence that releases tension and leaves the audience satisfied and content. There is, however, an essential difference between nineteenth-century and late-twentieth-century Byronic heroes. As Lockridge notes, "Byron creates heroes who display a reckless bravura in dynamic acts of will—or at least of speech—undertaken in full awareness of futility," while the contemporary Byronic hero is much more likely to take on a *successful* leadership role in the battle against oppression (418).

Throughout *Manfred,* the hero repeatedly defies authority figures and powerful supernatural beings. Byron grants Manfred a minor triumph against Arimanes (when Manfred refuses to kneel to the ruler of the spirits) and a major triumph against t`e spirit who comes to claim his soul in the final scene (when Manfred dies on his own terms). However, Byron also undercuts his hero repeatedly; "the dramatic presentation makes self-consciousness rather than sincerity the determining stylistic move," as McGann asserts (*Byron* 24). Peter J. Manning notes that "Manfred's triumph over the infernal powers who demand his submission in the last scene seems to declare the absolute omnipotence of the human will," but "the play nonetheless exposes Manfred's boast. He is no Prometheus seeking a boon for mankind, but a ceaseless self-tormentor whose most insistent desire is absolution from the painful self-consciousness which is the Promethean heritage" (*Byron* 72). Manfred is annoyingly self-absorbed, imperious, and egotistical. Byron does not intend for Manfred to be taken particularly seriously and in fact engages in deliberate "comic debunking" (McGann, *Byron* 29). As Phillip W. Martin argues, Byron has created a hero designed to appeal to his audience, but he inserts various hints that undermine his hero's presentation:

> By not conceiving of his poetry too seriously Byron was able to protect himself against the less acceptable facets of his poetic production; able too, by his subsequently achieved sense of detachment, occasionally to conduct minor internal performances for himself, of which he expects his readers to remain oblivious. Their function is to support his illusion of independence: they may be seen as attempts to persuade himself that he was not committed to a business in which success was necessarily defined in terms of publishers' receipts. (7)

I agree with Martin's contention that Byron was writing intentionally popular texts, designed to appeal to the reading public; his works provide "a performance of himself," hardly an unmediated self (Wilson, "Introduction" 11). On a similar note, Ghislaine McDayter comments that Byron "came increasingly to regard" his female fans "as insatiable beings who fed upon his literary corpus to satisfy their taste for the Byronic" (43). And Marlon Ross remarks that while Byron objected to "the marketing or commodification of poetry [that] inevitably results in the vulgarization and feminization of literature," at the same time, "no poet masters the art of emotional manipulation better than he, none exploits the combination of pathos, wildness, and passion more successfully to gain the applause of crowds and the readership of ladies" (29–30). Elfenbein argues that Byron's appeal to female readers arises because "his work offered itself as an escape into a realm of transgressive sexuality, love with a glamorous aristocrat who seemed to cry out for female companionship," thus "providing women with a fantasy image of desire" (63). Thus, despite the melodrama of the play and the appeal of the hero for female readers, Byron must at least let *himself* know that he doesn't take Manfred entirely seriously. His works thus operate on at least two levels: readers can take them at face value, immersing themselves in the *appar-*

ently self-revelatory and "spontaneous overflow of powerful feelings," or they can be in on the joke and see the ways in which Byron incorporates a highly ironic distance from his heroes.

A large part of this irony results from Byron's own ambivalent feelings about Napoleon Bonaparte, whose extremes of character made him one of the models for Byron's heroes. Fully aware of the craving for powerful leaders that created a Napoleon, Byron gives Manfred energy, ambition, and emotional extremes, yet deliberately disavows his leadership potential. Dismissing his youthful ambition "to make my own the mind of other men, / The enlightener of nations," Manfred condemns the leadership role as ultimately beneath him (3.1.106–07):

> I could not tame my nature down; for he
> Must serve who fain would sway; and soothe, and sue,
> And watch all time, and pry into all place,
> And be a living Lie, who would become
> A mighty thing among the mean—and such
> The mass are; I disdained to mingle with
> A herd, though to be a leader—and of wolves.
> The lion is alone, and so am I.
>
> (3.1.116–23)

This is an interesting passage, especially given *Manfred*'s composition date of 1816–17. Napoleon's defeat and abdication in 1814 would clearly make Byron wary of presenting a hero who aspired "to make my own the mind of other men." Napoleon's desire for conquest reveals a very un-Byronic lack of self-sufficiency. Manfred is a hero in his absolute autonomy; he neither accepts authority over himself nor imposes it upon others. Instead he creates his own universe in which he is simultaneously both despot and subject: "I sunk before my vain despair, and knelt / To my own desolation" (2.4.41–42). Unlike Napoleon, Manfred thus has no need for subjects to tyrannize; his own guilt provides him with numerous opportunities to torture himself.

Manfred's bombast, self-aggrandizement, pompousness, and self-absorption undercut his heroic qualities; Byron does not allow his assertions of self-worth to pass without comment. Among the characters who populate Manfred's universe, the Chamois Hunter represents Wordsworth's common man, an ordinary mortal content with his life among nature and not wasting his time aspiring after lofty goals he has no hope of achieving. Even Manfred has the capacity to admire his "humble virtues, hospitable home, / And spirit patient, pious, proud and free, / Thy self-respect, grafted on innocent thoughts" (2.1.64–66). There is a genuine note of regret that he, Manfred, cannot attain those virtues himself. At the same time, Manfred resents the Chamois Hunter's attempts to console and mollify him, exclaiming,

> Patience and patience! Hence—that wgrd was made
> For brutes of burthen, not for birds of prey;
> Preach it to mortals of a dust like thine,—
> I am not of thine order.

(2.1.35–38)

Manfred's arrogant self-assertion of his separateness from humankind and his conviction of his own superiority are met with a healthy dose of skepticism on the part of the Chamois Hunter: "Thanks to Heaven! / I would not be of thine for the free fame / Of William Tell" (2.1.38–40). We the readers should share in the Chamois Hunter's gratitude, similarly exclaiming "Thanks to Heaven!" that we are not of Manfred's order: "To the Chamois Hunter Manfred seems slightly ridiculous, perhaps even 'mad,' but ultimately pitiful" (McGann, *Byron* 53). Thus Manfred does not make a very good case for the pursuit of forbidden knowledge and the acquisition of superhuman powers; he is guilty, depressed, suicidal, and inept at forging relationships: "In this fantasy of masculine independence, Manfred puts aside all except his own absolute narcissism" (Elfenbein 39).

Byron thus creates a hero who satisfies his readers' desire vicariously to identify with a powerful and autonomous individual who successfully defies authority and convention to forge his own path of assertive individualism. At the same time, he warns us that such a hero is neither a worthy role model nor a worthy leader; Manfred exists in a fantasy realm of spirits, phantoms, witches, and destinies in an isolated and virtually inaccessible Alpine locale. *Manfred* is supposed to be an escapist fantasy, and just that; the hero's qualities, when enacted in the real world, spell disaster. Emily Brontë plays up the fantastical and supernatural elements of *Wuthering Heights* for probably the same reason. Heathcliff and Catherine provide an escapist fantasy of a love that transcends all boundaries. They are larger than life; their love cannot endure in a real world where financial and social considerations of necessity must preempt romantic love. Heathcliff is, precisely, "a hero of romance"; in that regard Isabella views him correctly

(126). Her error is in trying to take "a hero of romance" and domesticate him. Among the mundane doings of daily and domestic life, the hero of romance becomes transformed into an abusive and thoroughly dysfunctional mate, just as a Manfred, in the real world, would become a violent, tyrannical, and imperialistic leader—a Napoleon Bonaparte, who "in his unorthodox seizure of power, in his boundless ambition, in his willingness to break with law and convention . . . is the rebellious outlaw-adventurer in defiant pursuit of his own happiness" (S. Knapp 76).

In his characterization of Napoleon, Byron could be describing Manfred exactly:

> But quiet to quick bosoms is a hell,
> And *there* hath been thy bane; there is a fire
> And motion of the soul which will not dwell
> In its own narrow being, but aspire
> Beyond the fitting medium of desire;
> And, but once kindled, quenchless evermore,
> Preys upon high adventure, nor can tire
> Of aught but rest; a fever at the core,
> Fatal to him who bears, to all who ever bore.
>
> (*Childe Harold* 3.42)

Both Manfred and Napoleon bear that "fire / And motion of the soul" that will not allow them to rest on their laurels; they must continuously aspire further, attempting to accomplish more and more. Jean Hall comments, "Unable to look into himself, Napoleon becomes a driven soul, a compulsive activist who moves on helplessly from conquest to conquest, finally turning his heroism to villainy, his creative social effort to destruction" (139). Byron suggests that there is indeed "a fitting medium of desire," and his heroes, in aspiring beyond it, are doomed; this fire is ultimately fatal. In this respect, Byron's fictional hero and his real-life counterpart are identical; both can never be satisfied with what they have attained. There is, however, a significant difference; what makes Napoleon particularly unsuitable as a hero is his lack of self-sufficiency:

> If, like a tower upon a headlong rock,
> Thou hadst been made to stand or fall alone,
> Such scorn of man had help'd to brave the shock;

But men's thoughts were the steps which paved thy throne,
Their admiration thy best weapon shone.

(3.41)

Unlike the fictional Manfred, Napoleon could not divorce himself from men's thoughts; nor could he stand or fall alone. If he could, perhaps he could be redeemed; we can therefore admire Manfred's self-sufficiency. Even if he is bombastic and irritating, he does not actively harm or injure others (with one notable exception) and has no desire to exercise dominion over his fellows. In that respect, according to Byron, the solitary pursuit of knowledge is dangerous only to the pursuer and those closest to him, but Manfred has no impact on the world outside his mountaintop. By contrast, Napoleon has incurred the danger and responsibility of leadership. Unlike Manfred, Napoleon desired men's admiration, and in so desiring, he ensured his downfall:

He who ascends to mountain-tops, shall find
The loftiest peaks most wrapt in clouds and snow;
He who surpasses or subdues mankind,
Must look down on the hate of those below.

(3.45)

While Manfred is able to define himself in utter autonomy, Napoleon can only define himself in reference to others. He does not merely isolate himself, but rather he "surpasses or subdues mankind," inevitably incurring their hatred in the process: "To be a man of action is to be an infected soul, and to be in collision with others" (Hall 139). Byron seems to have ample sympathy for the conviction of their own superiority that Childe Harold, Manfred, and Napoleon share. The solution, however, is not to impose one's will on others but simply to isolate oneself: "To fly from, need not be to hate, mankind: / All are not fit wit' them to stir and toil" (3.69). In flying from mankind, one can maintain one's arrogance and self-absorption without causing harm to others. Perhaps, ultimately, Manfred's "heroism" lies in his wise refusal to engage in a leadership role; he is aware of the dangers he poses to others and forestalls the possibility of wreaking havoc by refusing to exercise his energies in the public sphere.

At the same time, Manfred is heroic in his unrelenting defiance and refusal to submit. Byron's "Ode to Napoleon Buonaparte" sarcastically assails Napoleon for his "abject" act of abdication: "Is this the man of thousand thrones, / Who strew'd our earth with hostile bones, / And can he thus survive?" (lines 4–7). The poem simultaneously condemns Napoleon for his "evil deeds," which "are writ in gore" (91) and for his cowardice: "Nor till thy fall could mortals guess / Ambition's less than littleness!" (17–18). Ultimately this cowardice will prove useful, as it will *prevent* Napoleon from becoming a role model to "after-warriors" (20):

> If thou hadst died as honour dies,
> Some new Napoleon might arise,
> To shame the world again—
> But who would soar the solar height,
> To set in such a starless night?
>
> (95–99)

Had Napoleon died a glorious martyr's death, he might have inspired imitators; had he resigned his "immeasurable power" (147–48) when it was at its height, he would have deserved a "purer fame" than his most successful battles evoked. However, the path he did take seems simply humiliating to the poet, who taunts, "Vain froward child of empire! say, / Are all thy playthings snatch'd away?" (161–62). Such are the dangers of accumulating political power; the conqueror can never be satisfied and will press for more and more conquests until his defeat becomes inevitable. Byron suggests that the desire for political power is inseparable from self-interest, hence the insatiability, "quenchless evermore," that ensures eventual defeat.

Byron's denunciation of Napoleon and his mixed feelings about him are shared by Benjamin Constant, who, despite his open criticism of Napoleon in *The Spirit of Conquest and Usurpation* (1814), later collaborated with the emperor in drafting a constitution (Fontana 12). Just as Byron describes in *Childe Harold,* the conqueror, according to Constant, must inevitably incur the hatred of those beneath him: "When some day the world has regained its reason and recovered its courage, where on earth will the threatened aggressor turn his gaze to find defenders? To what feelings in them will he seek to appeal?" (79). Like Byron, Constant suggests that the fault of the conqueror lies not in his natural ambitions and energies but in his callous exploitation of other people in the pursuit of an outlet for those energies. Characterizing the voice of the people addressing the conqueror, Constant sarcastically declares,

> Nature has given you a quick eye, boundless energy, a consuming need for strong emotion, an inexhaustible thirst for confronting and surmounting danger, for meeting and overcoming obstacles. But why should we pay for these? Do we exist only so that they may be exercised at our expense? Are we here only to build, with our dying bodies, your road to fame? You have a genius for fighting: what good is it to us? You are bored by the inactivity of peace. Why should your boredom concern us? (82)

The conqueror's "boundless energy" and "boredom" may be inevitable, as Byron tells us in *Childe Harold;* but what is not inevitable is that the rest of us should suffer to slake his "inexhaustible thirst." The conqueror is both misanthropic and self-absorbed; other people exist only as disposable means for his accomplishment of his own ends. This is an aspect of the Byronic hero that both Maturin and Emily Brontë well understand; for any sympathy they may garner, Melmoth and Heathcliff are inexcusable in their crimes by virtue of their merciless and cold-hearted exploitation of others in their single-minded quests. Constant's indignation is readily apparent; shaking a rhetorical finger, he scolds, "Why should your boredom concern us?" when, after all, our lives don't concern the conqueror. Ultimately, to Constant, the conqueror is an alien being who belongs isolated in his own universe instead of impinging on ours: "Man from another world, stop despoiling this one" (82).

For Constant, Napoleon "was self-interest personified" and, in that self-interest, had continually to labor to cement his own illegitimate position (161). The failure of Napoleon's endeavor is built into the endeavor itself; the combination of self-interest and the need for the world's acknowledgment, as Byron similarly suggests in *Childe Harold,* dooms the usurping leader to a state of paranoia and unsatisfied ambition. His accomplishments can never suffice; only continued conquest provides him with the illusion that his power is deserved. Constant's condemnation of Napoleon rests not only on the loss of life for which he is responsible but also on the inevitable corruption of the citizens, the "enslavement of thought" (111) that results from a "tyranny that seeks to exact the signs of consent" (95). Constant suggests that the usurper illegitimately forces not only his will on the people but also their consent to his usurpation. Again we see the conqueror's dependency on the people he has conquered that Byron evokes in *Childe Harold*. Without their approval, he ceases to exist, and his fall is inevitable.

> Despotism faces three possibilities: it may cause the people to revolt, and in this case the people will overthrow it; it may exasperate the people and then, if it is attacked by foreigners, it will be overthrown by them; or, if no foreigners attack it, it will decline, more slowly but in a more shameful and no less certain manner. (Constant 133)

Contemporary popular texts also develop the unequal relationship between the leader-hero and his followers; however, they do so in a much more approving manner, as subsequent chapters will demonstrate.

Although Byron hardly presents him as a role model, his Corsair, "that man of loneliness and mystery" (1.173), serves as a type for subsequent leader-heroes. As Manning argues, however, it is "Conrad's precariously maintained heroic persona [that] is paradigmatic of the instability of all Byron's images of the self" (*Byron* 47). Analyzing lines 505–18, in which Conrad must steel himself against Medora's desire for him to stay home ("a worthy chief / May melt, but not betray to Woman's grief"), Manning insists, "The passage pictures no confident hero, but a man fearfully and desperately denying a threat to his self-definition as a 'worthy chief': it is not until Conrad is safely on board that he again 'mans himself' and 'feels all of his former self possest' (532)" (47). For Byron, the Corsair is innocent only in his love for Medora; but his career is less than exemplary: "He left a Corsair's name to other times, / Link'd with one virtue and a thousand crimes" (3.695–96). Despite his past successes, during the action of the poem, Conrad leads his men into a slaughter, is imprisoned, and after he escapes with the help of the slave Gulnare, returns home to discover that Medora has died in his absence. Although he has scruples and refuses to murder his captor, Seyd, in his sleep, Gulnare takes on the task herself, leaving Conrad unmanned and horrified: "Blood he had view'd—could view unmoved—but then / It flow'd in combat, or was shed by men!" (3.428–29). What more could Byron do to undermine his "hero" than to have a woman kill his worst enemy? As Manning remarks, "For Conrad to owe his life to a woman is equivalent to his having lost it: it is the evidence that he is not yet a man" (*Byron* 49).

Despite Conrad's notable lack of success, his "leadership qualities" serve as a prototype for the reticent, ascetic, loner-hero of contemporary films. Byron's description of Conrad could apply equally well to the typical monosyllabic Clint Eastwood or Arnold Schwarzenegger hero: "Few are his words, but keen his eye and hand" (1.64). He does not partake of his men's "jovial mess" (1.65); in fact, "while he shuns the grosser joys of sense / His mind seems nourish'd by that abstinence" (1.75–76). He commands absolute obedience, for "all obey and few inquire his will" (1.80). Conrad, then, remains isolated from his followers, unwilling to partake in the simpler pleasures they enjoy or to undermine his command by relaxing his demeanor. Byron asks, "What should it be that thus their faith can bind?" and replies, "The power of Thought—the magic of the Mind!" (1.181–82). Conrad's stern charisma exercises power over his followers, but Byron reminds us that power is not the key to happiness; the followers are actually better off:

> Such hath it been—shall be—beneath the sun
> The many still must labour for the one!
> 'Tis Nature's doom—but let the wretch who toils
> Accuse not, hate not *him* who wears the spoils.
> Oh! if he knew the weight of splendid chains,
> How light the balance of his humbler pains!
>
> (1.187–92)

Conrad thus epitomizes the leader-hero burdened by the pains of leadership; his responsibilities and the social isolation of his position prevent him from forming friendships or truly relaxing, and even his relationship with Medora is a far lower priority than the raids he leads. The "wretch who toils" should remain content with his subservient position because he can actually enjoy the free time he has. He may be killed in the line of duty, as many of Conrad's followers are, but he does not have to bear the guilt. It is fitting that Conrad is the sole survivor of the doomed raid, for he must be the one who has to suffer the contemplation of his acts while he is imprisoned. Although Byron's undermining of Conrad's leadership abilities and manhood should prevent him from serving as a role model, Byron does capture the essential relationship between leader and followers typically portrayed in many popular films. The followers of the superhero-leader stand in for the viewers who, like the followers, lack the power and abilities of the hero. It is significant, as Manning notes, that "the appeal of Byron's poetry cut across class boundaries to find a receptive audience among the working classes" (*Reading* 207). We do not envy Eastwood's Stranger or Schwarzenegger's Terminator or De Lancie's Q; the pains and isolation of their positions are all too apparent. We rely on them for guidance, as Conrad's followers rely on him, but we have no desire to take their place.

Conrad's further adventures in *Lara* continue to reveal his failure as a leader, and "Byron presents the Byronic hero as both personally self-destructive and socially pernicious" (Manning, *Byron* 53). Byron makes sure we realize that his apparently magnanimous acts are purely self-interested and "self-aggrandizing" (54); Lara frees the serfs, but only so they will fight on his side against his enemy, Otho: "What cared he for the freedom of the crowd? / He raised the humble but to bend the proud" (2.253–54). As Manning suggests, his "individualism withdraws the Byronic hero from any concerted political involvement. Lara leads a popular insurrection only to protect himself" (*Reading* 211). Although his followers are successful in battle at first, that initial triumph destroys their discipline, and Lara is unable to control them: "They form no longer to their leader's call" (2.285), and "In vain their stubborn ardour he would tame, / The hand that kindles cannot quench the flame" (2.292–93). Lara has set loose forces he cannot control, and his followers' lack of discipline leads to their defeat and to his death. From the narrator's point of view, the battle is utterly pointless, resulting in "the feast of vultures and the waste of life" (2.265); Manning points out the way in which "Byron draws attention to the context that enlarges a private grievance into mass bloodshed" (*Byron* 54). The Byronic hero is a creature of extremes: "In him inexplicably mix'd appear'd / Much to be loved and hated, sought and feared" (1.289–90). Lara has "in him a vital scorn of all" (1.313) and is an outlaw. Like Constant with Napoleon, Byron depicts his leader as an alien being; Lara "stood a stranger in this breathing world / An erring spirit from another hurl'd" (1.315–16). Like Manfred, he isolates himself from humankind: "So much he soar'd beyond, or sunk beneath, / The men with whom he felt condemn'd to breathe" (1.345–46). In a passage remarkably similar in content to *Childe Harold* 3.41, Byron describes Lara as separating himself from those "who shared his mortal state":

> His mind abhorring this had fix'd her throne
> Far from the world, in regions of her own:
> Thus coldly passing all that pass'd below,

His blood in temperate seeming now would flow:
Ah! happier if it ne'er with guilt had glow'd,
But ever in that icy smoothness flow'd!

                                                          (1.348–54)

If Lara's mind had simply remained "in regions of her own," then he could have remained guilt-free; like Manfred he could have indulged his misanthropy in isolation. We might have cause to lament his "wasted powers" (1.326), but we have much more cause to lament the consequences of his "fiery passions" (1.327)—the deaths for which he, as a leader, is responsible.

In *The Corsair* and in *Lara,* Byron is appealing to his readers' desire for a powerful, charismatic, but gloomy outlaw-hero who can openly flaunt social conventions and institutional authority. Lara, after all, leaves his ancestral lands and becomes a pirate; the serfs are willing to follow him because "that long absence from his native clime / Had left him stainless of oppression's crime" (2.170–71). He *seems* like an alternative to the institutionalized oppression of the feudal lords, a rebel leader who will guide his followers to freedom. Byron does not, however, wish to leave his readers with a blind faith in outlaw heroes; Lara actually leads his followers to their deaths. And he does so for a purely selfish goal, not for his followers' benefit: "In his flamboyance the Byronic hero is . . . alien to any genuine political engagement" (Manning, *Reading* 211). At the same time, Byron concedes the public's fascination with this type of character. Describing Lara's apparent charisma, Byron actually characterizes the audience's response to the type of heroes he creates:

With all that chilling mystery of mien,
And seeming gladness to remain unseen,
He had (if 't were not nature's boon) an art
Of fixing memory on another's heart.

                                                          (1.361–64)

The readers may neither love nor hate Byron's heroes, but they *are* fascinated by such heroes, whether they will or no (1.365). Byron will cater to that fascination; he is, after all, a commercial author. His readers want to be haunted by Lara's presence; they want to participate vicariously in the thrill of his energetic and passionate lawlessness; and Byron gives his readers what they want. But he also wants to make sure that his readers do not mistake Conrad-Lara for either a role model or an appropriate leader.

Like Manfred and Conrad-Lara, Byron's Lucifer bequeaths several characteristics to the contemporary Byronic hero. The most significant are his omnipotence and his misanthropy, which I will discuss in detail in the section on *Star Trek*'s Q, the most explicitly satanic of all the heroes I will examine. Lucifer, in *Cain,* is the ultimate rebel; he rebels against the most powerful authority figure around: "I have a Victor—true; but no superior. / Homage he has from all—but none from me" (2.2.429–30). As such he becomes the emblem of the individualist who rejects institutional power; throughout the play he questions the legitimacy of God's authority over him and the humans God has created. Yet, as Peter A. Schock indicates, Lucifer is "enacting two conflicting roles, the traditional tempter and the Promethean metaphysical rebel" (182). While subverting God's authority, Lucifer tries to become an authority figure in his own right, demanding Cain's worship in exchange for knowledge: "Cain soon discovers that the promise of freedom Lucifer tenders him is only the illusion that enwraps an inescapable servitude" (Manning, *Byron* 148). Although he is openly contemptuous of humans' limitations and inferiority, Lucifer, like Napoleon, needs followers to sustain his sense of himself. He cannot simply rebel in isolation.

Lucifer *does* have a legitimate cause against God, and he does ask the right questions:

> Then who was the Demon? He
> Who would not let ye live, or he who would
> Have made ye live for ever, in the joy
> And power of Knowledge?

(1.1.207–210)

Byron undoubtedly has sympathy for Lucifer's denunciation of mindless faith and his advocacy of individualism: "Think and endure,—and form an inner world / In your own bosom—where the outward fails" (2.2.456–457). The individual who forms an inner world in his or her own bosom, like Manfred, is no longer subject to external authority. He or she could simply isolate him- or herself, engaging in an internal struggle, a struggle that presumably has the potential to be much more fruitful than a political one. Lucifer, however, *disregards his own advice.*

He does not simply form an inner world in his own bosom; he feels compelled to influence Cain's thoughts and behaviors, and in so doing, he utterly undermines his own claim to any kind of heroism. In addition, "he does not always tell the truth, in particular the truth about himself," and "he has promised Cain that he will satisfy his thirst for truth, but at the crucial stage of their dialogue he rebukes Cain for aspiring to know too much" (McGann, *Fiery* 255).

In taking on a leadership role, both advising Cain to rebel and providing him with superhuman knowledge, Lucifer reveals the destructive potential of the Byronic hero turned leader. Schock argues that Lucifer's ambiguous portrayal arose from Byron's attempt to undermine Christian myth yet avoid accusations of (and possibly prosecution for) blasphemy (197). I suggest, however, that the internal contradictions in Lucifer's character arise also from Byron's own ambivalence. On the one hand, he presents Lucifer's message of "autonomy, defiance, and metaphysical rebellion" (Schock 182), but he distrusts the power of charismatic leaders. Byron suggests that Cain's new knowledge of the inferiority of the human condition goads him to murder, that it is specifically Lucifer's interference that pushes Cain over the edge. Cain tells Adah,

> I had beheld the immemorial works
> Of endless beings; skirted extinguished worlds;
> And, gazing on eternity, methought
> I had borrowed more by a few drops of ages
> From its immensity: but now I feel
> My littleness again. Well said the Spirit,
> That I was nothing!
>
> (3.1.63–69)

Although Cain was discontented and rebellious before Lucifer's visit, there was no indication that he was capable of or planning murder. The conviction of his own "nothingness" that Lucifer has provoked brings him to the boiling point. When God rejects Cain's vegetarian sacrifice in favor of Abel's carnivorous one, Cain explodes. Unable to take out his anger on the real object of his wrath, he takes it out on a convenient victim, his brother. This act shows even more emphatically how pointless Lucifer's incitement of Cain to rebellion is. Cain can't win—not against this particular authority figure. But Lucifer has accomplished his own self-interested aim; he has won himself a worshipper in his own image.

Cain has become a miniature version of his tempter, and after committing murder, he is horrified at the transformation that has taken place:

> And who hath brought him there?—I—who abhor
> The name of Death so deeply, that the thought
> Empoisoned all my life, before I knew
> His aspect—I have led him here, and given
> My brother to his cold and still embrace,
> As if he would not have asserted his
> Inexorable claim without my aid.
>
> (3.1.371–77)

Cain's horror is that he has expedited the process he was most anxious to avoid—death. For all the moral force of Lucifer's verbalized objections to God's authority and unjust treatment of his own creations, Lucifer can be heroic only in *expressing* those objections, as the poet does, and in keeping his own mind free. When he tries to acquire a follower or worshipper, however, the effects of the guidance and leadership he offers Cain are fatal.

Byron consciously satisfies the desires of his public while providing hints that his heroes are neither to be taken entirely seriously nor viewed as role models. He gives them the powerful, charismatic, rebellious heroes they want, but he also deliberately and thoroughly undermines those heroes when they evolve from rebels to authority figures in their own right. We will see in subsequent chapters, however, that unlike Byron, the makers of contemporary popular texts applaud their heroes' transition into a leadership role. Maturin has the opposite problem. His intention in *Melmoth the Wanderer* is to create a portrait of a thoroughly malevolent character. Maturin examines the Byronic hero from a theological perspective to show the devastating consequences of his pride, ambition, and superhuman aspirations. His problem, however, is that he can't help making Melmoth attractive. Immalee is as hopelessly smitten with Melmoth as many fans can be with contemporary villain-heroes. Such heroes embody the irresistible appeal that Caroline Lamb attributes to Byron-Glenarvon in her roman à clef of her relationship with Byron:

> It was one of those faces which, having once beheld, we never afterwards forget. It seemed as if the soul of passion had been

stamped and printed upon every feature. The eye beamed into life as it threw up its dark and ardent gaze, with a look nearly of inspiration, while the proud curl of the upper lip expressed haughtiness and bitter contempt; yet, even mixed with these fierce characteristic feelings, an air of melancholy and dejection shaded and softened every harsher expression. Such a countenance spoke to the heart, and filled it with one vague yet powerful interest—so strong, so undefinable, that it could not easily be overcome. (120–21)

In fact Maturin's Immalee and Brontë's Isabella operate on the same "fabulous notion[s]" and "false impressions" Lamb's Calantha does in her infatuation with Glenarvon (Brontë 126–27). Like Maturin, Brontë has to struggle with her portrayal of Heathcliff. Unlike Maturin, Brontë has considerable sympathy for her hero's rebellion against society and his single-mindedness in love. But she is also aware of how dangerously tempting the Byronic male can be, and she works very hard to make Heathcliff's self-absorption, violence, and ruthlessness apparent.

Both Maturin and Brontë, then, warn their readers of the irresistible and dangerous sex appeal of the Byronic hero-villain. They assume an inherent masochism on the part of women; Melmoth and Heathcliff are "sexy" in their dangerousness, in the threat they pose to their lovers' independence, autonomy, and lives. Brontë emphasizes this masochism in both Catherine and Isabella, managing, like Byron, to satisfy and alert her readers at the same time, for "*Wuthering Heights* is no straightforward celebration of Byronic romance, although it has often been read as one" (Elfenbein 149). In the relationship between Heathcliff and Catherine, Brontë provides her readers with an idealized fantasy of a passionate and stormy love that consists of a complete identification with the other; at the same time, she insists that it *is* a fantasy—such a love can flourish only for ghosts wandering the moors, not for human beings with financial, domestic, and other concerns. She does, of course, embed a warning against investing too heavily in this fantasy; Catherine dies from an inability to prevent her fantasy love from encroaching on her real-life marriage. But the warning is more direct in the relationship between Heathcliff and Isabella. There Brontë explicitly notes that the Byronic male, attractive as he may seem, does not have a heart of gold and will make a thoroughly dysfunctional spouse. As Elfenbein argues, "Heathcliff's story suggests the consequences of taking Manfred's narcissism to an extreme within a realistic setting." He notes further, "The critique of Byronic romance is most evident in Heathcliff's behavior toward Isabella, whom he treats with relentless savagery" (154). Brontë has thus preemptively deconstructed the romance novel while contributing in large part to the conception of its archetypal moody, brooding, passionate, and dangerous hero.

Maturin makes clear that Immalee's attraction to Melmoth is masochistic and that his cruelty, ferocity, sadism, and "superhuman misanthropy" all magnify her love for him (303). Melmoth correctly anticipates that causing her pain is precisely what will conquer her: "She must learn to suffer, to qualify her to become my pupil, he thought" (288). The suffering and the violent emotions Melmoth causes become desirable to Immalee because they are more stimulating than anything else she has experienced: "But how delicious are these tears! Formerly I wept for pleasure—but there is a pain sweeter than pleasure, that I never felt till I beheld *him*. Oh! who would not think, to have the joy of tears?" (288). Isabella, similarly, undoubtedly bored and left out in her role as third wheel in her married brother's household, perceives Heathcliff as a source of emotional stimulation, with the added edge that she will be stealing her bad-tempered and indulged sister-in-law's true love away from her. Yet there has to be an element of masochism in Isabella's attraction to Heathcliff; in a brutal display of truth in advertising, Heathcliff makes very clear to Isabella just what she's getting herself into, *while she still has the chance to back out,* but she marries him anyway.

> She cannot accuse me of showing one bit of deceitful softness. The first thing she saw me do, on coming out of the Grange, was to hang up her little dog; and when she pleaded for it the first words I uttered were a wish that I had the hanging of every being belonging to her, except one: possibly she took that exception for herself. But no brutality disgusted her. (127)

Heathcliff's ruthless brutality should contain a warning to Isabella, but she sees in it an escape from a stultifyingly sheltered, smooth, and passionless existence. Compared with her brother's "milk-blooded" passivity, Heathcliff's intensity, even if sadistic, proves irresistible (100). In a similar fashion, Melmoth's sadism and Immalee's self-abnegating masochism perfectly complement each other. Melmoth feels "a glow of excitement" as he contemplates Immalee's "passive helplessness." Reflecting on the storm currently raging on the island, he "felt a wild and terrible conviction, that though the lightning might blast her in a moment, yet there was a bolt more burning and more fatal, which was wielded by his own hand, and which, if he could aim it aright, must transfix her very soul" (314). The phallic nature of Maturin's imagery here makes very clear that the threat Melmoth poses is rape, both sexual and spiritual.

Maturin and Brontë both make clear to their readers that devoting oneself to a Byronic male is a fatal mistake. Despite the extent of Immalee's humanizing influence on Melmoth, and despite his intermittent compassion for her and his attempts to protect her from himself, Melmoth cannot ultimately desist in his quest to victimize her. At the same time, he feels an intense contempt for her feelings toward him, as they have the potential to undermine his own dilated self-image:

> "And is it, then, in my power to confer happiness?" said her companion; "is it for this purpose I wander among mankind?" A mingled and indefinable expression of derision, malevolence, and despair overspread his features, as he added, "You do me too much honour, in devising for me an occupation so mild and so congenial to my spirit." (309)

Heathcliff similarly expresses contempt for Isabella's naïveté, passivity, and love for him, although those were the precise qualities that made her suitable for his purposes. When Nelly urges Heathcliff to treat Isabella kindly, for she abandoned her family for him, he retorts,

> She abandoned them under a delusion, . . . picturing in me a hero of romance, and expecting unlimited indulgences from my chivalrous devotion. I can hardly regard her in the light of a rational creature, so obstinately has she persisted in forming a fabulous notion of my character, and acting on the false impressions she cherished. (126–27)

Brontë could not have included a more explicit warning to her readers, many of them undoubtedly young women like Isabella, living comfortable but humdrum lives, possibly intended to marry a not particularly inspiring spouse, and longing for escape. Brontë provides them with a vicarious escape—the larger-than-life and supernaturally tinged fantasy of perfect love that Heathcliff and Catherine represent. In a fashion similar to Byron's, however, what she gives with one hand she takes away with another. She destroys Catherine, as if to emphasize the deleterious effects of pursuing such a passion, *and* gives her readers Isabella's fate to contemplate. She tells them, in effect, "Fantasize about heroes of romance all you want; JUST DON'T MARRY ONE!" Or as Lamb's narrator exclaims, "Woe be to those who have ever loved Glenarvon!" (264). Maturin also compares Immalee-Isidora's situation with that of a heroine of romance:

> Romances have been written and read, whose interest arose from the noble and impossible defiance of the heroine to all powers human and superhuman alike. But neither the writers or readers seem ever to have taken into account the thousand petty external causes that operate on human agency with a force, if not more powerful, far more effective than the grand internal motive which makes so grand a figure in romance, and so rare and trivial a one in common life.
>
> Isidora would have died for him she loved. At the stake or the scaffold she would have avowed her passion, and triumphed in perishing as its victim. The mind can collect itself for one great effort, but it is exhausted by the eternally-recurring necessity of domestic conflicts,—victories by which she must lose, and defeats by which she might gain the praise of perseverance, and feel such gain was loss. (372)

Self-abnegation and self-sacrifice for love are all very well in a romance novel, say Maturin and Brontë. The mistake Isidora and Isabella make is in trying to transplant the impossible passion of romance novels into real life. Had Isabella remained content to fantasize about the object of her imprudent desires, she would have been none the worse for wear. Had Immalee understood the seriousness of Melmoth's warnings about himself and been content to worship his image in her mind, she might have survived. Alternatively, had she rejected civilization entirely, she might have had a small chance of redeeming him. But romance heroes do not adapt well to domestic constraints. Maturin and Brontë both suggest that it is better to let them remain between the covers of a book. Should a young woman have the misfortune of encountering an individual who resembles a romance hero in real life, it would behoove her to give him a very wide berth.

Manfred, Melmoth, and Heathcliff all "exist" in a fantasy realm of supernatural occurrences and superhuman powers, and their creators are clear in their concurrence that this is where they should remain. Manfred must avoid human contact, for as he explains,

> I would not make,
> But find a desolation. Like the Wind,
> The red-hot breath of the most lone Simoom . . .
> Which seeketh not, so that it is not sought,
> But being met is deadly,—such hath been
> The course of my existence; but there came
> Things in my path which are no more.
>
> (3.1.125–35)

Melmoth and Heathcliff also spread devastation, but unlike Manfred, they do so intentionally. Melmoth will do anything to secure a victim, and Heathcliff is unremitting in the pursuit of revenge, not only on those who wronged him but on their innocent descendants as well. Maturin and Brontë are aware of how popular and appealing the Byronic hero has become as a literary figure, and they show the consequences of his egotism, self-absorption, and misanthropy in very real ways. Byron, too, understood the dangerous temptation the Byronic hero poses, and when he inserts such a hero into a public realm, as in his biographical accounts of Napoleon and his fictional accounts of Conrad-Lara, he makes clear just how deleterious such men prove as leaders. Contemporary creators of popular texts, however, seem not to share Byron, Maturin, and Brontë's reservations about the Byronic hero's detrimental effects on those he encounters. Although they frequently kill him off or otherwise remove him at the end of a film, they do so more as an injunction to the viewers not to emulate him rather than as a warning against the leader's own autocratic potential. We *are* supposed to accept his leadership and guidance, but we are *not* supposed to emulate him in his attacks on institutional authority. On his way to becoming reincarnated in contemporary forms, the nineteenth-century Byronic hero has had to make his way through the Victorian era, and in the process he has acquired some baggage best examined with a consideration of Thomas Carlyle's *On Heroes, Hero-Worship, and the Heroic in History* and John Stuart Mill's *On Liberty*.

While Carlyle's text is certainly an elucidation of the qualities to be found in a hero, or, more precisely, a hero-leader, what he repeatedly emphasizes is the stance ordinary citizens should take *toward* such a leader. Carlyle posits a kind of heroism in the followers who have the ability to recognize the hero's potential and thus willingly and submissively defer to his leadership. I believe this is precisely the stance the makers of the films and television shows considered in this study wish their viewers to adopt—an open-eyed, aware but passive, obedient, and grateful submission to his authority. Carlyle's formula for this successful hero-leader deserving of our reverence is simple: a Napoleon without self-interest. Napoleon certainly has the necessary ingredients to be a great leader: "There was an eye to see in this man, a soul to dare and do. He rose naturally to be the King. All men saw that he *was* such" (206). But he is hampered by his self-interest:

> *Self* and false ambition had now become his god: *self*-deception once yielded to, *all* other deceptions follow naturally more and more. What a paltry patchwork of theatrical paper-mantles, tinsel and mummery, had this man wrapt his own great reality in, thinking to make it more real thereby! (206)

Carlyle has no problem with autocratic, tyrannical, and powerful leaders—*as long as they are motivated by the good of their subjects.* He insists that they be allowed to use whatever methods are necessary, for the end justifies the means:

> I care little about the sword: I will allow a thing to struggle for itself in this world, with any sword or tongue or implement it has, or can lay hold of. We will let it preach, and pamphleteer, and fight, and to the uttermost bestir itself, and do, beak and claws, whatsoever is in it; very sure that it will, in the long-run, conquer nothing which does not deserve to be conquered. What is better than itself, it cannot put away, but only what is worse. (53)

According to Carlyle, it is when the ambitious quest for power in and of itself takes over that the leader sets himself up for failure: "The heavier this Napoleon trampled on the world, holding it tyrannously down, the fiercer would the world's recoil against him be, one day" (207). For Carlyle, the truly great leader does not pursue power for selfish ends: "We exaggerate the ambition of Great Men; we mistake what the nature of it is. Great Men are not ambitious in that sense; he is a small poor man that is ambitious so" (191). He states further that "The selfish wish to shine over others, let it be accounted altogether poor and miserable" (193).

According to Carlyle, the followers of a heroic leader *without* self-interest should subordinate their wills and "loyally surrender" to him (169); their glory lies in recognizing his ability:

> Find in any country the Ablest Man that exists there; raise *him* to the supreme place, and loyally reverence him: you have a perfect government for that country; no ballot-box, parliamentary eloquence, voting, constitution-building, or other machinery whatsoever can improve it a whit. It is in the perfect state; an ideal country. The Ablest Man; he means also the truest-hearted, justest, the Noblest Man: what he *tells us to do* must be precisely the wisest, fittest, that we could anywhere or anyhow learn;—the thing which it will in all ways behoove us, with right loyal thankfulness, and nothing doubting, to do! (170)

Carlyle's notion is, of course, profoundly nondemocratic. Carlyle, like Mill, seems to see democracy as leading to a type of paralysis, what contemporary political candidates in the United States refer to as gridlock. As subsequent chapters discuss in detail, the hero of the western, of the science fiction film, of the action-adventure movie is that "Ablest Man," the one who can cut through the paralysis, ineptitude, and corruption that surrounds him and cleanse his societq of evil with purgative violence. The contemporary Byronic hero has no respect for such trivia as civil liberties or the criminal justice system; he is simultaneously judge, jury, and executioner to the villains, while imposing the equivalent of martial law on everybody else until justice is served. For Carlyle, progress is furthered not only by Great Men ("The history of the world is but the biography of Great Men" [26]) but by the willingness of the people to offer their allegiance to such a leader: "Faith is loyalty to some inspired Teacher, some spiritual Hero. And what therefore is loyalty proper, the life-breath of all society, but an effluence of Hero-worship, submissive admiration for the truly great? Society is founded on Hero-worship" (12).

To Carlyle, submission to the leadership of a great man is ennobling. We cannot hope to emulate the insight or the deeds of great men; thus, for the rest of us, our only real hope for heroism lies in surrendering our wills to our proper leader: "We all love great men; love, venerate, and bow down submissive before great men: nay can we honestly bow down to anything else? Ah, does not every true man feel that he is himself made higher by doing reverence to what is really above him?" (14). This submission is the only form of heroism, of making him- or herself "higher," available to the common person. This notion is critical to contemporary depictions of the Byronic hero. He is so far above what we as the audience can achieve that we have no hope of emulating him, particularly if he is given some kind of supernatural or superhuman quality. We do not have the capacity to make the decisions or perform the acts that he does. We simply have to accept that the hero knows better. At the same time, his creators increase our reverence for him by humanizing him. By admiring ordinary peoples' capacity for simpler pleasures he cannot share, the hero reinforces the worth, in their own eyes, of the viewers' subordinate and powerless position. Although the leader may be a revolutionary, overthrowing institutional authority, we followers owe him our loyalty, because, Carlyle reminds us, his intentions are good even if the means are distasteful:

> It is a tragical position for a true man to work in revolutions. He seems an anarchist; and indeed a painful element of anarchy does encumber him at every step,—him to whose whole soul anarchy is hostile, hateful. His mission is Order; every man's is. He is here to make what was disorderly, chaotic, into a thing ruled, regular. He is the missionary of Order. Is not all work of man in this world a *making of Order*? (175)

The process of making order often necessarily involves what appears to be anarchy. In many contemporary popular texts, the hero violates the law and rebels against institutional authority; but it is all toward a larger good, a higher order in which corruption and self-interest have been banished. He defines his own moral code, but it is in the cause of a worthy goal or purpose; the hero will use any means necessary, because what makes him a leader is precisely that ability to use any means necessary in pursuit of the goal: "he, as every man that can be great, or have victory in this world, sees, through all entanglements, the practical heart of the matter; drives straight toward that" (205). And as Napoleon (in Carlyle's example) or the contemporary Byronic hero drives straight toward the practical heart of the matter, who are we to question him?

Although Mill disavows Carlyle's notion of hero worship, his notion of progress also depends on a profoundly antidemocratic faith in the leadership of an extremely talented individual. It is precisely Napoleon's restless energy that Constant condemns; he insists that the conqueror has no right to use others to cure his boredom and provide him with a release for his energy. Mill, by contrast, suggests that such energetic individuals should be encouraged:

> Strong impulses are but another name for energy. Energy may be turned to bad uses; but more good may always be made of an energetic nature, than of an indolent and impassive one.... The same strong susceptibilities which make the personal impulses vivid and powerful, are also the source from whence are generated the most passionate love of virtue, and the sternest self-control. It is through the cultivation of these, that society both does its duty and protects its interests: not by rejecting the stuff of which heroes are made, because it knows not how to make them. (60)

Strong impulses benefit society because it is only someone with such strong impulses who can slice through the dead weight of custom and conventionality, the evils of his age, according to Mill, in order to initiate progress. For Mill, democracy is but another form of that dead weight which impedes society's advancement. The only true road to progress is following the lead of an energetic, talented, superior individual:

> No government by a democracy or a numerous aristocracy, either in its political acts or in the opinions, qualities, and tone of mind which it fosters, ever did or could rise above mediocrity, except in so far as the sovereign Many have let themselves be guided (which in their best times they always have done) by the counsels and influence of a more highly gifted and instructed One or Few. The initiation of all wise or noble things, comes and must come from individuals; generally at first from some one individual. The honour and glory of the average man is that he is capable of following that initiative; that he can respond internally to wise and noble things, and be led to them with his eyes open. I am not countenancing the sort of 'hero-worship' which applauds the strong man of genius for forcibly seizing on the government of the world and making it do his bidding in spite of itself. All he can claim is, freedom to point out the way. (67)

Mill does not agree with Carlyle's contention that any means necessary are acceptable as long as the end is worthwhile; according to Mill, the most the leader can do is "point out the way." He is not entitled to use force.

The principal similarity in Carlyle's and Mill's arguments lies in their conception of the role of ordinary citizens. Mill defines "the honour and glory of the average man" as following the leadership of "the strong man of genius." It is not a blind obedience that Mill requires; instead he explicitly posits an ability on the part of the average man to recognize "wise and noble things," to offer his allegiance "with his eyes open" to the most talented and capable individual. In contemporary popular texts, the audience cannot long identify with the hero himself; he represents too unattainable an ideal. The audience can, however, identify with the "average man" who recognizes the hero's potential and offers him support and allegiance. These willing followers are then contrasted with the representatives of institutional power who refuse to recognize the hero's legitimacy, who fight desperately to hold on to their own power. The average man in such texts usually takes on the role of a sidekick, an admirer, a protégé, or some combination thereof: the midget Mordecai in *High Plains Drifter;* Hull Barrett, Sarah Wheeler, and her daughter Megan in *Pale Rider;* the little girl Sarah and Officer Albrecht in *The Crow;* Sarah and Johf Connor in *Terminator 2;* Jean-Luc Picard in *Star Trek: The Next Generation (TNG);* and Call in *Alien Resurrection.*

Although some of these characters begin by resisting the hero-leader's self-proclaimed authority, they come to realize that he really does know better than they do and has a competence at rectifying wrongs that far surpasses their own. The audience, too, accepts the hero's authority, questioning neither his violent deeds nor his autocratic demeanor. Like Byron's Conrad and Lucifer, and like Napoleon himself, the contemporary Byronic hero makes his "own the mind of other men"; but unlike Conrad, Lucifer, and Napoleon, he ultimately succeeds in his goals. In his usurpation of authority, the contemporary Byronic hero is applauded, not condemned.

2

"Not Such a Dork"
The Rehumanization of the Byronic Hero

T he Byronic hero, nineteenth-century or contemporary, provides a satisfying vicarious experience for his audience because of his invulnerability and his successful defiance of institutional authority. In his self-sufficiency, he creates a law unto himself and refuses to be subject to any external authority or conventional values. Yet, as Frederick Garber argues, "the attitude of the hero toward society is paradoxical and ambivalent, rarely if ever as pure and unequivocal as it is usually said to be" (324). According to Garber, Romantic heroes manifest an "unresolved ambivalence toward those values of society that seem continually to press against the boundaries of the self and demand recognition" (325). As he points out, "The hero is free, presumably, to choose what values he sees fit for the role he has assumed," yet he "broods, agonizes and suffers remorse, never adopting the complete freedom apparently available to him. Why does he feel sinful if he can, as it seems, choose to be otherwise? Obviously, responsibility had not been waived at all; it has become guilt" (330–31). I take Garber's insight a step further; the authors who create such heroes are writing for an intended audience who is, of course, a segment of the society the hero appears to reject out of hand. The ambivalence that Garber notes results, in part, from a need for the *author* not to alienate the audience. The hero's superhuman abilities, defiance of institutional authority, and declared autonomy all provoke the audience's awe and admiration. But, however much the audience wants to share those qualities, they know they cannot live independently of other people and institutions. And the hero's human aspirations remind the audience that he is not a role model to emulate or imitate. Therefore the creators of texts with heroes who rebel against governmental authority and corporate or institutional power wish to *satisfy* the audience's own rebellious urges, I suspect, not encourage them. To win the audience's sympathy, identification, and allegiance and to discourage viewers from taking up his outlaw stance, the authors or filmmakers must create a hero who, in some ways, aspires to the condition of ordinary people. When John Connor asks whether the Terminator can be "more human and not such a dork all the time," he speaks also for the members of the audience who desire to see human traits in the hero with which to identify. And if the Terminator is becoming more like us, we are precluded from wanting to become more like him. Byron's Manfred and Emily Brontë's Heathcliff both evince an apparent invulnerability to and defiance of society's values. Yet Manfred reaches for the Abbot's hand before dying, and as Garber notes, his conviction that his act of incest was a sin reflects "the values of society" (331). And Heathcliff, despite all his efforts to dominate and destroy the Linton and Earnshaw families, ceases his efforts at the moment when he could make his revenge complete: "My old enemies have not beaten me; now would be the precise time to revenge myself on their representatives; I could do it, and none could hinder me. But where is the use? I don't care for striking, I can't take the trouble to raise my hand" (Brontë 255). Brontë, I believe, wishes to indicate the ultimate futility of Heathcliff's obsession with revenge; she wants to rehumanize him before he dies by not allowing him to complete the execution of his plans.

In our contemporary culture, the western hero is one version of the Byronic hero who embodies the qualities of invulnerability and defiance, and the western landscape, according to Jane Tompkins, "implies—without ever stating—that this is a field where a certain kind of mastery is possible, where a person (of a certain kind) can remain alone and complete and in control of himself, while controlling the external world through physical strength and force of will" (75). Autonomy and force of will thus define the western hero *and* his Byronic predecessor. Rita Parks also characterizes the western hero in terms that resonate with Byronic qualities:

> The Western hero, then, is generally a loner. He is, however, a man in command of things, persons, and events, handling them skillfully but with a certain aloofness that preserves his integrity. He is a man of mysterious and frequently melancholy past; his future is tenuous and foreboding. (58)

Or, as Henry Sheehan observes, Clint Eastwood's "Westerners are loners, outcasts, and outlaws who have to forge some coherent ethical code in a world dominated by hypocritical adherence to money, power, and force, and defined by an implacable landscape" (17). And Paul Smith describes Eastwood's heroes as "rebellious, Western, sometimes Promethean" (88). John Cawelti could well be describing the Byronic hero when he characterizes western heroes in terms of "their reluctance to commit themselves to any particular social group, their ambivalence about who was right and wrong, and their strong desire to retain their own personal integrity and the purity of their individual code" (250). Ultimately, *The Crow* (1994) and *Terminator 2: Judgment Day* (1991) are westerns in Gothic and science fiction guises, respectively. Like the western hero, Eric Draven and the Terminator figuratively ride into town, dressed all in black, eliminate the bad guys, restore justice, and ride off into the sunset.

Yet the descendants of the western hero reveal cracks in their surfaces of stereotypical impervious masculinity. Eric Draven reveals a romantic vulnerability in his overwhelming grief for his murdered fiancée; and the Terminator becomes a kinder, gentler killing machine, one who stops killing, shares his heroic function with a woman and a child, thus forming a quasi family, and is presented as the ideal surrogate father. This chapter, then, analyzes the rehumanization of the Byronic hero in three Clint Eastwood westerns, the *Crow* films, and the *Terminator* films while exploring the ways in which the Byronic hero is modified to appeal to a late-twentieth-century viewing audience, particularly in being given a Carlylean hero-leader role, one eventually relinquished so that the hero does not become the very oppressive force he is fighting. This voluntary relinquishment again affirms the status quo by assuring the viewers that the job of fighting the Establishment is now complete. They need not take up the banner themselves. While Byron's heroes do not succeed at leadership—Manfred rejects it, Conrad-Lara fails at it, and Lucifer alienates his only potential follower—these film heroes succeed in saving society from itself. In all of these films, to use Cawelti's words, "because society is violent and corrupt, the only solution lies in the private action of a good leader who is able to overcome the outlaw's evil aggression and society's own endemic violence and corruption by superior ruthlessness and power of his own" (256). And to maintain his moral stance *and* not lose his edge, the hero must then isolate himself from the society he protects. Edward Gallafent notes that Eastwood is interested "in the quality of the isolation conferred by closeness to violence and death" (133). His heroes are outside society with no possibility of being reintegrated into it.

Three Clint Eastwood films made over the course of approximately twenty years illustrate the range of late-twentieth-century incarnations of the Byronic hero. Laurence F. Knapp's description could readily apply to Byron's heroes: "Eastwood's latent style of acting accentuates a major theme that runs throughout his work—the motif of the individual and the difficulty of being one" (18). Not satisfied with the apparent invulnerability, isolation, and perfect aim of the typical western hero, Eastwood emphasizes these qualities by making the heroes of his *High Plains Drifter* (1973) and *Pale Rider* (1985) ghosts or archangels. Similarly, Manfred's superior abilities have allowed him to be almost entirely self-sufficient. Byron deliberately disavows the bargain Faust made with Mephistopheles by insisting that Manfred has acquired his supernatural powers on his own.

> my past power
> Was purchased by no compact with thy crew,
> But by superior science—penance, daring,
> And length of watching, strength of mind, and skill
> In knowledge of our Fathers.
>
> (3.4.112–17)

If only "superior science" could enable the rest of us to declare a state of utter independence! Manfred can get away with his arrogance toward figures of authority because he does not owe anything to anyone. The western hero displays a similar quality of self-reliance, although it has a somewhat different origin. Both the Stranger and the Preacher were betrayed by institutional authority during their lifetimes; both were murdered by the powers that be in their communities. At that point, all bets were off, and they both were free to exact whatever revenge was appropriate. They would not compromise with corrupt authority during their lifetimes, and as ghosts, they had the ability to destroy their tormentors. In each case, the hero is in a place of existential isolation, one that allows him to operate entirely autonomously. The supernatural aura of both Eastwood heroes is hinted at throughout both movies, and in *Pale Rider,* the camera lingers over the multiple bullet wounds in the Preacher's back further to enhance our impression of his supernatural qualities. As Knapp suggests, "the more mythic Eastwood's persona is, the more inhuman, invulnerable, and abstract he becomes. The Stranger and the Preacher are archangels anointed by God to punish the wicked and/or shepherd a chosen flock or group of people" (19).

Yet in his most recent western, Eastwood goes out of his way to re*humanize* his hero; William Munny of *Unforgiven* (1992) is anything but superhuman. Richard Combs remarks that the film "convincingly describes a western town as a violent muddy hellhole, without pretending that it really is hell and that only an avenging angel can put the world to rights" (14). Dennis Bingham suggests that *Unforgiven* is "a revisionist Eastwood film" that "attacks the notion of the western man's gun as a reflection of the phallus" (9). *Unforgiven* seems a deliberate attempt to undercut the superhuman heroes of Eastwood's earlier films. In certain respects, *Unforgiven* almost appears to apologize for attitudes in the earlier films; while the Stranger in *High Plains Drifter* unapologetically rapes one woman and commits adultery with another, and the Preacher of *Pale Rider* commits adultery as well, Munny remains faithful to his deceased wife, even declining a prostitute's offer of a "free one." The fact that Munny is named at all testifies that Eastwood is consciously recasting his hero into a more human, flawed, and fallible form:

> That persona is for the first time turned into a fully developed character—which means it is then opened up to other doubts and ambiguities, because for the first time this persona joins the same world as the other characters and is compared with (and even doubled by) them. (Combs 16)

William Munny, like Heathcliff at the very end of *Wuthering Heights,* has been effectively "deByronized."

Eastwood continues to revise his conception of the hero. Just as his secret service agent in *In the Line of Fire* (1993) is a more human and more vulnerable version of Dirty Harry (his most heroic act being to place his body in front of an assassin's bullet, instead of firing one himself), William Munny in *Unforgiven* is a more human and less competent version of the Stranger. *High Plains Drifter* takes the notion of the hero as an antisocial outcast to an extreme, yet as Bingham observes, "the figure's narcissism and isolation lead to reactionary if not fascist fantasy and nostalgia" (169). His callousness and violence make him closely resemble his murderers; "Eastwood's antiheroes behave in ruthless or calculated ways that nullify the romantic traditions associated with or ascribed to heroism" (L. Knapp 19), yet could not the same be said of Byron's Conrad-Lara or Lucifer? The Stranger rapes a woman and kills at least seven men *before* the climactic and violent conclusion. Like Brontë's Heathcliff, who successfully appropriates the means of oppression that were used against him, eventually controls both the Earnshaw and Linton houses, and becomes a wealthy property owner, a capitalist, and "a cruel hard landlord to his tenants" (162), the Stranger has his revenge on the town of Lago by instituting a twisted and parodic version of the town's civic authority. "He reigns as virtual dictator of Lago" because "the town needs protection, and this deadly Stranger is the only obvious candidate for the task" (Downing and Herman 107). During his lifetime, as hired marshal Jim Duncan, he was ineffectual in preventing corruption in the form of a private mine on government-owned property, a mine that is Lago's principal source of livelihood. Returning as the mysterious and ghostly Stranger, he is no longer impotent. Although Eastwood reportedly said that "the Stranger is just a relative of the late sheriff Jim Duncan," numerous readings of the film suggest that the Stranger is indeed a ghost, and one of the flashbacks of the bullwhipping that killed Duncan is from the Stranger's point of view. His hint about his identity to the Stranger's admiring follower, Mordecai, at the end of the film is also more consistent with the reading that he is a ghost or avenging angel. Even Sheehan, reporting Eastwood's comment, made the same assumption: "It's been widely assumed (by yours truly too) that he was literally an avenging angel" (24). Bingham offers a similar reading:

> In *High Plains Drifter* the audience learns only at the end of the film
> that the stranger is an avenging angel, the ghost of a marshal who

had been conspired against and put to death by the town of Lago. It is obvious, however, that he has appeared in a different incarnation, a changed body, because no one knows him. (171)[1]

I find the reading that the Stranger is a ghost more plausible than Eastwood's denial and more in keeping with the evidence the text itself presents.

Because the townspeople are so eager to protect themselves from three troublemakers, Stacy Bridges and the Carlin brothers, they offer the mysterious gunman anything he wants. The Stranger, of course, intends to revenge himself on the entire town, which had colluded in his brutal murder, but does so by turning the machinery of institutional authority against the town itself. He makes a great show of reluctance, accepting the townspeople's offer only when they promise him anything he wants. In addition to stocking up on material goods, such as new boots, the Stranger imposes himself as sole authority, making gratuitous displays of his power. As Laurence Knapp observes, "having been appointed the de facto warrior-king of Lago, the Stranger makes a mockery of capitalism and usurps the Invisible Hand of avarice and duplicity" (62). He orders that the barn of hotel owner Belding be torn down to provide wood for picnic tables, insists that Belding empty his entire hotel of guests, and has the entire town literally painted red, adding the finishing touch himself: the appellation "Hell" on the town sign. The Stranger's antisocial behavior and flaunting of authority create objections, of course. Belding complains,

> That stranger's got everybody in this town at each others' throats. He's set himself up like a king. He's got you all snake-fascinated. Every damn one of you. This crazy picnic. Two hundred gallons of blood-red paint. Couldn't be worse if the devil himself had ridden right into Lago.

As with many Byronic heroes, it is not clear whether the Stranger is a devil or an avenging angel. Just as Heathcliff's mysterious origins, dark complexion, and vindictive behavior prompt those around him to speculate that he is a demon, not a human being, the Stranger prompts similar speculation. At the same time, Eastwood makes a point of trying to humanize his dark hero. Using Lago's newly offered bounty, the Stranger gives a pile of blankets and two jars of candy to a poor Indian family. He also wins the allegiance of the dwarf Mordecai (Billy Curtis), himself a frequent victim of bullying, and the innkeeper's wife, Sarah Belding (Verna Bloom), the only person who protested the marshal's brutal murder. She goes to bed with the Stranger after only perfunctory protests, and we see her the next morning squarely on his side, saying, "Mister, whatever you say is fine with me." The Stranger's autocratic methods are further vindicated by the portrayal of the town's men as weak, corrupt, and cowardly and the institutional authorities as incompetent. As Cawelti notes, "Westerns and hard-boiled detective stories affirm the view that true justice depends on the individual rather than the law by showing the helplessness and inefficiency of the machinery of the law when confronted with evil and lawless men" (35). In a drill to prepare for the ambush of Bridges and the Carlin brothers, the townsmen all prove utterly inept, while the Stranger has perfect aim, effortlessly shooting off the heads of the three dummies. The incompetent sheriff exclaims, "Damn, can you do that every time?" In the actual ambush, the townsmen flee their sniper posts almost as soon as the trio rides into town. To illuminate their cravenness even further, Eastwood includes two relivings of the bullwhipping, one from the Stranger's point of view and one from Mordecai's. In each case, the scene is portrayed in vivid detail, from the sound of the three whips to the bloody gashes on the marshal's face. The townspeople stand around watching silently, ignoring the marshal's plea for help. As Downing and Herman observe, "this No Name's amoral behaviour is sanctioned by others' immoral behaviour. He can do whatever he wants because he has been wronged before the film even begins. . . . The situation has been created to legitimise the hero" (111).

Yet the supposed good guys are equally callous. Mordecai delightedly watches the Stranger rape Callie, who had earlier gratuitously insulted him. Bingham suggests, "While a sequence such as the rape scene . . . does not initiate in a male spectator the impulse to rape, it perpetuates misconceptions that continue the culture's tacit tolerance of rape by reaffirming the ideological construction brought to the film by a male in patriarchy" (165–66). Making a typically antifeminist statement, the film portrays Callie as enjoying the rape, moaning and breathing heavily, while the Stranger remains silent. Later when she attempts to shoot him in the bath, the Stranger laconically remarks, "Wonder what took her so long to get mad," and in manly collusion, Mordecai leers, "Because maybe you didn't go back for more." Callie's demands to prosecute the Stranger for "forcible rape in broad daylight," which is "a misdemeanor in this town," are ignored in favor of hiring the Stranger for protection against Bridges and the Carlin brothers. Gallafent, in fact, argues that "the rape becomes a kind of replay of the death of Duncan, another outrage that the town will ignore" (115). And the Stranger's murder of three troublemakers who harassed him is dismissed by the sheriff, who genially says, "Forgive and forget; that's our motto." As Laurence Knapp remarks, "by not responding nor reacting to the Stranger's crime spree, the people of Lago tacitly condone it. The Stranger's antisocial and criminal behavior becomes excusable; rape and murder become an everyday occurrence" (59). The Stranger's antisocial attitudes seem the only viable alternative to a society in which corruption, venality, and self-interest are so pervasive, yet he is almost as callous and brutal as his murderers, treating the acts of rape and killing with utter casualness.

If the audience cheers the Stranger, it is because he satisfies their own resentment of institutional authority, portrayed `ere, as in so many other films, as corrupt and ineffective. It is fitting that he orders the town painted red, "especially the Church," as the preacher was also a silent and acquiescent witness to the marshal's murder. The Stranger's terseness, laconic attitude, and impeccable aim seem a refreshing antidote to the cowardice and ineffectuality of the townspeople, just as the Terminator's indifference to the act of killing provokes laughter in the moviegoing audience. Like Byron's Conrad, the Stranger may be described with "few are his words, but keen his eye and hand" (1.64). The film's denouement is satisfying precisely because the viewers are unable to achieve retribution against corrupt and impersonal forces in their own lives and because the Stranger is so effortlessly competent. When he efficiently dispatches the trio of troublemakers one at a time, against the backdrop of the flaming town of Lago-Hell, the viewers have a satisfying sense of justice restored. Parks notes,

> The less civilized aspects of the hero—his wildness bordering on savagery and his often marginal position as a reformed outlaw—were particularly thrilling to the popular audience. The possibility of being both good and bad at the same time was a fascinating prospect even in pre-Freudian times; it met the eternal need for a vicarious taste of forbidden fruit. (41)

The Stranger rides out toward the shimmering desert just as he rode in but smiles at Sarah Belding on his way out of town, while she beams back.

And Mordecai is completing work on a grave marker for Marshal Jim Duncan, saying, "I'm just about done here. I never did know your name." The Stranger replies, in an uncharacteristically gentle tone, "Yes you do. Take care," before riding off. The Stranger must be seen to have made a human connection, with Mordecai and Sarah standing in for the audience. Both are powerless themselves to achieve justice; Sarah is prevented from speaking out against the marshal's murder, and Mordecai views it from a hiding place, where he goes to escape being bullied. Despite apparently overlooking Sarah's sympathy for the stranger, Bingham astutely argues,

> A male spectator is encouraged to identify with a fantasy projection of himself as a socially constructed male. This projection lures an irresistible narcissism. At times, however, the spectator seems to occupy the position of Mordecai, the dwarf, the only character sympathetic to the stranger. Mordecai is often explicitly a voyeur, burrowing into tight spaces to watch the stranger. He lights his cigars, enjoys his threat to the town, and lives vicariously through him, just as the spectator can. (164)

But Mordecai *and* Sarah become the conduit for the viewers' feelings of sympathy for the Stranger; if he can secure the affection of others, despite his brutality, then he is worthy of redemption. As the grave marker attests, the Stranger can now rest in peace.

Eastwood's Stranger is a quintessentially Byronic outlaw, rejecting society as unworthy of him. As Cawelti suggests, "in the classic western . . . the hero's violence is primarily an expression of his capacity for individual moral judgment and action, a capacity that separates him from society as much as it makes him a part of it" (251). Like Brontë's Heathcliff, the Stranger is a victim of society who returns to take revenge, by using the very institutional powers that originally failed him. Yet while Byron and Brontë render their heroes ineffectual—Conrad-Lara fails as a leader, and Heathcliff loses interest in revenge just at the point when he can achieve it completely—the Stranger triumphs over all his enemies. He succeeds in making "a mock of this whole town," punishing Lago for its culpability in his murder, dispatching his three killers, and leaving the surviving townspeople to pick up the pieces. As Sheehan observes, "when the scourging Stranger finally leaves town, we discover that the administration of true justice means nearly absolute destruction" (24). When Mordecai asks about the aftermath of the planned ambush—"What about after we do it? What do we do then?"—the Stranger responds, "Then you live with it." He cannot acquiesce to Mordecai's implicit request for his continued leadership; then he would indeed be no better than the authority he overthrew. Remaining in Lago would taint the purity of his victory, and Eastwood grants his hero a triumphant and graceful exit, his own crimes and brutality forgotten or excused by the malignancy of those he killed. His first three victims taunted him for no good reason with the appellation "Pigshit," and Callie goes out of her way to confront and insult him as "just trash, a bottle of whiskey for courage, and the manners of a goat"; he retaliates by raping her. In effect, they were all "asking for it," according to the value system the film sets up:

> The film's construction of violence, however, does require a disavowal on the part of the spectator who derives pleasure from it: 'She deserved it,' or, 'Those guys asked for it.' The absence of character and motivation, combined with the identification techniques the film employs from the beginning, relieves the spectator of moral responsibility for enjoying the rape and murders—even though it's enjoyment the spectator must disavow. . . . In both events desire is justified by threat and thus displaced onto law: The gunmen are 'justly punished' by the gun; the woman, the sexual threat, is 'justly punished' by sexual violence. (Bingham 166)

While Brontë undermines her audience's sympathy for Heathcliff by having him pursue revenge against innocent victims (Linton, Hareton, and young Cathy), Eastwood makes clear that none of the Stranger's victims were innocent. The film establishes that they all, in some sense, "deserve" their fate, as Sarah Belding attests when she says, "Yes, they're my neighbors and they make me sick. Hiding behind words like *faith, peace,* and *trust*." She condemns the townspeople as hypocrites, thus justifying the Stranger's revenge, a revenge she won't suffer, as we see her leaving town at the end of the film. When she earlier warns him, "You're a man who makes people afraid, and that's dangerous," he answers, "Well, it's what people know about themselves that makes 'em afraid." Thus, "in *High Plains Drifter,* the powers of a community must be punished for violating the individual" (Bingham 178–79). The satanic Byronic hero has been modified into an avenging angel who achieves justice with purgative violence. Downing and Herman argue, "This individual *can* act as social judge, jury and executioner. And as if that wasn't enough he himself is as invulnerable as only a ghost can be." But, they note, "all-power-ful ghosts full of Old Testament fervour are no answer to the social dis-eases of contemporary America, no matter how stylish their *modus op-erandi*" (111). But Eastwood understands the appeal of a wrathful ghost with a stylish m.o.; his viewers must all have versions of the cowardly and corrupt townspeople in their own lives upon whom they fantasize about exacting a Biblically proportioned revenge.

The Preacher of *Pale Rider* takes on an even more overt leadership role than the Stranger does, and "he works smoothly and effectively against the men in power" (Cawelti 254). He is the charismatic force that holds the "tin pans" together in their fight against the wealthy miner, Coy LaHood (his name not too subtly suggesting his character). The inde-pendent miners readily and willingly accept the Preacher's understated yet charismatic leadership, expecting him to solve their problems and rid them of the encroaching LaHood (Richard Dysart). His charisma is fur-ther attested to by the crushes of both Sarah Wheeler (Carrie Snodgrass) and her teenage daughter, Megan (Sydney Penny). As in *High Plains Drifter,* the hero must execute justice in the absence of any credible legal authority. The independent miners know that no legal authority is avail-able to protect them from LaHood's raids; if they are driven off their claims, they forfeit them to LaHood. The only institutional authority is utterly corrupt—Marshal Stockburn (John Russell) and his six deputies, who "uphold whatever law pays them the most."

Also like the Stranger, the Preacher (who, not coincidentally, is referred to as a stranger several times) has a supernatural aura. He has returned from the dead, with bullet holes visible in his back and a clear implication that he had been a victim of Stockburn and his men. He appears in the mining colony after Megan Wheeler prays for a miracle and just as she is reading from the book of Revelation, "And behold a pale horse, and his name that sat on him was Death." Conveniently, the Preacher rides a pale horse, and as he rides in, Megan reads, "And Hell followed with him." When Sarah later asks "Who are you? Who are you really?" he replies, "Well, it really doesn't matter, does it?" As the typical Eastwood Man with No Name, he is larger than life, a mysterious outsider. But as François Guérif points out,

> there is one slight difference. The high plains drifter was full of
> contempt and scorn for the town of cowards which had abandoned

him to be brutally murdered. The "pale rider" has come to help a community in need. He becomes a part of it for the length of his stay. Revenge will come as a bonus. (184)

Although his character is not as ambiguous as the Stranger's—the Preacher becomes part of the community, as Guérif notes, and has women throwing themselves at him, unlike the rapist Stranger—Megan's Bible reading gives him the satanic associations of the Byronic hero. He eventually sheds his role as Preacher, placing his clerical collar in a safe-deposit box while retrieving his holster and guns. Hell literally follows with him as he uses dynamite to blow up LaHood's mining operation in retaliation for LaHood's dynamiting of the mining colony's stream. Like the Stranger, he is impeccably proficient with his weapons, disabling a gang of LaHood's men with "a nice piece of hickory" and killing LaHood's thugs, Stockburn, and all six of the deputies in the final shoot-out. His reflexes are supernaturally fast; he shoots Stockburn before the marshal can even draw his gun. And his aim is perfect: when Josh LaHood tries to rape Megan, the Preacher shoots young LaHood's gun out of his hand, fires a couple more bullets at the gun to push it away from him, then finally drills a hole in LaHood's hand.

The Preacher takes the law into his own hands, but the film justifies his violence by making the villains absolute exemplars of self-interest and evil. They deliberately kill Megan's dog in the raid at the beginning of the film, and we learn that LaHood's hydraulic mining methods are destroying the environment, unlike the benign panning methods of the independent miners. We know that Stockburn and his men deserve to die because of their sadistic and drawn-out murder of Spider Conroy, a murder intended to send a message to the Preacher. Although seemingly more of an outlaw than a preacher (Spider Conroy remarks, "Preacher, my ass."), he elicits the audience's wholehearted support. The law is corrupt, and big corporations (represented by LaHood's company) ruthlessly pursue profit with no consideration for the environment, human lives, or small-business owners. They are racing to acquire as much gold as possible before the state government in Sacramento bans hydraulic mining for environmental reasons. The hapless tin pans serve as stand-ins for the audience; it is made clear that they are powerless to change their own fate. Tompkins argues that the western "is about men's fear of losing their mastery and hence their identity, both of which the Western tirelessly invents" (45). This notion is apropos to *Pale Rider* and is exemplified in the character of Hull Barrett (Michael Moriarty). His inspiring speech to the others, urging them to refuse LaHood's buyout, is effective only because of the implied promise of the Preacher's help. Barrett is shown as a powerless victim of LaHood's thugs, and the Preacher consistently refuses his aid, only reluctantly allowing him to participate in the dynamiting expedition. He then uses a ruse to leave Barrett behind when he rides off to confront Stockburn. Barrett arrives when the shoot-out is over and is granted only the boon of killing LaHood, who is himself helpless with his hired guns all dead. The Preacher eradicates evil and restores justice single-handedly. He is a kind of benevolent despot, dedicated to serving others and refusing LaHood's offered bribes. The Preacher thus meets Carlyle's criteria for a hero-leader or "Ablest Man"; he is not motivated by self-interest and conquers only that which deserves to be conquered.

Despite his supernatural aura and superhuman abilities, the Preacher is portrayed as wanting to partake of the ordinary pleasures of regular folks. His rejection of Megan's overtures is rather wistful, as he says, "A young girl, a young woman like you, you wouldn't want to spend your future on a man like me." But such a domestic future is not for him: "The dialogue underlines . . . that for Megan sex is tied up with a vision of the future, the ongoing community of which the Preacher isn't a part" (Gallafent 136). He tries to project himself as just one of the guys; when LaHood asks, "Do you imbibe?" the Preacher answers "Only after nine in the morning." He bonds with Barrett and the other miners by helping to break up a large boulder, having explained, "Spirit ain't worth spit without a little exercise." While the Preacher seems to long for the simple pleasures of the miners and their families, just as Manfred admires the "humble virtues" and "hospitable home" (2.1.64) of the Chamois Hunter, it is clear that he cannot remain to partake of them. The miners must find their own way, once the immediate evil is eradicated, just as the surviving citizens of Lago must rebuild. Cawelti remarks that the western hero's

> climactic violence, though legitimated by its service to the community, does not integrate him into society. Instead, it separates him still further, either because a community so pacified has no need of his unique talents, or because the new society cannot aid him or do him honor. . . . In the classic Western, the hero increasingly moves toward isolation, separation, and alienation. (247)

Similarly, the Byronic hero cannot be integrated into the human community. The Preacher rides off into the distance to the echoing call of Megan's declarations of love: "Preacher! We all love you, Preacher! *I* love you." Despite his satanic overtones and efficient violence, the Preacher's role is salutary and redemptive. The bright, sunny northern Californian backdrop into which he rides off leaves a promise of optimism and hope. The corrupt "lawmen" and the ruthless businessman have been eliminated; presumably, Sarah Wheeler will marry Hull Barrett, and the Preacher can rest, having settled his score with his murderers. It is a satisfying denouement for the miners and the audience alike, except for Megan's wistful longing that the Preacher would remain. Like her, we are susceptible to his charisma and admire his take-no-prisoners approach to getting things done; like her, we long for an Ablest Man to restore order and justice. But that way lies dictatorship, and the Byronic hero-leader must depart the scene.

Eastwood's most recent western, *Unforgiven* (1992), does not share *Pale Rider's* optimistic tone. It is relentlessly dark and bleak; all are unforgiven at the end, and no redemption is available. It is, as Len Engel characterizes it, both "de-romantic and revisionist" (261). Christopher Frayling comments, "It's as if Eastwood is going back over his career as a western hero to take stock of how far he has traveled, eventually arriving at the heart of darkness" (58). And Laurence Knapp describes *Unforgiven* as "an elegy, a sad and uncompromising farewell to a persona that has bedeviled Eastwood for 30 years" (164). As Munny puts it, "We all have it coming, kid." No one is innocent, except perhaps the prostitute Delilah (Anna Thomson), whose only sin was giggling at a cowboy with "a teensy little pecker," and "most of the men in the film are depicted as selfish, boastful, cowardly and unheroic—for the most part, they are (or have been) wastrels and drunks" (Engel 262). The unnamed and supernatural stranger is now rendered as a very human and flawed William Munny, introduced as "a man of notoriously vicious and intemperate disposition." Engel notes that "De-romanticizing of the gunslinger is clear early in the film" (261). Essentially, Eastwood reveals what happens when the Byronic hero does not ride off into the sunset, die heroically, or appear as a wrathful ghost. *Unforgiven* shows what happens when a Byronic outlaw grows old, and it isn't pretty. Shortly after the movie begins, Munny clumsily tries to separate some pigs but ends up falling down into the mud; "he is a haunted, impoverished man who is at odds with nature and himself, an unshaved and disheveled man knee-deep in muck and misfortune" (L. Knapp 167). Throughout the film, Munny has trouble mounting his horse. And his attempts at target practice are inept; he "is a has-been, a schmuck who cannot shoot a canister 20 yards away or mount a horse without being thrown to the ground" (167). As the Schofield Kid (Jaimz Woolvet) remarks, "You don't look like no rootin'-tootin' sonofabitch and cold-blooded assassin." As Bingham observes, "Munny/Eastwood's tag line, 'I ain't like that any more,' is complemented by the view of the heroic horseman—a pose from Eastwood's filmic past—from which Munny/Eastwood turns away to attend again to his pigs" (234–35). Unlike the Stranger and the Preacher, who are terse but say precisely what they mean, Munny is hesitant; his speech is peppered with "Maybe," "I guess," and "I don't suppose." When he is delirious from fever, Munny reveals that he is afraid of dying, a fear the Stranger and Preacher don't share, as they are dead already. Far from a savior, Munny in his heyday was a killer of innocents; he can't remember whether he was scared or not because "he was drunk most of the time," and he is haunted by memories of his victims:

> Eastwood's Western career takes him from the supernatural Man with No Name to the undead who wreaks vengeance to the unforgiven whose veneer of renunciation gives way to revelations of guilt and terror. Far from having killed people who "had it comin'," Munny is haunted by those he killed. (Bingham 237)

High Plains Drifter and *Pale Rider* get the viewers on the heroes' sides by emphasizing the brutality and thoroughly evil natures of the villains. In *Unforgiven*, by contrast, everyone is venal and self-serving in some way: the cowboy who cut Delilah's face; Sheriff Little Bill Daggett (Gene Hackman), who is brutal and abusive in the extreme; English Bob (Richard Harris), who is a boastful liar as well as a cowardly killer; the Schofield Kid, who wants the reputation of a fearless killer; and Strawberry Alice (Frances Fisher), who pushes the other prostitutes into setting up the murders of an innocent man and the knife-wielding cowboy. Eastwood deliberately undermines any sort of climactic shoot-out; it is, instead, "nothing more than a cold-blooded assassination" (Tibbetts 12). As Engel reminds us, "in previous Eastwood Westerns, and, generally, in most Westerns, climaxes are characterized by specific, stylized imagery and the gradual building of dramatic tension" (264). Munny's murder of the innocent cowboy is drawn out and pathetic, culminating in Munny's demand that someone give the cowboy some water before he dies. The Schofield Kid kills the other cowboy, Mike, while he sits in an outhouse—"another stark example of how the executions in the world of this film consist not of gunfights but of brutal encounters between the armed and the defenceless, and having nothing to do with skill" (Gallafent 226). The Kid then falls apart, weeping and insisting he'll never kill again. After Little Bill's brutal bullwhipping of Munny's partner, Ned Logan (Morgan Freeman), to death and his grisly display of Ned's corpse, the viewers might find Munny's quest for vengeance satisfying, but we learn that Munny can harden himself to the killing only with alcohol. Drunk, he kills not only Little Bill but all his deputies and the unarmed brothel owner, Skinny. He tries to present himself as the avenging angel in a quest for justice; as he rides out of the town of Big Whiskey, he yells, his former hesitancy gone, "You'd better bury Ned right. You better not cut up nor otherwise harm no whores, or I'll come back and kill every one of you sons of bitches." We know, however, that his threats are empty, the product of a bravado fueled by whiskey. We learn in the closing written titles that it was rumored he "prospered in dry goods," hardly the stuff of western legend. The Preacher's neat and precise elimination of Stockburn and his deputies in *Pale Rider* and the Stranger's confrontation with his murderers in *High Plains Drifter* are suitably satisfying climaxes, like Manfred's triumphant defiance of the Spirit who comes to claim him. Munny's killings, by contrast, are sloppy and drawn out. Little Bill isn't killed in the original barrage; Munny has to shoot him point blank while he lies on the floor injured: "The scene violates the cardinal rule of all westerns—the good guy (no matter how provoked) can't just shoot a man in cold blood" (Tibbetts 10–11). Cawelti observes that in the western,

> the action of legitimated violence not only affirms the ideology of individualism but also resolves tensions between the anarchy of individualistic impulses and the communal ideals of law and order by making the individual's violent action an ultimate defense of the community against the threat of anarchy. (35)

However, Munny's actions in *Unforgiven* do nothing to defend the community. He is a force of anarchy, not a defense against it.

Munny is not entirely without redeeming qualities, however. His late wife Claudia had some success in reforming him. He tries to avoid drinking, and as he explains to his children, he learned not to be cruel to animals. When Delilah offers him "a free one," he gently declines: "You're a beautiful woman, and if I was to want a . . . free one, I'd want it with you, I guess, more than them other two. It's just that I can't on account of my wife." Ned, by contrast, collects "free ones," although his wife, Sally, is still alive. Munny insists he has changed from the "crazy sonofabitch" he used to be: "I'm just a fella now. I ain't no different than anyone else. No more." Little Bill also tries to live the life of a regular "fella." He is building a house himself and plans a patio where he can smoke a pipe, drink coffee, and watch the sunset. He is completely inept as a carpenter; his roof leaks like a sieve, and his house lacks a single straight angle. About to be killed by Munny, Little Bill whines, "I don't deserve this, to die like this. I was building a house," as if building a house is a sufficiently domestic endeavor to negate his brutality. Disavowing any moral high ground, Munny drawls, "Deserve's got nothing to do with it." Little Bill's house does nothing to make his character more endearing, and Munny's few redeeming qualities are far outweighed by his fundamentally flawed character. Munny is either timid and incompetent or drunkenly violent. Little Bill is a sadist, enjoying his abuse of those in his power in the name of law enforcement; he tells Ned, in a respite between whippings, "I'm going to hurt you, and not gentle like before, but bad." Little Bill won't physically punish the cowboy who assaulted the prostitute, fining him instead, but he enforces the no-gun rule in Big Whiskey with brutal beatings and bullwhippings. Eastwood captures the gunman's desire to be "just a fella," but he insists that the gunman—on either side of the law—is beyond redemption. Money is enough to lure Munny out of his retirement from the gunslinging business, and whiskey is enough to steel him to commit murder. Engel characterizes an unholy bond between Little Bill and Munny: "Each has revealed the truth about the past, especially the past of the gunfighter, and has demythologized western stories extolling male heroes" (266).

In *Unforgiven,* the Byronic hero has been thoroughly humanized and stripped of his outlaw glamour, and Eastwood radically undercuts the mythology of his earlier films, showing the diminished capacities and moral bankruptcy of the aging action-adventure hero. And William Munny was no 'ero but rather "the same William Munny that dynamited the Rock Island and Pacific in '69, killing women and children and all." Both Munny and Ned are becoming crotchety, missing their beds and their roofs while camping out; they are hardly images of the tough gunman, oblivious to hardship. Eastwood further parodies the western mythos in the characters of English Bob and his biographer, W. W. Beauchamp (Saul Rubinek), who is so terrified of guns he urinates in his pants the first time he has weapons pointed at him. Beauchamp writes exaggerated narrations of English Bob's feats, trusting Bob's unreliable accounts. Little Bill swiftly destroys English Bob's aura by beating him up and transforming the moniker "the Duke of Death" to "the Duck of Death," henceforth referring to English Bob as "the Duck." Beauchamp switches allegiances and begins taking notes on Little Bill's history and philosophy, yet, as Engel notes, Little Bill is "the living embodiment of the anti-myths he's been mouthing to Beauchamp"; he is "living the life of a cruel outlaw . . . but now doing it in the name of the law" (265–66). And when Little Bill is shot, Beauchamp turns to Munny for material. Thus, "when the dime-novel writer views Munny/Eastwood with awe, he makes clear who the male spectator is: one who draws strength from transforming the violence of madmen into feats of mettle and courage" (Bingham 240). Even the gratuitous violence that both Little Bill and Munny perpetrate does not cure him of his desire to mythologize the West. He is impressed that Munny "killed five men, single-handed" and is mentally taking notes about the event for his next book. Similarly, both the Schofield Kid and Munny exaggerate Delilah's injuries in ludicrous fashion to enlist assistance in the planned killing. Beauchamp's purple style and glorification of the western myth of the gunfighter contrast starkly with the ironic tone of the written titles at the beginning and end of the film, a rather dry, almost Austenian voice:

> Some years later, Mrs. Ansonia Feathers made the arduous journey to Hodgeman County to visit the last resting place of her daughter. . . . And there was nothing on the marker to explain to Mrs. Feathers why her only daughter had married a known thief and murderer, a man of notoriously vicious and intemperate disposition.

Killing is not a heroic endeavor. As Munny reflects, "it's a hell of a thing, killing a man. You take away all he's got and all he's ever gonna have." Like the Terminator, Eastwood's gunslinger apparently begins to comprehend the value of human life, enough that he must numb himself with alcohol to steel himself to murder. Film audiences, however, seem to want their heroes both violent *and* vulnerable, impervious killers with human hearts. Cawelti describes westerns as "allegories with strong implications for the contemporary scene" (249). The appeal of the western hero—and his predecessor, the Byronic hero—is apparent in the way he is recast into new forms: the hard-boiled detective hero, the Dirty Harry–esque action-adventure hero, and the science fiction hero, to name a few.

The Byronic hero remains glamorous to filmgoing audiences, as does the quest for vengeance pursued outside the law. *The Crow* essentially consists of a western in an urban setting, with Gothic trappings such as the eponymous crow that serves as the ghost-hero's guide. Eric Draven (Brandon Lee) even walks like a cowboy, with bowlegs and his arms dangling at his sides, sometimes firing with a gun in each hand like a western gunfighter. As in *High Plains Drifter,* the hero is the Romantic outlaw modified into a force for justice and a higher law. The videotape version of *The Crow* features an interview with the late Brandon Lee in which he neatly sums up the appeal of the film. Eric is a dark hero, who "in a sense is quite mad sometimes and in a sense is completely insane." Lee explains,

> I think that the appeal of Eric's mission is that it is a very pure one. He has come back to seek justice. I've done other films that have had violence in them, but I must say I've never done anything where I felt that the violence was as justified as it is in this. There's very little need to worry about compassion for the victims. This is justice, you know, and I truly feel that it is, and I truly feel that if I were in the same situation I would do the same thing. He has something he has to do, and he is forced to put aside his own pain long enough to go do what he has to do. (Lee)

Without irony, Lee insists that the vigilante justice performed by the film's hero is fitting because Eric's victims were all bad. Thus they merit no compassion. As in *Pale Rider,* the villains are portrayed as supremely evil men who delight in rape and mayhem, and murder cold-bloodedly with no compunction. They are even casual about the deaths of their associates; Top Dollar (Michael Wincott) announces that "our friend T-Bird won't be joining us tonight because of a slight case of death." The scenes of Shelly's violent rape and assault, her hospitalization, and the hours of suffering she endures before her death are graphically replayed as flashbacks, further emphasizing the heinousness of the crime Eric seeks to revenge. Eric's madness only increases his audience appeal; the viewers sympathize in his grief and rage at his loss. There is little in the way of ambiguity; Eric's quest is presented as purely heroic and in the cause of justice. The presence of Sarah (Rochelle Davis), a young girl who knew Eric and Shelly in their lifetimes, further emphasizes Eric's appeal and likability. He treats her with gentleness and respect, and her role is greatly expanded from that of the little girl, Sherri, in the graphic novel (O'Barr). Furthermore, Eric acquires an ally in the person of Officer Albrecht (Ernie Hudson), a beat cop who comes to see that Eric is on the side of justice. Sarah and Officer Albrecht represent the ordinary viewers, people who are powerless against evil and oppression in their lives.

Eric is the quintessence of the Byronic hero. He is dark, tortured, and moody, if not mad altogether. He has risen from the dead and has superhuman strength and a supernatural ability to withstand injury. He declares in the graphic novel, "Bullets don't stop me . . . Knives don't hurt me" (n. pag.). Embodied in O'Barr's black and white drawings, he is a Goth vision in black, complete with black and white makeup, somewhat reminiscent of Robert Smith, lead singer of the band the Cure. Calling attention to his nineteenth-century origins, O'Barr has a witness describe him as "this seven foot vampire, like Dracula or somethin'" (n. pag.). He also has the half-mad moodiness of a Childe Harold. O'Barr characterizes him as "grey and despairing, strong as steel but collapsed inside" (n. pag.). And he has the wry understated sarcasm of the western hero. When Fun Boy says, "Pal, something is seriously wrong with you," Eric, casually straddling a chair, deadpans, "Atrocity has that effect on me" (n. pag.). The filmmakers have enhanced Eric's outlaw appeal by recreating him as "the rocker as avenging angel" (Travers 105), and two scenes of the film show him sitting on a rooftop at night, playing chords on an electric guitar (fig. 1). The guitar returns throughout the film. Eric dramatically leaps from rooftop to rooftop, following his guiding crow, to the chords of Goth rock favorite Nine Inch Nails; and in the climactic scene when Eric kills Top Dollar's gathered associates, the guitar wails in the background while bullets fly and glass shatters. While the graphic novel begins with Eric's first act of revenge, the film shows Eric's grave opening and Eric emerging into a rainy night. He howls in agony, then staggers through the night, led bq the crow to his former apartment, where he has flashbacks of the murder scene. After reminiscing about Shelly (Sofia Shinas), he punches a mirror, then ritualistically applies his makeup, effecting a deliberate transformation from victim to a satanic avenging angel. He alternates between a bitter, wry, sardonic humor (while he kills Fun Boy, he tells the old joke about Jesus arriving at an inn and asking to be put up for the night) and a righteous rage (after retrieving Shelly's engagement ring from a pawnshop, he tosses rings at the owner, Gideon, yelling, "Each one of these is a life, a life you helped destroy").

O'Barr's graphic novel is an ode to the stages of grief, interspersed with poetry (particularly poems by Rimbaud), song lyrics, and chapter titles like "Irony & Despair." The narrator tells us, "Tonight, Hell sends an angel bearing gifts" (n. pag.). Eric's memories of times with Shelly are drawn in a softer style, without the harsh outlines of the scenes in Eric's present. While the violence is presented with all the gore and graphic detail comic books demand, the pictures are black and white, which mitigates the grotesqueness. At the end are several stylized color portraits of the hero, who is given an unearthly beauty. And O'Barr presents him almost as an abstraction, a symbol: "I am pilot error, I am fetal distress, I am the random chromosome . . . I am complete and total madness . . . I AM FEAR" (n. pag.). The contest is purely between good and evil; the murderers attack Eric and Shelly when their car is stalled on a lonely road, beating and raping Shelly before killing her (one, in fact, rapes her body after she is dead). It is simply a sadistic and gratuitous act of violence. In the film, by contrast, as in so many western, action-adventure, and science fiction films, the evil is institutionalized. The creators of the film are aiming for a wider demographic than comic-book readers, and thus they draw on proven popular themes. Top Dollar owns the apartment building where the couple lives, and Shelly is murdered for fighting an eviction notice. Thus the very fabric of institutional power in Detroit is enmeshed with gangs, drug dealers, and murderers. The police force is both inept (unable to secure any convictions in the murder case after a year) and corrupt, removing Albrecht from the case in favor of an arrogant and incompetent detective. As a ghost and an outlaw, Eric transcends the law and moral codes of ordinary people; like the Byronic hero, he achieves an almost total autonomy. In his initial encounter with Albrecht, who tries to arrest him, when Albrecht yells, "Don't move!" Eric mockingly remarks, "I thought the police always said 'Freeze.'" Albrecht insists, "Well, I am the police, and I say don't move, Snow White. You move, you're dead." Eric raises his arms, announcing, "And I say I'm dead, and I *move*." As a ghost, he can act with total impunity, killing his victims in any number of gruesome ways in the cause of a justice that transcends the law.

The contest is between the superior individual and the institutions; we learn that even the arson spree on "Devil's Night" has been institutionalized. Top Dollar himself is discontented with the institutional blandness of the criminal life; there are even Devil's Night greeting cards. He tells his men, "I want you to set a fire so God damned big the gods will notice us again. That's what I'm saying. I want all you boys to be able to look me straight in the eye one more time afd say '*Are we having fun or what?*'" He is no longer having fun and appreciates the contest with Eric: "I'm sorry if I spoiled your wedding plans there, friend. But if it's any consolation to you, you have put a smile on my face. You got a lot of spirit, son." The film's stylized violence seems a purifying antidote to the web of institutionalized crime and corruption that permeates the city. It is not coincidental that the climactic confrontation takes place at a church; Top Dollar is satisfyingly impaled, and Eric has presumably purified the city in a ritual of consecration.

In the graphic novel, Eric remains invulnerable to his enemies, vulnerable only in his grief. The filmmakers, on the other hand, chose to humanize him in a different way, nearly stripping him of his powers toward the end. His friend Sarah has been kidnapped by Top Dollar, whose girlfriend-sister Myca (Bai Ling) understands the source of Eric's power. The crow that serves as Eric's guide is shot and injured, and Eric becomes susceptible to injury. Albrecht says, "I thought, you know, you were invincible," and Eric replies, "I was. I'm not anymore." With the help of Albrecht and the crow itself, however, he is able to triumph. A hero with supernatural powers wins the viewers' admiration; a hero with supernatural powers who is also the underdog fighting an apparently superior force wins their sympathy as well. Eric's autonomy turns out *not* to be his most effective weapon against evil. When Albrecht says, "Then I guess you really will need my help, won't you?" we learn that the apparently invincible hero needs human connection. And like the western hero, he must take his leave, returning to the cemetery and reunion with Shelly. Sarah's voiceover narration shifts the film's focus from revenge to love: "If the people we love are stolen from us, the way to have them live on is to never stop loving them. Buildings burn, people die, but real love is forever." At the beginning of the film, her voiceover sets up the theme of revenge:

> People once believed that when someone dies a crow carries their soul to the land of the dead. But sometimes something so bad

happens that a terrible sadness is carried with it, and the soul can't rest. Then sometimes, just sometimes, the crow could bring that soul back to put the wrong things right.

The revenge theme drives the film, but the ending, with the embrace between Shelly and Eric, suggests that what we've been watching is a love story. We can identify with Eric the grieving lover in a more intimate way than we can identify with Eric the invincible avenging angel. And Brandon Lee's untimely death on the film's set created an additional overlay of pathos.

Like the western hero, Eric is not the type of hero who serves as a role model. The audience hardly wants to share his madness and rage and isolation. We are content to sit back and let Eric eradicate evil in our stead, yet it is satisfying to know he would gladly exchange his supernatural powers for ordinary life with his fiancée. We are incapable of fighting institutionalized corruption ourselves; Shelly is murdered for protesting an eviction notice. We must leave that battle up to the Byronic hero, with his supernatural powers and tormented soul. The film presents a reactionary vision of "eye for an eye" revenge, glorifying vigilante justice. It is a form of packaged rebellion; the rock soundtrack (featuring such popular and apparently antiestablishment performers as Nine Inch Nails, the Cure, and Stone Temple Pilots) and Eric's dressed-in-black-outlaw, Goth-rock persona create a surface veneer of youthful subversion. The film does nothing to change the status quo, however, encouraging passivity in the viewers and their support of corporate America in buying copies of the soundtrack and associated products. The videotape version even includes an advertisement for a book about the making of the film, no doubt appealing to a morbid curiosity about Brandon Lee's death on the set. The subversiveness of the film is as packaged and institutionalized as the Devil's Night greeting cards that so offend Top Dollar. Eric may achieve his western-style justice, but the institutional forces that control the viewers' lives roll on.

The Crow: City of Angels (1996) essentially repeats the plot of the first movie but in a more ponderous fashion. A murder victim, Ash (Vincent Perez), awakes underwater where his body was tossed, is guided by a crow, has flashbacks of the crime (a brutal murder of himself and his son), and pursues vigilante justice against a group of callous, sadistic, unredeemably evil murderers and drug dealers with the encouragement of a grown-up Sarah (Mia Kirshner). A homeless child, Grace, also evokes Sarah of the previous film. The villain, Judah Earl (Richard Brooks), has a female companion who sees the future and understands the nature of the hero's power; the only difference is that in this film, she turns against the villain at the end. As in the first film, the hero moves "up the food chain," killing off Judah's lieutenants and thugs before going after the man himself, setting up a dramatic final showdown. And as in the first film, the hero is temporarily rendered vulnerable by the removal of his supernatural powers. The contest is, even more than before, one between simple good and evil; Judah Earl is explicitly linked to "a darker world" and supernatural forces. He is a two-dimensional caricature of a power-mad, thoroughly inhuman villain. Perez's Ash also never transcends the two-dimensionality of a symbol and is never convincingly humanized. Lee's performance in the first film is much more believable; he seems very human in his madness, grief, and wry humor. While *City of Angels* lacks the focus on institutional corruption of *The Crow,* the depravity is pervasive. Judah (both a large-scale pimp and a drug dealer) grandiosely announces that "our products feed this entire city," and Sarah, in a voice-over, says, "All I see around me are victims. It's the city of drugs and of darkness. The city of Judah Earl." The pervasiveness of Judah's power is visually enhanced by the height of the tower that serves as his headquarters, while the all-permeating corruption is indicated by the putrescently greenish-yellow filters through which the story is filmed. Like Top Dollar in the first film, Judah appears to be the entire power structure; but in contrast to the first film, the police are entirely absent from *City of Angels.* Ash, thus, is not doing the work of the police for them (in *The Crow,* it is repeatedly emphasized that the Detroit police had failed to obtain a conviction in Eric's and Shelly's murders); he is fighting the devil, pure and simple. The film lacks any semblance of subtlety; the female killer of Ash's child is named Kali, and Judah receives prophecies of the future from the oracular Sybil.

Ash is a much grimmer version of the ghost-hero; unlike Eric Draven, he lacks any sense of sardonic humor or delight in his pursuit of revenge. Lee's Eric had considerably more style. Ash's statements are stilted: "I have to find the others. I have to finish what I started." His appearance, however, is suitably Byronic. He sports a toned-down version of Eric's black and white make-up and wears a long, dark trench coat, which flaps behind him like a cape as he rides his motorcycle, the vehicle symbolizing his rebel nature and outlaw status, which are otherwise unexplored. We know that Sarah is an outcast and rebel as well, as she works in a tattoo parlor, another unexplored and unsubtle signifier of youthful rebellion. Ash, however, lacks Eric's Goth rock star glamour but makes a quintessentially Romantic statement at the climax of the film. When Judah gloats over Ash's loss of power (his guiding crow having been tortured and killed) and threatens, "There's nothing but pain for you now," Ash screams, "Pain *is* my power!" It is a statement of Byronic autonomy; just as Manfred insists that he kneels to no authority but his own desolation (2.4.42–43) and acquired his powers without selling out to the devil, Ash can operate independently of his guiding crow.

Although both films present vigilante justice as desirable and necessary, suggesting that only a being of supernatural power can defeat the forces of evil, they both subtly (and I believe unintentionally) undermine their own message. Eric passionately grieves Shelly's death, and Ash laments the loss of his son, repeatedly looking at his son's last drawing. Both have flashbacks of good times with their loved ones as well as of their brutal murders. Yet both films emphasize the message, as the second film's voiceover tells us, that "sometimes love is stronger than death." Both films conclude with a joyful reunion between the hero and his loved one; if death allows such togetherness, it doesn't seem like such an undesirable state. For the sake of a happy ending with redemption for the hero, the horror of the villains' crimes is undermined. Ash's pursuit of vengeance is also undermined by Sarah's murder by Judah. She would be alive if not for her involvement in Ash's quest. The film, however, never overtly questions whether her death is a suitable price for the elimination of Judah and his gang. Ash may, as the voiceover tells us, "set the wrong things right" to be reunited with the one he loves, but Sarah is sacrificed in the process. In fact, her death is necessary, as it is the catalyst that allows Ash to summon his own power, in the form of a "murder" of crows (some of which emerge from his chest) that attacks and destroys Judah. Ash gets his revenge, but only at the cost of another murder of an innocent victim.

As at the end of the first film, the status quo is unchanged. The villain, Judah, is a purveyor of pleasure in the forms of flesh and drugs, and he witnesses a sadomasochistic (S-M) scene that is staged for him. Yet the film itself appeals to the same dark sensibilities that Judah's kinkiness evokes. The tattoo parlor that employs Sarah is named the Gargoyle, and the soundtrack features such bands as Hole and White Zombie, both associated with youthful rebellion and darker themes. The repeated flashbacks of the murder scene are there to stimulate viewers' fascination with the pleasure of horror (the boy Danny is killed by a beautiful Asian woman, Kali [Thuy Trang], who sings a twisted version of "Hush, Little Baby"); and there are several scenes in an S-M club, featuring bound women and hot candle wax. The S-M association presumably is there to indict Judah, but the scenes also exist to titillate the viewers, including them as voyeurs. Both films are marketed to appeal to listeners of a particular type of music, and advertising for them featured their soundtracks. Thus the filmmakers, like Judah, sell darker pleasures; the rebellion against the commodification of pleasure in the film is merely a surface rebellion. The viewer is encouraged to remain passive and to continue purchasing pleasure in marketable form. The film is itself an example of the commodified dark pleasure that it, on the surface, condemns. At least *The Crow* is more honest in its embrace of the dark side; Eric, for all his melodrama and grief, clearly enjoys his role, smiling at his victims, cracking jokes, and gloating at his abilities. Unlike the second film, *The Crow* aims for laughs. After his first encounter with Eric, Albrecht remarks, "Guy shows up looking like a mime from hell, and you lose him right out in the open. Well, at least he didn't do that walking against the wind shit. I hate that." The humor makes Eric's grief and his pronouncements ("Believe me, nothing is trivial") more believable and more moving; by contrast, Ash's grief and anger simply become tedious. *The Crow* knowingly shares a joke with its viewers—we all enjoy the dark side, or we wouldn't be watching the film—while *City of Angels* takes itself unrelentingly seriously, with no acknowledgment of the hypocrisy of the film's message. In works like *Manfred* and the Turkish Tales, Byron appeals knowingly to his readers, giving them what they want while reminding us he doesn't take his heroes' Romantic posturing too seriously; *The Crow*, I believe, is a more successful film than its sequel in that it, too, can laugh at itself and its Gothic trappings and Romantic sensibility.

While Eric Draven is a Goth rock version of the western gunslinger, the cyborg villain-hero of the *Terminator* films not only is another updating of the western formula but also, like Eastwood's ghost-heroes and the heroes of the *Crow* films, has much in common with the Byronic hero, modified for a contemporary audience.[2] In fact, the Terminator embodies all the qualities that Tompkins attributes to the western hero: "self-discipline; unswerving purpose; the exercise of knowledge, skill, ingenuity, and excellent judgment; and a capacity to continue in the face of total exhaustion and overwhelming odds" (12). What makes the Terminator a particularly intriguing "hero" is his development from his original role as a villain. Just as Byron, in his conception of the Byronic hero, adapted the qualities of the Gothic villain, recognizing the appeal and interest this villain had for Radcliffe and Lewis's audience, James Cameron transformed the villain of the first film, *The Terminator* (1984), into the hero of the sequel, *Terminator 2: Judgment Day* (1991). What struck him was that the villain played by Arnold Schwarzenegger in the first film, a superhuman, emotionless, ruthless, indefatigable killer, had proved very popular with movie audiences. Jonathan Goldberg notes,

> If as social psychopath, the Terminator seems simply outlaw, the figure also taps into right wing fantasies of vigilante control (the weapons purchased are for home defense); but also underclass opposition to police oppression. . . . Everyone loves to see the police massacred. (186)

The audience had, in effect, turned the killing machine (a half-human, half-machine cyborg) into a hero anyway; Cameron's adaptations of the character for the second film played on his audience's fascination wit` this villain figure. Similarly, Byron recognizes that the villain is the most interesting character in Gothic novels, and he transforms the villain's isolation, pride, and aspiration into admirable, if self-destructive, attributes. But Cameron goes a long way toward humanizing the Terminator in *Terminator 2*. Tompkins sees the robotized hero, such as the Terminator, as an extension of the ethos of "the need for numbness" required of the western hero (217–18). Yet in *Terminator 2*, the cyborg repudiates numbness in favor of human feeling.

The Terminator features two heroes of the ordinary-person type—Sarah Connor (Linda Hamilton) and Kyle Reese (Michael Biehn)—who are forced by extraordinary circumstances to draw on every resource available to them to battle a much more powerful foe, the Terminator (Arnold Schwarzenegger), who is, literally, "a stranger in this breathing world / An erring spirit from another hurl'd" (Byron, *Lara* 1.315–16). Kyle, in fact, travels through time from the future to give Sarah a message from her son John, telling her "you must be stronger than you imagine you can be." The scenario contains the typical paradoxes of time-travel stories. A sentient computer, Skynet, had started a nuclear war to eliminate human beings. The survivors were rounded up into camps for forced labor, disposing of dead bodies. We learn that the disposal units ran night and day, and the human race would have been eliminated if not for the leadership of John Connor, who organizes the humans' resistance against the machines. This war is continuing forty years into the future (the film is set in its present, 1984), and Skynet has attempted a preemptive strike against its enemy, sending a cyborg "infiltration unit" in human form (to the extent that Arnold Schwarzenegger can be said to resemble a human) to destroy John Connor before he is born by killing his mother, Sarah. Connor also sends someone back in time: a protector, Kyle Reese.

Throughout the film, the Terminator relentlessly pursues Sarah, killing anyone who gets in the way with emotionless efficiency, while she and Kyle run away and fight back, falling in love and conceiving John along the way. Sarah and Kyle are appealing characters, ones to whom the audience can easily relate. When the movie begins, Sarah is a ditzy waitress who can't even balance her checkbook, and Kyle is a lovesick admirer of the legendary Sarah Connor, who "taught her son to fight, organize, prepare from when he was a kid." They have our sympathies, as they are so completely outmatched by the seemingly invincible Terminator; when Sarah finally triumphs over him (after he has killed Kyle), her declaration "You're terminated, fucker!" resonates. This nice girl, with her pink shirt and fluffy hair, has managed to rise to the occasion and destroy a superhumanly strong figure of institutionalized power. (It is not accidental that the Terminator drives a police car in much of the film.)

Yet it is the figure of the Terminator that fueled the audience's imagination and led to sales of action figures. Imagining ourselves in Sarah's position, we suspect that we too would try to refuse "this great honor." She demands, "Do I look like the mother of the *future*? Am I tough? Organized?" Sarah's triumph occurs only after the death of her protector-lover and only after he has disabled the Terminator with a Molotov cocktail. The metal endoskeleton of the Terminator is reduced to a head, torso, and arms. Nonetheless, it nearly catches Sarah before she crushes it with industrial equipment in the warehouse where the climactic scene takes place. The inspirational hero, or Ablest Man, of this film is behind the scenes: John Connor (initials not accidental). Kyle describes him in worshipful terms: "There was one man who taught us to fight, to storm the wire of the camps, to smash those motherfuckers into junk. He turned it around. He brought us back from the brink." He later tells Sarah, "He's got a strength. I'd die for John Connor." John Connor takes on an almost supernatural aura, the hero of the resistance against the ultimate in impersonal, institutional authority—a machine. As Anne-Marie Harvey points out, "The plots of both *The Terminator* and *T2* depend on the belief that the course of history hangs on the birth of a single man (John Connor) and that resistance and salvation cannot originate with anyone else" (34).

But it is not John Connor, the resistance leader, who inspires the sequel, *Terminator 2: Judgment Day.* We can't really count on the Sarah Connors and Kyle Reeses of the world to free us from institutional oppression. What we need is a superhero. The Terminator of the first film is a figure of autonomy, superhuman strength, and single-mindedness. He is seemingly invincible, unstoppable, and so appealing to the viewers that his menacing threat "I'll be back" became a necessary staple of most subsequent Schwarzenegger films. As Kyle describes it, "It can't be bargained with. It can't be reasoned with. It doesn't feel *pity*, or *remorse*, or *fear*, and it absolutely will not stop, *ever*, until you are *dead*." The Terminator's inhuman nature is reinforced by the scenes of it operating on itself with an exacto knife to make repairs, even cutting open its own eye, which had been damaged. He kills without compunction, murdering his first victim by pulling his heart out, and killing thirty cops inside a police station while searching for Sarah. Kyle exclaims, "He'll find her! That's what he *does*! That's *all* he does! You can't stop him!" The Terminator is finally rendered entirely machinelike toward the end of the film; its flesh has been burned away in an explosion, and what is left is a walking metal skeleton, "a hyperalloy combat chassis." He shows no vulnerabilities nor a spark of emotion throughout the film; he is simply determined and methodical, unable to deviate from his programmed goal. This cyborg is the nightmare vision of a technological future; a human form encasing a machine. Yet some of the machine's qualities seem desirable; the Terminator appeals to a fantasy of autonomy and invulnerability. As in *High Plains Drifter* and *The Crow*, the institutional forces are impotent. The police can't protect Sarah and refuse to believe Kyle's story, trusting the callous and uncaring assessment of the smirking psychiatrist Silberman (Earl Boen) that "in technical terminology, he's a loon." Lieutenant Traxler assures Sarah, "You'll be perfectly safe. They got thirty cops in this building." We know then that he and the others are doomed.

Terminator 2 more clearly defines the villains as institutional forces: the Skynet computer (given free rein by the government and the Pentagon), uniformed police officers, and the authorities in charge of the mental hospital where Sarah is confined, particularly the smug and unsympathetic Silberman: "For *T2* medico-juridical-corporate-military, and sometimes familial, formations are both frighteningly malevolent and pitifully ineffective" (Harvey 34). The Terminator, like Byron's heroes, is an outlaw, standing up to oppressive institutional power. As Tony Rayns observes, "*Terminator 2* is less a sequel to *The Terminator* than a benign revision of the earlier film, a parable in which Arnold Schwarzenegger's matchless T-800 is transformed from an unstoppable killing machine into man's best friend and an ideal father figure" (50). Manfred's supernatural powers and the Terminator's awesome strength and speed give the audience a vicarious opportunity to triumph over those institutional forces before which they feel helpless. Manfred, as a sorcerer, triumphs over the threats of Arimanes and the summons by the hellish spirit at the end of the play. The cyborg similarly triumphs over powerful forces, including, especially, the villain, an advanced Terminator, the T-1000 (Robert Patrick), not coincidentally disguised as a uniformed police officer.[3] What member of the film's audience has not fantasized about blowing away some representative of an impersonal governmental or other institution with a casual "Hasta la vista, Baby"? Like the Preacher and Eric Draven, the Terminator embodies "the fantasy of a superior father figure who can protect the innocent and wreak vengeance on the guilty, a fantasy that reflects a profound disbelief in the modern agencies of law and justice to serve their proper function" (Cawelti 259). Sarah's ill-treatment in the asylum and the inability of an entire police force to subdue the Terminator imply that neither justice nor law prevails in Los Angeles in the 1990s. The construction of the Skynet computer reveals a recklessness on the highest levels of authority—the government and the Pentagon—that would lead to nuclear destruction if not for the Terminator and his companions; "whereas individuals like Sarah or the Terminator master whatever technology they use (or embody), the corporate-military formation that produces Skynet is so ineffective as to be mastered by its own machine" (Harvey 36). Yet the Terminator's technological origins create a more layered father figure–individualist than Cawelti's description here can account for. Harvey argues,

In its Arnold Schwarzenegger character, *T2* dreams up its own version of a masculinity defined by contradiction, an internal split that is mapped onto the Terminator's status as, in his own words, "living tissue over metal endoskeleton." In *T2*, flesh versus the technological part in Arnold Schwarzenegger's oh-so-masculine body come to represent not only vulnerability versus strength, but also rebellious individualism versus disembodied institutional power. These two physical parts come to represent the Terminator's individual fatherliness versus the power he borrows from corporate/military/government patriarchy. *T2* articulates a desire for reconciliation of the two opposite poles that constitute ideal masculinity, embodying them in a fantasy father who is both soft and supremely potent, both human and non-human. The paternal masculinity represented in the Terminator is both humanly impossible to attain, and ultimately impossible to sustain: at the movie's end, the Terminator itself recognizes that its death is necessary to preclude universal destruction. It must die to save us all. (26–27)

Like the Stranger, the Preacher, Eric, and Ash, the Terminator represents an unattainable heroism, one consisting of superhuman or supernatural capabilities. The Byronic hero's powers command our respect and admiration. His superadded human qualities and vulnerabilities evoke our identification. Yet, as Harvey notes, this combination is "ultimately impossible to sustain," and our hero must terminate himself or depart.

Both Manfred and the Terminator are defined by their assertive individualism, by their ability to transcend petty human concerns. Manfred evokes "the Promethean spark" (1.1.154), which gives him power over the spirits, and he disdains human contact: "My Spirit walked not with the souls of men, / Nor looked upon the earth with human eyes" (2.2.51–52). The Terminator is a representative and exemplary action-adventure hero, for he embodies the most deliberate development of the rugged individual. He is not only excessively strong but superhumanly so, because he is half-machine: "The machine becomes the trickster/messiah/frontiersman to lead us from an inhuman technological wilderness. He is thus in body and cultural mythos our perfect champion against postmodern, postindustrial society" (Larson 62). Like Manfred, who has acquired forbidden and supernatural knowledge, the Terminator masters information (a skill his information-overloaded audience would appreciate); his CPU contains detailed files on just about everything, and he instantaneously becomes expert at such skills as riding a motorcycle and operating advanced weapons. He embodies Roger R. Rollins's speculation that "as information-retrieval, processing and transfer assume more and more importance in modern society, it is likely that popular culture will respond by offering its audiences more heroes who rely less on physical prowess and more on information-storage and application," although the Terminator, of course, relies on physical prowess as well (34). In the film, "mastery of technology confers power, implying penetration and taming of what is, to most, impenetrable and untamable" (Harvey 33). The Terminator operates outside the law, determinedly helping Sarah escape from the oppressive mental hospital, firing on police officers, and helping to blow up an entire office building, all in the name of a higher cause.

In the first film and the first part of the sequel, the Terminator carries Manfred's disdain for humankind to an extreme; he has no respect for human life whatsoever. His companion, John Connor (Edward Furlong) as a boy, is shocked at the Terminator's callousness: "You were going to kill those two guys!" The Terminator replies casually, "Of course, I'm a Terminator." When told "You can't just go around killing people," he asks, simply, "Why?" As a fantasy, this callousness allows the audience a vicarious sense of power, autonomy, and control. Just as Byron's audience was fascinated with the isolated and self-absorbed figures of his heroes, today's audience is intrigued by the figure of the violent and powerful loner. At the same time, these audiences need to have it both ways; they want a vicarious escape from their daily lives, but they do not want those daily lives utterly dismissed. As Larson neatly puts it, "we say that, so long as the recognizable man-machine envies our humanity, we have not sold it away" (69). Manfred cannot be allowed to exist without human contact, and the Terminator must gradually become more human. The product of a supercomputer whose goal is to exterminate the human race, the Terminator learns to value human life and, in the warped logic of time travel, even assists in his own "self-termination" in order to prevent the Skynet computer from being built. *Manfred* and *Terminator 2* both conclude with the heroes simultaneously proving their superhuman abilities by defeating a powerful enemy while tentatively affirming their humanity. Manfred, having defeated the demons in his most concrete victory, finally sees the need for human contact, asking for the Abbot's hand and remarking, "'Tis not so difficult to die" (3.4.151). Discussing the binary distinctions evident in *The Terminator*, Larson observes, "The difference between man and machine, between Christ-like human and satanic trickster, is incarnateness itself, particularly the presence or absence of an organ of mercy or empathy, the presence or absence of a heart" (60). By the finale of *Terminator 2*, the machine has apparently acquired a heart. The Terminator, having defeated the T-1000 and about to sacrifice himself for the benefit of humankind, apologizes to the weeping John Connor, "I'm sorry, John, I'm sorry. I have to go away," and adds, in the typical monosyllabic style of an Arnold Schwarzenegger role, "I now know why you cry, but it is something I can never do." This statement reveals the Terminator's growing humanity and empathy but also insists that he can never cross the line entirely. Harvey notes,

> The Terminator cannot elucidate the contradiction in which it functions: that as a machine, it can have no emotions, yet as a potential father, not to mention movie star, it must simultaneously encourage longing for its warmth. It can only tantalize us with the suggestion that it *can* learn. (30)

But he will remain something Other. Like the lone gunman in the western, he must remove himself from the scene.

It is this simultaneous separation from and affirmation of humanity that I find the most intriguing parallel among Manfred, the Terminator, and Eric Draven, but the quality is most pronounced in the Terminator. Referring to the Terminator and *Star Trek*'s Mr. Spock, Harvey remarks, "It is these creatures' alien coldness that leads their audiences to desire so intensely proof of their hidden or nascent humanity and warmth; it is their sterile rationality that leads to fantasies of their involvement in erotic or family connections" (30). In creating this balance of humanity and superhumanity, the filmmakers render the Terminator systematically less and less human in appearance and more and more human in behavior, simultaneously emphasizing both his mechanical origins and his glimmerings of humanity: "The Terminator ostensibly feels no emotions, but in fact exhibits them at moments when remaining emotionally blank would set him beyond the pale of his viewers' desire" (Harvey 29). His appearance is completely human (though of superior and apparently impressive physique, as the women's appreciative glances attest during the scene in the bar) at the beginning of the film, and leather clothes, sunglasses, and a motorcycle give him the appearance of an outlaw, a romanticized figure outside the conventions of society. This figure is, however, not taken entirely seriously; newly attired, the Terminator emerges from a biker bar to the strains of George Thoroughgood and the Destroyers' "Bad to the Bone," a deliberately overstated and humorous ode to machismo. Like the creators of the first Crow film, Cameron realizes that a tongue-in-cheek, cartoonish approach makes the Terminator's violence all the more appealing to the viewers. In fact the Terminator casually defeats a host of contemporary fears, and the viewers' laughter arises partly from their own complicity in his triumphs. When he single-handedly unmans a group of macho bikers, we can't help but enjoy the moment, particularly when he advances on one biker, snatches his rifle with one hand, and then neatly removes the man's sunglasses from his pocket and puts them on. The outlaw cool image is complete, and Cameron self-consciously plays on our conventional expectations of the outlaw figure.

On the one hand, as the film progresses, the Terminator becomes more human in behavior and "not such a dork." He even becomes a type of surrogate father to John Connor. Sarah says,

> Watching John with the machine it was suddenly so clear. The Terminator would never stop; it would never leave him, and it would never hurt him, never shout at him, or get drunk and hit him, or say it was too busy to spend time with him. It would always be there, and it would die to protect him. Of all the would-be fathers who came and went over the years, this thing, this machine was the only one who measured up. In an insane world, it was the sanest choice.

Harvey thus remarks that "*T2* leaves its viewers with little doubt that we are to conceive of the Terminator as a bizarrely desirable father uniquely suited to the contemporary world" (27). From killing machine to ideal father is a stretch, but the human interest is necessary to further the viewers' identification with the cyborg hero. The Terminator exemplifies Cawelti's notion that "in the case of the superhero, the principle of identification is like that between child and parent and involves the complex feelings of envious submission and ambiguous love characteristic of that relationship" (40). As a ten-year-old child, John can reveal only glimpses of his future greatness, and Sarah is a very flawed potential savior of the world (more on this in chapter 5). They are ordinary people in extraordinary circumstances, but their heroism serves also as a contrast to the

Terminator's greater abilities, insight, and eventual self-sacrifice. In addition to becoming the father figure in a quasi nuclear family, the Terminator learns such essential expressions as "No problema" and "Hasta la vista, Baby." In the first film, the Terminator responds to a pestering motel manager with "Fuck you, asshole" after finding the phrase (one that had been aimed at it earlier) in a directory of "Possible Responses" in its processor; in the sequel, he learns slang from John, then apparently uses it in a more spontaneously human fashion. There is a comic incongruity in the Terminator being introduced as "Uncle Bob" and then hoisting up a toddler by the child's overalls to inspect it. As he becomes progressively more human, he clearly relishes his role, posing with a massive gun and a lethal grin, while John comments, "It's definitely you." It is a knowing nod to the audience that refers to Schwarzenegger's superhero image but also shows us that the Terminator is developing a very human sense of self.

At the same time that Cameron humanizes his hero, more and more of the Terminator's "metal endoskeleton" and machinelike qualities emerge: he is impervious to bullets, and he dramatically cuts away the flesh of his arm to reveal his metal hand and arm to the computer programmer, Dyson. At various points, we are given a Terminator's eye view of the world, complete with infrared vision and continuous computer-generated information. By the end of the movie, the Terminator barely retains any human appearance; one of his eyes is gone, leaving a cameralike lens, and one arm is a mass of tangled metal; yet at the same time, it is at this point that he reveals himself to be the most human, embracing his human companions and sacrificing himself to ensure the preservation of the human race. After the exhausting battle with the T-1000, the Terminator even deadpans, wearily, "I need a vacation."[4] We also see the Terminator's growing humanity in his newly acquired ability to *think* for himself. Despite being programmed to obey John, he ignores his commands to stay and proceeds with his self-sacrifice. Yet he needs Sarah's assistance; like Manfred, he cannot "self-terminate," and like Eric Draven, he needs the assistance of his companions. Our last view of the Terminator is a determined and very human thumbs-up as he sinks into a vat of boiling, liquid steel.

The director's cut of the film included a scene that more explicitly deals with the Terminator's developing humanity. The Terminator, Sarah, and John are taking shelter in a service station garage for a night. Sarah coldly declares, "If you can't pass for human, you're not much good to us." It is not the threat of the T-1000 that she must be considering here; the Terminator's appearance is irrelevant, as the T-1000 already knows what to look for. Instead, she is reflecting on the threat posed by institutional power—police forces and the judicial system that incarcerated her in a mental hospital. Not only must he "pass for human" in appearance, but he must act human as well, not simply for the benefit of John and Sarah's cause but to increase his appeal to the audience. John asks, "Can you learn stuff that you haven't been programmed with? So you can be, you know, more human and not such a dork all the time?" The Terminator answers "My CPU is a neural-net processor, a learning computer." That portion of the scene appeared in the theatrical release. But the director's cut includes the information that "Skynet presets the switch to read-only when we're sent out alone," and Sarah remarks, "Doesn't want you to do too much thinking, huh?" Here Skynet is presented as a force not only oppressive to humans but to its own creations, standing in the way of the Terminator's personal development. The Terminator coaches his human companions on how to reset the switch. Sarah, not trusting the Terminator after her prior experiences, wants to smash the CPU, leaving the Terminator shut down. She insists on referring to the Terminator as "it," while John prefers "him." She reluctantly agrees to replace the reset CPU at John's insistence, and the Terminator awakes. His first lesson in becoming more human occurs (a scene in the theatrical release as well) when he smashes a car window and begins to hot wire the car. John reveals the keys resting on the visor and teases, "Are we learning yet?"

Ultimately, it is the Terminator who must provide leadership to the group. He figures out Sarah's plan to eliminate Miles Dyson (Joe Morton), the inventor of the chip that would lead to the development of the Skynet computer; he explains the nuclear war and its aftermath to Dyson; and he leads the assault on the Cyberdyne plant as well as the escape from the police. By the end of the film, he has developed sufficient concern for human life that he willingly sacrifices himself to prevent his CPU from being used by a future developer (as Dyson had used the chip from the first Terminator). The Terminator, designed as a tool by the ultimate in impersonal authority—Skynet—certainly has the potential to be misused as a tool of authoritarian oppression again. Of course the moral tone of the concluding voiceover is a little absurd. Sarah intones, "If a machine, a Terminator, can learn the value of human life, maybe we can too." I don't believe most viewers attend Schwarzenegger films to hear a sermon on the value of human life. Cameron has given his audience "Arnold remade in the mold of a kinder, gentler America—no murderer, now, just a maimer" (Goldberg 195). Cameron has appealed to our delight in cinematic violence throughout the film (although in a stylized, cartoonish fashion, much less gory than another Schwarzenegger vehicle, *Total Recall* [1990]), and has done so with a tongue-in-cheek humor typical of action films. To append a concluding moral, as at the end of a children's fable, seems to take away with one hand what he gives us with the other. Larson observes, "It is no mystery that we are witnessing the cynical populism of Hollywood: presenting Arnold Jr. as a champion of individualism set against the extension of precisely those global forces which could *afford* to create *T2*" (66). And, as in the *Crow* films, "we are also offered the moral satisfaction of demonizing precisely that cycle of consumerism (sequelization) in which we are caught" (67).

Up until the conclusion, the film has been a knowing and self-conscious piece of packaged rebellion. The Terminator's attire, motorcycle, elaborate (and *big*) weapons, and deadpan demeanor are all clichés of the genre that are gaven a new life in their very self-consciousness. To suggest, as the voiceover does, that the Terminator is our guide and moral leader into a new and nonviolent future is absurd. But Rollin suggests,

> Popular culture heroes are *gestalts* of the popular mind, symbolic figures whose totality is greater than the sum of their parts. Though they are often death-dealers themselves and defined and deified amidst death, they are ultimately life-affirming. Life is what they are out to preserve, even at the risk of their own lives. And their victories over death, either through their survival or their transfiguration, are our intimations of immortality. (44)

And Cameron is also aware of the appeal of a charismatic and powerful guide who ruthlessly and efficiently solves problems and dispenses with obstacles. When Dyson's entry code no longer works on the Cyberdyne lab's door, the Terminator raises his weapon, saying drily, "Let me try mine." He assures the others that he can "take care of the police," and when John worries that he might kill, he grins, saying "Trust me." We can trust the Terminator to solve our problems because he both masters and embodies the technology wielded by institutional power: "By placing technology inside the body of this father who thus 'measures up,' *T2* grapples with the dangerous desire to pull abstract patriarchal power from its pan-institutional existence and place it inside a familiar person" (Harvey 33). And Larson argues that the *Terminator* films "not only replicate . . . dependence upon the status quo of corporate capitalism but present the loss of popular control of political institutions as itself desirable" by "endear[ing] us to the cyborg" (64). The notion of *trusting* such a reliably competent and superhumanly powerful guide is tempting; that is why the Terminator, like his western counterparts and the heroes of the *Crow* films, must take his leave. Like the Stranger, the Terminator has the potential to commit Heathcliff's sin—oppressively wielding the very institutional power he originally rebelled against. Harvey argues that

> *T2* exemplifies the distinctively U.S. sense that power should originate within the individual self, and it attempts to disavow any recognition that paternal power flows from patriarchal institutions. But this attempt to disengage paternity from patriarchy, summoning it to rise from patriarchy's ashes, is from the start rife with problems. (36–37)

She continues,

> Thus, the rebel Terminator is by implication divorced from the mainstream-standard U.S. family, here figured as hypocritical and emasculating, but the kind of paternity he eventually adopts is endowed with its sentimental weight precisely by that family. He's a tough guy, but he does trade his Harley for a family car. (37)

The problem, as Harvey convincingly characterizes it, is that

> *T2* may go out of its way to figure legitimate institutions as impotent, but it also, unwittingly, reinscribes their power. *T2*'s audiences are encouraged to desire precisely that which is here fatally threatening, a strong paternity whose strength derives from the only source of power *T2* can imagine: organized patriarchy. (37)

The viewers' desire to rebel against oppressive institutional authority and corporate rapacity must be contained within the parameters of the film; they must leave the theater with a satisfied sense that the problems are all solved or are about to be—hence Sarah's reassuring voiceover.

Of course, Byronic heroes in popular films are not limited to the examples discussed in this chapter. From Robocop to Dirty Harry to Martin Riggs of the *Lethal Weapon* films, heroes with the Byronic traits of a self-declared autonomy and an assertion of the individual over law and custom abound. But it is not only action heroes who embody Byronic traits. Eric Draven's Goth rock persona and his romantic grief over his lost lover play on an image cultivated by certain real-life performers, particularly musicians.[5] In fact rock stars such as Kurt Cobain, Morrissey (formerly of the Smiths), and Trent Reznor of Nine Inch Nails appeal to fans partially because they create the image of wounded, sensitive souls battered by an uncaring world. Cobain's untimely death, in particular, seemed to embody a certain Romantic sensibility: a restless discontent despite tremendous success, a persistent melancholia, an all-consuming self-destructiveness, and a monolithic self-absorption. That type of the Byronic hero, the moody, melancholy, self-absorbed, and self-tormented individual, is the subject of the next chapter. It is entirely fitting that Anne Rice's vampire Lestat becomes a rock star and Neil Gaiman's Dream dresses like one.

Fig. 1. Brandon Lee as Eric Draven in *The Crow* (© 1994 by Miramax/ Dimension Films)

Fig. 2. Dream from *The Sandman: Brief Lives* (Sandman no. 42; © 1992 DC Comics; all rights reserved; used with permission)

Fig. 3. Portrait of George Gordon, Lord Byron, by Thomas Phillips, 1814

(John Murray)

Fig. 4. John de Lancie as Q
in *Star Trek: The Next
Generation*

Fig. 5. Arnold
Schwarzenegger as the
Terminator in *Terminator 2:
Judgment Day*

Fig. 6. Linda Hamilton as Sarah Connor in *Terminator 2: Judgment Day*

Fig. 7. David Boreanaz as Angel from the eponymous television series

3

"I Just Want Something I Can Never Have"
Angst, Egoism, and Immortality

A Romantic desires what is unattainable. Should that desire become attained, it becomes, by definition, no longer desirable. This situation provides the Romantic with an infinite capacity for self-pity, lamenting both the unattainability of his or her desires *and* the undesirability of his or her goals, once attained. In "To a Skylark," Percy Shelley envies the "unbodied joy" (line 15) that is the skylark, whose poetry far surpasses any human creation:

> Better than all measures
>   Of delightful sound,
> Better than all treasures
>   That in books are found,
> Thy skill to poet were, thou scorner of the ground!
>
> (96–100)

If the poet could learn "half the gladness" of the skylark (101), he would create such "harmonious madness" that his intended audience would be compelled to listen, just as he is compelled to listen to the skylark. His goal to create perfect poetry is an impossible one, however. Shelley tells us, in "A Defence of Poetry," that "when composition begins, inspiration is already on the decline, and the most glorious poetry that has ever been communicated to the world is probably a feeble shadow of the original conception of the poet" (504). Mary Wollstonecraft Shelley astutely analyzes the desire for the ultimate in unattainability—Godhood—in *Frankenstein*. Victor Frankenstein not only wishes to create new life, without the contribution of a woman, but hopes also to conquer death, "to renew life where death had apparently devoted the body to corruption" (83). When Frankenstein succeeds in his original goal of creating life, he is horrified by the flaws and imperfections of his creation: "Now that I had finished, the beauty of the dream vanished, and breathless horror and disgust filled my heart" (86). His creation is but a "feeble shadow" of his original conception.

The Romantic desires to soar beyond earthly and fleshly constraints, to attain perfect love, to write perfect poetry, and to remain in an unlimited flight of the imagination. Keats joins with the nightingale, escaping the limitations of an existence defined by "the weariness, the fever, and the fret" (23), but the flight cannot last, and he must be reluctantly returned to his "sole self" (72). He complains, "the fancy cannot cheat so well / As she is fam'd to do, deceiving elf" (73–74). It is not that the fancy cheats which bothers him; it is that she is not very good at it. He must return to reality. For Keats, as for Byron and Shelley, the quest to transcend the limitations of the human condition is ultimately a death wish. Keats is "half in love with easeful Death" (52), but he knows that death will not bring him what he desires: "Still wouldst thou sing, and I have ears in vain— / To thy high requiem become a sod" (59–60). Keats knows that his longing is an unavoidable condition—attainable desires quickly lose their luster. In *Lamia,* the lovers live in an apparent paradise, a luxurious house created by Lamia's magic. They do not need to exert themselves for any purpose but loving each other (they rest "with eyelids closed, / Saving a tythe which love still open kept, / That they might see each other while they almost slept" (2.23–25), yet the narrator notes, "For all this came a ruin" (2.16). The lovers begin to quarrel, if only to introduce some novelty into their relationship, which has begun to bore them. Lycius "took delight / Luxurious in her sorrows, soft and new" (2.73–74), and Lamia "lov'd the tyranny" (2.81). Even perfect love in a perfect environment cannot suffice to sate Romantic desire, which flags as soon as it is achieved.

Byron's poetry also evokes unlimited desire. Manfred despairs at being "half-dust, half-deity" (1.2.40), wishing instead that he could shed his human limitations to become "a bodiless enjoyment" (1.2.55). Byron's Childe Harold, "the wandering outlaw of his own dark mind" (3.3), lives to create, "and in creating live / A being more intense" (6). Yet this ability to create is limited by the gravity pull of mortal flesh:

> Like the Chaldean he could watch the stars,
> Till he had peopled them with beings bright
> As their own beams; and earth, and earth-born jars,
> And human frailties, were forgotten quite.
> Could he have kept his spirit to that flight
> He had been happy; but this clay will sink
> Its spark immortal, envying it the light
> To which it mounts, as if to break the link
> That keeps us from yon heaven which woos us to its brink.
>
> (3.14)

His imagination allows him to forget "human frailties," and in such a state "he had been happy" if not for the clay which must "sink / Its spark immortal." The ability to people the stars "with beings bright / As their own beams" does not suffice to satisfy Childe Harold's desire, which must be of infinite proportion to be worthwhile. Ultimately, he desires to escape the limitations of his condition as a human being, to be free of the constraints of clay:

> And when at length the mind shall be all free
> From what it hates in this degraded form,
> Reft of its carnal life, save what shall be
> Existent happier in the fly and worm,—
> When elements to elements conform,
> And dust is as it should be, shall I not
> Feel all I see, less dazzling, but more warm?
> The bodiless thought? the Spirit of each spot?
> Of which, even now, I share at times the immortal lot?
>
> (3.74)

He anticipates a time when the bodiless mind shall be free "from what it hates in this degraded form," longing for a bodily death that would allow an immortality of spirit. In this passage, the speaker's body is better suited to be food for "the fly and worm," but it prevents the unlimited apprehension of the bodiless realm of pure thought and spirit that he desires. He shares "at times the immortal lot" of pure spirit, but must return to his body's "carnal life."

It is not surprising that, in popular fiction, vampires embody Byronic desire. They undergo a bodily death, emerging as creatures that, though not bodiless, have achieved immortality, along with a superhuman strength and enhanced perceptions. This association is made explicit in Tom Holland's *Lord of the Dead,* a novel which posits that Byron became a vampire on his visit to Greece and Albania. Vampires also embody the perpetual questioning and despair of the Byronic hero. In *Childe Harold,* Byron tells us, "My springs of life were poisoned" (3.7). Harold is weary, jaded, and disillusioned: "He of the breast which fain no more would feel / Wrung with the wounds which kill not, but ne'er heal" (3.8). He can no longer partake of "life's enchanted cup" because

> His had been quaffed too quickly, and he found
> The dregs were wormwood; but he filled again
> And from a purer fount, on holier ground,
> And deemed its spring perpetual; but in vain!
> Still round him clung invisible a chain
> Which galled forever, fettering though unseen,
> And heavy though it clanked not, worn with pain,
> Which pined although it spoke not, and grew keen,
> Entering with every step he took through many a scene.
>
> (3.9)

The Romantic egoist cannot find a cure for his perpetual angst. Childe Harold tries refilling life's cup from "a purer fount . . . but in vain"; he is perpetually weighed down by his despair and thwarted hopes. Life, for the Romantic, is a perpetual quest to transcend and escape the limitations that make up its essence:

> Our life is a false nature, 't is not in
> The harmony of things,—this hard decree,
> This uneradicable taint of sin,
> This boundless upas, this all-blasting tree
> Whose root is earth, whose leaves and branches be
> The skies which rain their plagues on men like dew—

Disease, death, bondage—all the woes we see—
And worse, the woes we see not—which throb through
The immedicable soul, with heart-aches ever new.

(4.126)

Caught between the earth and the poisonous skies, men are plagued by "disease, death, bondage." Byron wishes to escape, "spurning the clay-cold bounds which round our being cling" (3.73), but the escape may not be all it's cracked up to be either. The only possible escape is death, and the outcome is uncertain: "we die you know—and then— / What then? I do not know, no more do you" (*Don Juan* 1.133–34). Immortality may well turn out to have its own sorrows and terrors; even immortality cannot suffice to quench Romantic desire.

This chapter examines two types of the self-pitying Romantic egoist: the vampires Louis and Lestat of Anne Rice's series The Vampire Chronicles and the immortal Lord Morpheus, or Dream, of Neil Gaiman's *Sandman* graphic novels. Such heroes have certain characteristics in common with the more action-oriented heroes of the previous chapter. They define themselves by their autonomy, and they exhibit superhuman powers. But the difference lies in that they *do* less and *suffer* more. They are interested not in righting the wrongs of the world but in contemplating themselves. They embody the self-centeredness and melancholy of the Romantic hero, continually made aware of the discrepancy between their aspirations and reality. They fear death and long to embrace it, learning that immortality contains the same miseries and disillusionment as mortal life does, only without surcease.

Anne Rice consciously makes use of Byronic themes, explicitly acknowledging her debt to the Romantic period, or as Jennifer Smith argues, "Rice is a twentieth-century Romantic writer" (9). She understands the continuing appeal of the Byronic hero for a popular audience. Lestat even describes Magnus's tower, his first home as a vampire, as "a dark and dreary place fit for all the Byronic horrors of this strange age" (*Vampire Lestat* [henceforth *VL*] 503). The vampires themselves are "Byronic horrors," yet they are irresistibly attractive at the same time to Rice's large reading audience. She evokes the Romantic period as the very embodiment of the psychological and spiritual state she wants to embody. The vampire Louis, in a typically self-pitying mode, protests, "Don't you see?

I'm not the spirit of any age. I'm at odds with everything and always have been! I have never belonged anywhere with anyone at any time!" Amused, the older vampire Armand counters, "This is the very spirit of your age. Don't you see that? Everyone else feels as you feel. Your fall from grace and faith has been the fall of the century" (*Interview with the Vampire* [henceforth *IWTV*] 286). Louis describes his reaction as "stunned." Caught up in his self-pity and self-proclaimed alienation, he doesn't realize that he is, in fact, the spirit of his age, the nineteenth century. The readers seem to find Louis' angst and alienation as fascinating as Armand does. Rice realizes that the spirit of the Romantic period still speaks volumes to late-twentieth-century readers. As Bette B. Roberts indicates, "in confirming the awful truths of his own existence, Louis clearly is not just a spirit who represents Armand's nineteenth century but a voice for late twentieth-century readers as well" (31).

Both Louis and Lestat partake of the melancholy, brooding, introspective nature of the Byronic hero; both suffer a burden of "guilt and self-loathing" (*VL* 498) that throws its shadow over their immortality. In the same manner that it does for Byron's heroes or Mary Shelley's Victor Frankenstein, this guilt becomes more a catalyst for narcissistic self-examination than a concern for others. Their guilt is significant in how it affects *them,* not as a remorse for harm done to others. Louis, more so than Lestat, wallows in guilt and introspection. As the author says of *Interview,* "it's a book about disappointment, disillusion, and bitterness. Every single question that comes up has a disappointing answer. Everything Louis looks for, everywhere he goes, doors close, or darkness is revealed to be at the core, or death results, or things burn down" (Riley 23). He introduces himself to his interviewer as beset with guilt for the suicide of his brother, insisting "I felt that I'd killed him" (*IWTV* 10). Similarly, Manfred feels responsible for the death of Astarte, although he did not perform the deed himself, and Frankenstein condemns himself for the death of Justine, saying, "I listened to this discourse with the greatest agony. I, not in deed, but in effect, was the true murderer" (122). Frankenstein's own agony is of more interest to him than Justine's suffering. Louis, in a similar fashion, broods over this guilt, unable to take action to alleviate it: "I lived like a man who wanted to die but who had no courage to do it himself" (*IWTV* 11). Louis' feelings of guilt extend to his career as a vampire; he cannot reconcile himself to the deaths he causes. Lestat grows impatient with Louis' self-pity, exclaiming, "You whining coward of a vampire who prowls the night killing alley cats and rats" (*IWTV* 51). Louis does whine throughout Rice's novel, yet the immense popularity of the book suggests that readers are drawn to the idea of an emotional and sensitive Shelleyan vampire.

In the film version of *Interview*, Louis (Brad Pitt) is provided with a recently deceased wife and child, who died in childbirth, and explains, "I would have been happy to join them. I couldn't bear the pain of their loss." He says, "Most of all I longed for death. I know that now. I invited it. A release from the pain of living." Lestat (Tom Cruise) frames his temptation to Louis in almost irresistible terms:

> I've come to answer your prayers. Life has no meaning any more, does it? The wine has no *taste*. The food sickens you, and there seems no reason for any of it, does there? But what if I could give it back to you? Pluck out the pain, and give you another life. One you could never imagine. And it would be for all time, and sickness, and death could never touch you again.

The film (with a screenplay written by Rice herself) provides Louis with a more universally identifiable sorrow than his guilt over the death of his brother, while, not coincidentally, heterosexualizing him in the process, as one analysis points out (Reep, Ceccio, and Francis 126–27). The grief over the loss of a spouse or child is something any viewer can readily imagine if he or she has not experienced it. Who hasn't had her moments of feeling that life has no meaning and the wine has no taste? Lestat offers Louis (and the viewer for a couple of hours) the possibility of an existence without emotional pain and without the ravages of sickness and death. When Louis tells the interviewer (Christian Slater) that he doesn't mind his cigarettes, the interviewer bokes, "It's not like you're going to die from cancer or anything, is it?" What Lestat doesn't tell Louis, of course, is that the vampires are as miserable as the mortals they supposedly transcend.

Louis is introspective, continually questioning his state: "Am I damned? Am I from the devil? Is my very nature that of a devil?" (*IWTV* 73). He continues, "What have I become in becoming a vampire? Where am I to go?" He cannot rely on conventional authority for answers. The institutions of his day, like the Abbot in *Manfred*, have no answers. He searches for knowledge, wanting "the answer to why under God this suffering was allowed to exist—why under God it was allowed to begin, and how under God it might be ended" (*IWTV* 168). Like Byron's heroes, he can achieve momentary peace but knows it is fleeting. Manfred attains a moment of "calm" and "inexplicable stillness" (3.1.6–7) but knows "it will not last" (3.1.14). Louis describes a similar experience:

> Over the long, low row of pointed roofs were the massive shapes of oak trees in the dark, great swaying forms of myriad sounds under the low-hung stars. The pain for the moment was gone; the confusion was gone. I closed my eyes and heard the wind and the sound of water flowing softly, swiftly in the river. It was enough, for one moment. And I knew that it would not endure, that it would fly away from me like something torn out of my arms, and I would fly after it, more desperately lonely than any creature under God, to get it back. (*IWTV* 88)

Louis describes a continual psychic pain, one that is alleviated only for the briefest of moments. He suffers "the great awful sadness of all the things I'd ever lost or loved or known" (*IWTV* 331) and knows "that happiness is not what I will ever know, or will ever deserve to know" (203). Like the speaker of Keats's "Ode to a Nightingale," he will be flung back on his "sole self" and emerge longing to return to this state of peace and communion with the world outside him.

Although Lestat does not flaunt his suffering in the same fashion as Louis, he, too, has his guilts and terrors and vulnerabilities. While still a human, he develops a "malady of mortality" (*VL* 69) and a horror at the apparent lack of ultimate meaning. He is horrified by the realization that "even when we die we probably don't find out the answer as to why we were ever alive." He laments, "We'll never know, and all this meaninglessness will just go on and on and on" (*VL* 55), demanding, "How do you live, how do you go on breathing and moving and doing things when you know there is no explanation?" (*VL* 57). It is a terror that never leaves him, as he confides to the reader, "And let me tell you a little secret. It *never did pass, really*" (58). Just as Lestat grows impatient with Louis' self-pity, Lestat's friend Nicholas tires of Lestat's Shelleyan "talk of the eternal, the immutable, the unknowable" (*VL* 65). Lestat suffers loneliness, "bitterness at being shut out of life, . . . bitterness that I'm evil, that I don't deserve to be loved and yet I need love hungrily" (*VL* 355) and is acutely aware of his own isolation: "I was alone among humans, and my writing to Marius couldn't keep me from knowing my own monstrosity" (*VL* 331). Rice's vampires allow her readers a vicarious experience of immortality and superhuman strength, but at the same time, they evoke the reader's sympathy with their sufferings and longings.

Rice's vampires are particularly human in their constant search for a meanang extrinsic to themselves, and they partake of a Byronically nihilistic despair that no such meaning is possible. As Waxman argues, "like Stoker, Shelley, Maturin, and other Romantic writers, Anne Rice embraces the Gothic, and in particular the vampire, as a vehicle for philosophic speculation" (82). Louis hopes that the older vampire, Armand, will have answers for him, some knowledge of God or the devil or the reason for the vampires' existence. When he learns that Armand has no such answers, he reflects, "It was as I'd always feared, and it was as lonely, it was as totally without hope. Things would go on as they had before, on and on. My search was over" (*IWTV* 238). He must face "the most fantastical truth of all: that there is no meaning to any of this!" (239). Louis explains, "And so I sought for other vampires, for God, for the devil, for a hundred things under a hundred names. And it was all the same, all evil. And all wrong. Because no one could in any guise convince me of what I myself knew to be true, that I was damned in my own mind and soul" (*IWTV* 337). Louis' search for significance and purpose reveals to him that his significance and purpose begin and end in himself. In the film of *Interview*, Louis accuses Lestat, "You condemned me to hell," but Lestat retorts, "I don't know any hell." Louis later tells the interviewer, "But there *was* a hell. And no matter where we moved to, I was in it." He is faced with the painful autonomy of the Byronic hero, the realization that

> The mind which is immortal makes itself
> Requital for its good or evil thoughts,
> Is its own origin of ill and end,
> And its own place and time.
>
> (*Manfred* 3.4.389–92)

To Louis it doesn't matter whether he finds God or the devil—he wants any external validation of the significance of his experiences. Even a force that punishes his crimes would allow him the comfort of belief. But as Manfred insists, "there is no future pang / Can deal that justice on the self-condemn'd / He deals on his own soul" (3.1.76–78). The mind of the vampire, like the mind of the Byronic hero, is sufficient unto itself. If

Louis is damned, it is because he has damned himself, and his angst-ridden questioning of the meaning of his existence strikes a chord in readers who find themselves in a similar position of lacking easy answers.

Lestat also searches for some kind of answer to the riddle of his purpose for existence, but he is, ultimately, "an immortal being who must find his own reasons to exist" (*VL* 380), because there are no reasons extrinsic to himself. Lestat sees himself "as a hungry, vicious creature, who did a very good job of existing without reasons, a powerful vampire who always took exactly what he wanted, no matter who said what" (380). As such, he provides a powerful vicarious experience for readers who *can't* always take exactly what they want. The vampires are appealing characters because they allow readers a vicarious experience of what they cannot have themselves *and,* at the same time, despite their power, they validate the readers' own longings for purpose and meaning in a confusing world.

The Romantics' longing for an unattainable transcendence of the limitations of a mortal existence often shapes itself as a death wish. Since they cannot conquer mortality, their only hope to transcend it is in death. Byron's Manfred attempts suicide; when thwarted, he achieves peace only when he learns he will die the next day. Rice's vampires are, by definition, fascinated with death. Suffering the pangs of immortality, they literally drink death at every opportunity. As Nina Auerbach argues, "They embody not fear of death, but fear of life: their power and their curse is their undying vitality" (5). Occasionally, they commit suicide, unable to achieve any other end to their sufferings. Lestat's creator Magnus, a Promethean rebel who stole the "Dark Gift" of vampirism from an unwitting vampire, deliberately burns himself to death after leaving his legacy to Lestat. Lestat explains that he has learned that "immortals find death seductive and ultimately irresistible, that they fail to conquer death or humanity in their minds" (*VL* 317). Louis' death wish forms a part of his mortal character—he admits that he succumbed to Lestat's temptation because of his "wish for self-destruction . . . [his] desire to be thoroughly damned" (*IWTV* 17). He is horrified by his first experience of killing and moans, "This is unbearable. I want to die. You have it in your power to kill me. Let me die" (*IWTV* 17). Echoing Keats's "Ode to a Nightingale" ("Now more than ever seems it rich to die"), Louis thinks, "It would be sweet to die. . . . Yes, die. I wanted to die before. Now I wish to die. I saw it with such sweet clarity, such dead calm" (*IWTV* 71).

The act of killing another becomes for the vampires a way to reenact their own bodily deaths and satisfy, temporarily, their own death wish:

> Killing is no ordinary act. . . . One doesn't simply glut oneself on blood. . . . It is the experience of the loss of that life through the blood, slowly. It is again and again the experience of that loss of my own life, which I experienced when I sucked the blood from Lestat's wrist and felt his heart pound with my heart. It is again and again a celebration of that experience: because for vampires that is the ultimate experience. (*IWTV* 29)

Killing is a way to relive the act of suicide repeatedly through the death of another. As Rice describes the act of draining a victim, a bond is formed between vampire and victim, and the vampire experiences his or her victim's death. Vampires have attained the ultimate in Romantic transcendence: immortality and the continual reenactment of suicide. Louis explains, "I knew peace only when I killed, only for that minute; and there was no question in my mind that the killing of anything less than a human being brought nothing but a vague longing" (*IWTV* 87). That minute of peace arises from the vampire's identification with his victim, from the longing to experience his own death. Lestat, in fact, is tempted to destroy Enkil and Akasha, the original vampires, because that act will destroy all vampires everywhere: "I understood the irresistible madness of trying to destroy them. Of going out, in a blaze of light with them that would take all our doomed species with it" (*VL* 467). Lestat contemplates the ultimate murder-suicide, one that would eradicate himself and his entire species.

The vampires' fascination with death arises from their ambivalence about their own immortality. As Kathryn McGinley points out, "For Byronic heroes . . . particularly the Ricean version, immortality can be simultaneously desirable and intolerable" (86). On the one hand, immortality is desirable because it allows them to transcend human limitations and human mortality—in Byron's words, that "the mind shall be all free / From what it hates in this degraded form / Reft of its carnal life" (*Childe Harold* 3.84). The purging of bodily wastes that Rice describes for newly fledged vampires represents this new freedom from the limitations of the "degraded" human body. Along with immortality, vampires acquire a superhuman strength and a certain psychic power over humans, and their abilities increase with age, rather than declining as humans' abilities do.

On the other hand, immortality has its horrors as well. As Louis complains, "but it wasn't that which made me weary. It was something else, something far worse. It was as if this night were only one of thousands of nights, world without end, night curving into night to make a great arching line of which I couldn't see the end, a night in which I roamed alone under cold mindless stars" (*IWTV* 68–69). Bette Roberts compares Rice's vampires to Tennyson's Tithonus, who, "caught in the meaninglessness of an eternal existence, sees himself as a 'grey shadow, once a man.' Instead of creatures to be destroyed, her weary vampires also complain of being consumed by 'cruel immortality' and run the risk of their own self-destruction" (23). For Louis and some of Rice's other vampires, immortality represents unending dull pain. It is a desire that, once attained, turns out to be a torment, what Lestat describes as "the vast untasted horror of my own immortality" (*VL* 276).

Rice explores the ramifications of immortality in practical terms. The four-hundred-year-old vampire Armand explains,

> How many vampires do you think have the stamina for immortality? They have the most dismal notions of immortality to begin with. For in becoming immortal they want all the forms of their life to be fixed as they are and incorruptible: carriages made in the same dependable fashion, clothing of the cut which suited their prime, men attired and speaking in the manner they have always understood and valued. When, in fact, all things change except the vampire himself, everything except the vampire is subject to constant corruption and distortion. . . . One evening a vampire rises and realizes what he has feared perhaps for decades, that he simply wants no more of life at any cost. That whatever style or fashion or shape of existence made immortality attractive to him has been swept off the face of the earth. And nothing remains to offer freedom from despair except the act of killing. And that vampire goes out to die. (*IWTV* 283)

The practical downside of immortality is that the world around one will continue to change while one remains unchanging oneself. In the inflexibility that Armand describes, the vampires reveal themselves to be psychologically very human. Their discomfgrt with change mirrors that of humans who find political and technological change bewildering. The disillusionment sets in quickly. Lestat reports, "And already at the age of thirty mortal years, I have some understanding as to why so many of our kind have wasted it, given it up" (*VL* 338). Like Louis, Lestat insists on "grieving for my lost mortality" (476).

Despite these warnings of the perils of immortality and its accompanying angst, Rice realizes just how powerful a temptation it represents. After hearing all the horrors of Louis' miserable life, including Armand's description of the dreariness of immortality, the boy reporter in *Interview* still wishes to receive the Dark Gift. And in a later novel, *The Tale of the Body Thief*, we learn that given the opportunity to regain mortal status, Lestat chooses immortality. The vampires are torn between the transcendence their condition offers them and their attraction to the simplicity of human life. In a similar fashion, in their erotic glamour and superhuman power, vampires are a very attractive fantasy for Rice's readers. A routine existence and the sensation of powerlessness in the face of institutional authority makes the vampires' transcendence of the fears and concerns of daily life very appealing. As Lestat describes it, "nothing would be ordinary now. Not joy or pain, or the simplest memory. All would possess this magnificent luster, even grief for the things that were forever lost" (*VL* 104). While Louis remains paralyzed with self-doubt, Lestat proves to be resourceful and adaptable in a way that would strike a chord with readers adapting to the continuous technological advances and complexities of their time. Lestat acquires a motorcycle and "a little Sony Walkman stereo in my pocket that fed Bach's Art of the Fugue through tiny earphones right into my head as I blazed along" (*VL* 6), finds a lawyer to procure him necessary identification, and effortlessly masters the instruments and equipment of a rock band. With his powers and his "preternatural and remorseless ambition," he can simply remake himself as a rock star.

Just as the viewers of the *Terminator* films enjoy the title character's casual violence and callousness, Rice's readers may envy the vampire's state of "detachment." On the one hand, their senses are heightened, providing them with more vivid experiences; but on the other hand, they have a detachment that provides them with a state of godlike indifference, like Stephen Dedalus's vision, in Joyce's *Portrait of the Artist as a Young Man*, of the godlike artist who "remains within or behind or beyond or above his handiwork, invisible, refined out of existence, indifferent, paring his fingernails" (215). As Louis describes the sensation,

> I saw my life as if I stood apart from it, the vanity, the self-serving, the constant fleeing from one petty annoyance after another, the lip service to God and the Virgin and a host of saints whose names filled my prayer books, none of whom made the slightest difference in a narrow, materialistic, and selfish existence. I saw my real gods . . . the gods of most men. Food, drink, and security in conformity. Cinders. (*IWTV* 14)

From the vampire's perspective, human life is petty and trivial, an endless procession of dealing with annoyances and bowing to authorities, all in the service of "a narrow, materialistic, and selfish existence." Readers could well envy the ability to walk away from the concerns of daily life. A similar desire motivates people to participate in elaborate role-playing games in which they take on a vampire persona.[1] The combination of detachment and heightened awareness is intoxicating for Louis. While Lestat accuses him of being "dead to [his] vampire nature," Louis responds,

> My vampire nature has been for me the greatest adventure of my life; all that went before it was confused, clouded; I went through mortal life like a blind man groping from solid object to solid object. It was only when I became a vampire that I respected for the first time all of life. I never saw a living, pulsing human being until I was a vampire. I never knew what life was until it ran out in a red gush over my lips, my hands! (*IWTV* 81–82)

Louis describes the paradox of the Byronic hero. On the one hand, he asserts his superiority to ordinary mortals who don't share his gifts of perception; but on the other hand, he develops a fuller appreciation for human life after he is no longer a part of it, has in fact, become a predator of it.

For Lestat, this transcendence of human nature takes on godlike dimensions. He asserts that vampires can "see death in all its beauty, life as it is only known on the very point of death." He adds, "You alone of all creatures can see death that way with impunity. You . . . alone . . . under the rising moon . . . can strike like the hand of God!" He goes on to explain that vampires are "predators. Whose all-seeing eyes were meant to give them detachment. The ability to see a human life in its entirety, not with any mawkish sorrow but with a thrilling satisfaction in being the end of that life, in having a hand in the divine plan" (*IWTV* 83). While

Louis is horrified by what he sees as Lestat's cruel toying with his victims, Lestat describes himself in terms of the godlike role of supreme judge: "I hunted almost exclusively among the gamblers, the thieves, and the killers, being more faithful to my unspoken vow to kill the evildoer than even I had hoped I would be" (*VL* 499). When he emerges from his underground hibernation in 1984, he kills "drug dealers," "pimps," and "murderers," resolving not to drink "innocent blood" (*VL* 11). Like the temporarily undead heroes of the *Crow* films, Lestat decides who should live and who should die. As a part in the "divine plan," he enforces his own brand of justice outside the law, which, to him, is utterly irrelevant. Always mercurial, however, Lestat periodically mocks his self-appointed role: "What a sublime idiocy that I had dragged that paltry morality with me, striking down the damned ones only—seeking to be saved in spite of it all? What had I thought I was, a righteous partner to the judges and executioners of Paris who strike down the poor for crimes that the rich commit every day?" (*VL* 135). Lestat realizes that he is not really motivated by any humanly identifiable morality, which is "paltry" and trite. Instead, he must acknowledge his own self-interest. The divine plan he participates in is an aesthetic one, and it is the beauty of the moment of death that he relishes. Like Victor Frankenstein, Lestat also asserts the power to create as well as to destroy. Planning to turn the dying five-year-old child Claudia into a vampire, Lestat argues,

> God kills, and so shall we; indiscriminately He takes the richest and the poorest, and so shall we; for no creatures under God are as we are, none so like Him as ourselves, dark angels not confined to the stinking limits of hell but wandering His earth and all its kingdoms. I want a child tonight. I am like a mother . . . I want a child! (*IWTV* 88–89)

With reference to this passage, Waxman notes, "By seeing evil as a concept defined according to one's perspective, by implicitly criticizing God's decision-making as random and indiscriminate, and hence by subverting the concept of a God who sanctions moral beliefs and conduct, Lestat is articulating existentialism's central tenet" (86). Lestat is, of course, justifying his own "random and indiscriminate" decision making and subjecting himself to his creations' condemnation of his actions. Like Victor Frankenstein, Lestat incurs the wrath of his creations for his irresponsibility. Louis and Claudia rebel against Lestat, and Claudia attempts to murder him. Claudia, in particular, hates her creator for thoughtlessly giving her "immortality in this hopeless guise, this helpless form!" (*IWTV* 262). Lestat's godlike powers allow him, like Frankenstein, to take actions without considering their consequences, and the tragic consequences of his arrogance and thoughtlessness result in Claudia's gruesome death by burning. In response to her murder, Louis also takes on the role of judge, jury, and executioner to punish Claudia's killers: "And they are the only deaths I have caused in my long life which are both exquisite and good" (*IWTV* 312). That particular scene in the film version of Rice's novel is one of the few where Brad Pitt's Louis is roused from his usual state of passive misery. He becomes a fury in motion, long hair flying as he sets the fires that will kill the theater vampires. He is animated by the same revenge motif that we see in western and action-adventure films; it is one of the few moments when Louis is shown as an actively heroic figure rather than the passive object or vehicle of others' intentions. Even the moping Louis has the means to obtain revenge on his enemies, and he provides the viewers with a satisfying vision of Byronic power.

Self-consciously aware of his glamorous appeal, Lestat boasts, "There is great romance in what I am!" (*VL* 229). Rice's readers seem to agree with him that "there was a grace in sleeping in the crypt. There was a romance to rising from the grave" (*VL* 337). Sleeping in coffins and rising from the grave, the vampires nightly conquer death. Lacking the fear of death, the vampires attain an autongmy humans can only fantasize abgut. Having no external authority to fear, they are self-sufficient unto themselves and have no need of a human moral code. As Armand tells Louis, "I am evil with infinite gradations and without guilt" (*IWTV* 285). For readers bound by the conventions and rules of ordinary human intercourse, to be evil "with infinite gradations and without guilt" may seem an attractive prospect, or as Armand (Antonio Banderas) says in the film, "We must be powerful, beautiful, and without regret." Rice dispenses with many of the superstitions attendant on earlier vampire stories, particularly Stoker's *Dracula*. Lestat proves that he can enter churches and touch crucifixes without being harmed, and he delights in the "proof that God had no power over me" (*VL* 103). Lestat craves a complete autonomy: "I hate those who make me feel fear, those who know things that I need to know, who have that power over me" (*VL* 249). As Lestat ages and his powers and knowledge increase, he can free himself from any dependence on the wisdom of older vampires; in fact, he must continually prove his autonomy by rebelling against such rules as vampires have agreed on for themselves.

In addition to self-sufficiency, immortality also provides the vampires with an immunity to political upheavals, which they regard with indifference: "As moral aesthetes, Rice's vampires are beautifully devoid of social consciousness, another major attraction for disaffected readers" (Auerbach 154). Lestat carelessly remarks of the impending French Revolution, "Talk in the shadows of intrigue. Who cares? Kingdoms rise and fall. Just don't burn the paintings in the Louvre, that's all" (*VL* 273). He is indifferent to matters of political equity and justice; again, aesthetics are all that matter. If the paintings in the Louvre survive, Lestat doesn't care how many heads roll or why. Yet his attachment to human artifacts reveals the flip side of the vampires' transcendence of human mortality and limitations. They cannot help missing their human nature and are often dismayed by the extent of their alienation from humans. As Lestat wistfully remarks, "I'll never know what it is like to be human in any way, shape, or form again" (*VL* 145). For the vampires, it takes the transcendence of the human condition to allow an appreciation of what one has lost. Louis thus attempts to teach Claudia "that our eternal life was useless to us if we did not see the beauty around us, the creation of mortals everywhere" (*IWTV* 100). While Lestat mocks Louis' love of humans, he too shares the appreciation of human beauty possible only with his heightened vampire senses:

> How to describe what humans look like to us! I've tried to describe it a little, when I spoke of Nicki's beauty the night before as a mixture of movement and color. But you can't imagine what it's like for us to look on living flesh. There are those billions of colors and tiny configurations of movement, yes, that make up a living creature on whom we concentrate. But the radiance mingles totally with the carnal scent. Beautiful, that's what any human being is to us, if we stop to consider it, even the old and diseased, the downtrodden that one doesn't really 'see' in the street. They are all like that, like flowers ever in the process of opening, butterflies ever unfolding out of the cocoon. (*VL* 133–34)

Of course Lestat's appreciation of human beauty is the appreciation of a predator; his use of the phrase "a living creature on whom we concentrate" has a sinister ring that reminds us *why* he concentrates on particular humans. Vampires are the ultimate objectifiers—the beauty of their victims enhances the experience of drinking their blood. Yet Lestat insists that his feeling for humans is not purely exploitive: "From the first nights when I held them close to me, I loved them. Drinking up their life, their death, I love them. Dear God, is that not the very essence of the Dark Gift?" (*VL* 231). Lestat's love for humans differentiates him from other vampires, even his mother, Gabrielle, who wishes to isolate herself from civilization entirely and dreams of destroying it, so that humans serve *only* as vampires' prey. She is contemptuous of Lestat's financial assistance to his human family and his filial devotion to his abusive father, but he insists "I need these things, I tell you. This is what life is to me!" (*VL* 332). He is attracted to Louis precisely because Louis was "the most beguilingly human fiend I have ever known" (*VL* 499). For Lestat, the ideal would be to "be both human and inhuman" at the same time (*VL* 232). It is as if Manfred had managed to supersede the condition of being "half dust, half deity" and realized that he missed the very qualities of which he was so eager to rid himself.

One aspect of the Romantic hero's quest for an unattainable ideal that loses its luster once attained involves the pursuit of romantic love. In a Romantic text, the loved one is frequently the hero's sister or is in a sisterly relation to him. The Romantic hero is a narcissist, capable of loving only a mirror of himself, yet unable to sustain such a love for long, unless his beloved conveniently dies, her permanent inaccessibility rendering her forever perfect. The very act of creating a new vampire as a companion literalizes the Romantic process of imagining a perfect lover, dramatized particularly in P. B. Shelley's *Alastor* and *Epipsychidion*. Lestat's first "fledgling" is his mother, Gabrielle, "flesh and blood and mother and lover and all things beneath the cruel pressure of my fingers and my lips, everything I had ever desired" (*VL* 157). It almost goes without saying that "Lestat's life story, beginning with 'his great and unshakeable love' for his mother, Gabrielle, is so 'Freudian' that one hardly needs to tease out the repressed content" (Doane and Hodges 428). He wishes a companion who will serve as his perfect mirror, lover, and mother all at once, "the one I had needed all of my life with all of my being. The only woman I had ever loved" (*VL* 168). During Lestat's mortal life as the youngest son of a declining French aristocratic family, his mother was the only family member who expressed any understanding of him or connection to him; when she is dying, making her a vampire seems to him the perfect solution. Gabrielle was a capricious mother, alternately lavishing her son with sympathy and withholding affection. In recreating her as a vampire, Lestat attempts to contain her power and form her in his own image, but his attempt fails, and Gabrielle asserts her independence and leaves him in a fashion that devastates Lestat perhaps more than her natural death would have done.

Lestat's creation, Louis, of course, also proves to be a disappointment. While they are both representations of the Byronic hero, they have very different world views. As McGinley suggests, "Lestat and Louis are polar opposites, each displaying different sides of the Byronic hero" (85). She categorizes Louis as the Hero of Sensibility and Lestat as the Noble Outlaw. Offering another perspective, Bette Roberts suggests, "Louis's counterpart is surely the Romantics' cast-out Cain and Lestat the modern Prometheus" (25). While Louis broods and mopes in Shelleyan fashion ("I fall upon the thorns of life, I bleed" indeed!), Lestat engages in reckless and defiant action. Roberts argues that

> both characters seek knowledge, but while Louis's quest is for moral significance and a way to endure despair when he discovers the amorality and insignificance of his immortal existence, Lestat challenges his fate. Louis is the long-suffering melancholic; Lestat is the supervampire rebel, the rule breaker with Dionysian energy and ebullience. (40)

Louis resents Lestat for not drawing his attention to the stages of his transformation from human to vampire "with reverence" (*IWTV* 22). Louis is continually offended by Lestat's irreverence, much as the young hero of Byron's *Don Juan* might be at the cynicism with which the narrator describes Juan's youthful romantic exploits. Of course, Lestat had his self-pitying stages and his "malady of mortality," but that was in a time before he knew Louis. Louis is still engaged in "his self-communion with his own high soul" like the young hero of *Don Juan* (1.91), but Lestat, like the narrator, has learned that "the sad truth which hovers o'er my desk / Turns what was once romantic to burlesque" (4.3). From Louis' perspective, Lestat takes "cataclysmic" experiences "for granted": "He felt nothing. He was the sow's ear out of which nothing fine could be made" (*IWTV* 31). From Lestat's perspective, Louis is whiny and immature, refusing to accept the reality of his situation, desperately romanticizing his experiences in the hope of lending them significance and meaning, much as Lestat himself did in his early days as a vampire. The cynical narrator of *Don Juan,* of course, is the young lover grown up. While Louis "plague[s] himself" with "longings sublime and aspirations high" (1.93), vowing to go through his existence "delicately and reverently" because "what I'd felt as a vampire was far too powerful to be wasted" (*IWTV* 32), Lestat learns to accept the lack of meaning in his existence. Claudia's death freezes Louis' character into immobility: "I never changed after that. . . . I was dead. And I was changeless" (*IWTV* 321). Lestat, by contrast, although he continues making mistakes, is infinitely resourceful and adaptable, emerging from an underground hibernation to become a rock star, possibly the most appropriate identity a vampire–Byronic hero can assume: "By turning the vampire into a rock star, Rice presents, therefore, an image of rebellion rather than despair in response to a 1980's existential milieu" (B. Roberts 43).

Like the creators of the film *The Crow,* Rice plays on the rebellious aspects of her outlaw hero to increase his popular appeal, for "the anti-establishment messages of rock music contribute to the vampire's freedom from conventional moralities and the power of this subversive appeal" (B. Roberts 52). Lestat is not only an outlaw to human society by virtue of being a vampire but is also a rebel among vampires, disregarding their rules and conventions. He conceives of his planned rock concert at the Cow Palace in San Francisco as "an unprecedented rebellion, a great and horrific challenge to my kind all over the world" (*VL* 14). He knows he will be an instant success as his rock band's "sinister and reckless star" (15). From Jim Morrison of the Doors in the 1960s to Trent Reznor of Nine Inch Nails in the 1990s, "sinister and reckless" rock stars have an irresistible audience appeal. Lestat's androgyny and queer associations make him an even more attractive singer for 1984, the setting of the beginning and end of the novel.[2] Rice's choice of rock star for Lestat's contemporary career is inspired, and she effectively capitalizes on her hero's multifarious rebel appeal. Thus, in performing in his concert and in rock videos and in publishing his autobiography, Lestat sets out to break the "law that all vampires hold sacred . . . that *you do not tell mortals about us*" (*VL* 16). Lestat defiantly announces, "Old rules didn't matter to me now, either. I wanted to break every one of them," and he instantly appeals to every reader who ever wanted to break all the rules but didn't have the will or the means. As Jennifer Smith points out, the vampires are "representatives of the power of the rule-breaker, the being that can flaunt all the rules of society and still flourish" (53). As a vampire, Lestat has the means to break rules in the most spectacular fashion possible.

Lestat portrays himself from the beginning of the novel as an outcast, the one who never fit into his family: "I'd been born restless—the dreamer, the angry one, the complainer" (*VL* 23). Smith, like other commentators on Rice's novels, notes "a possible reference to the homosexual's outcast status in our homophobic society" (35). The novelist herself explains, "I've always been fascinated by the vampire, the elegant yet evil Byronic figure. It's easy to say it's a metaphor for the outsider, the predator, anyone who feels freakish or monstrous or out of step but appears normal" (Beahm 135). Rice's vampires have an undeniable homoerotic appeal, and their status as Byronic outsiders and outcasts draws fans from a wide variety of persuasions. Rice constructs them in a way that speaks to the yearnings of a very large audience. As Smith notes,

> Since so many of us see ourselves as the powerless Other, hopelessly out of step with the world we live in, the popularity of Rice's vampires is easily explained. We read her vampires, and see not murderous blood-sucking immortals but sexually free, societally free, powerful beings who live life to the fullest. Lestat, the great vampire/rock star, is our metaphor for social anarchy and sexual freedom, the ultimate powerful Other. (53)

The power and alienation of the Byronic hero appeals precisely to those who feel alienated and power*less*. As Margaret L. Carter observes, "today, creators of fictional vampires often choose the Romantic path of identification with the 'alien' supernatural being rather than with the superstitious majority bent on excluding and destroying him or her" (28). Those of Rice's readers who feel constrained by authority figures and impersonal institutions can identify with and admire a hero who defies every authority and institution he faces.[3] Rice consciously plays on the outcast appeal of her characters, telling an interviewer,

> The Chronicles are about how all of us feel about being outsiders. How we feel that we're really outsiders in a world where everybody else understands something that we don't. It's about our horror of death. It's about how most of us would probably take that blood and be immortal, even if we had to kill. It's about being trapped in

the flesh when you have a mind that can soar. It's the human dilemma." (Rice, Interview 57)

Thus she includes Lestat's conflicts with his brutal and obtuse father and brothers; Lestat's desire to choose his own career independently of his father's wishes (first by studying in a monastery and later by joining a theater troupe) is a theme to which many readers can relate. He contrasts himself with Armand by saying, "I've been a rebel always. . . . You've been the slave of everything that has ever claimed you" (*VL* 308). Lestat defies every attempt to enslave him, from leaving home and his father's wishes to fighting the superstitious band of vampires in Paris, the Children of Darkness. In his usual flippant tone, he tells us, "After all, I had never been very good at obeying rules" (*VL* 320). As the author suggests, Lestat forms his own moral code: "I think the novels are about a refusal to be doomed. They're about assuming the guilt for killing, assuming the guilt for having all kinds of advantages that human beings don't have, and bearing that guilt, and refusing to behave as if one is doomed" (Riley 161). Lestat is represented as taking responsibility for his actions and refusing to give in, which makes him a more appealing hero than the despairing and passive Louis.

His mistakes, as well as his successes, arise from his perpetual defiance. He admits that the creation of Claudia was a disastrous error on his part, as well as a monumentally selfish act, and explains simply, "But why was it that for purely selfish reasons, I didn't listen to some of the advice given me? Why didn't I learn from any of them—Gabrielle, Armand, Marius? But then, I never have listened to anyone, really. Somehow or other, I never can" (*VL* 501). Lestat must be defined by his rebelliousness, even when it invites disaster. Invoking a prototypically Byronic trait, Lestat relates that "sheer will had shaped my experience more than any other human characteristic. And advice and predictions notwithstanding, I courted tragedy and disaster as I have always done" (*VL* 497). The novel serves as underpinning to set up Lestat's grand project of rebellion against his own kind—the rock concert. In the face of threatened punishments by other vampires, he says, "I realized that I possessed a new concept of loneliness, a new method of measuring a silence that stretched to the end of the world" (*VL* 520). The technology of the modern world has made the vampires' self-imposed rules even more stringent to avoid detection by mortals; yet even the vampires wish to imitate Lestat's style: "I loved being the outlaw, the one who had already broken every single law. And so they were imitating my book, were they?" (*VL* 530). Lestat's rebelliousness and glamour are irresistible even to the very vampires who feel threatened by him.

Lestat's planned rock concert has as much to do with a Byronic "craving for sensation" (McGinley 84) as it does with rebellion against vampire rules. What Laurence S. Lockridge says of Childe Harold can apply equally to Lestat: "Given a human being's continuous slow decay ending in ruin, a last-ditch imperative one can give oneself is to fight off entropy through sensation, desire, and act, not directed toward goals, but for the sake of life's intensity" (432). Lestat may not suffer from decay and entropy, but his projects are initiated for the sake of intensity, not goals, and perhaps his immortality gives him an even stronger imperative toward sensation. Lestat's "malady of mortality" and his understanding of why so many vampires choose to end their lives reveal to him that there are no ultimate answers. Immortality can be as terrifying as mortality, if not more so, because it allows the vampires to take everything for granted: "Heightening sensation to give ourselves the impression we exist is one way of avoiding the characterless state of being most of us occupy most of the time" (Lockridge 433). If this is true for humans, how much more so it must be for immortal beings. Lestat pursues sensation for its own sake, seeking out intense experience just to give some variety to his endless days: "Describing himself as someone who does not engage in moral battles, Lestat confronts the uncomfortable realities of vampirism and explores its mysteries to sharpen his own vampiric powers, enhance his reputation, and stir up some romantic excitement in an otherwise dull and predictable eternal life" (B. Roberts 43). He is not alone in this exploration. The vampires need "the impetus, the excitement. They feed upon it like blood" (*VL* 525). Louis learns that the killing of other vampires has to be expressly "forbidden under penalty of death" for the reason that it is "very exciting" (*IWTV* 256). The brief but intense moment of fulfillment and communion achieved in drinking a human's blood can only be magnified in the murder of another vampire. In the film, we see a similar lust for danger in Armand's playing with a candle flame and reacting with an erotic rush to one of the few things that could destroy him. Lestat plans to use his book, concerts, and rock videos to reveal himself because he "wanted mortals *to know* about us" (*VL* 17). Although he realizes they won't believe him, he imagines the possibilities if they do:

I mean what if they really believed it, really understood that this world still harbored the Old World demon thing, the vampire—oh, what a great and glorious war we might have then!

We would be known, and we would be hunted, and we would be fought in this glittering urban wilderness as no mythic monster has ever been fought by man before.

How could I not love it, the mere idea of it? How could it not be worth the greatest danger, the greatest and most ghastly defeat? Even at the moment of destruction, I would be alive as I have never been. (*VL* 17)

The last sentence is telling—to feel alive would be worth sacrificing his immortality, just for the sensation, a sensation lacking in his vampire existence. Lestat conceives of excitement in epic terms: a war between vampires and humans or a war among vampires themselves—"the one in which we'd all come together, or they would all come to fight me" (*VL* 17). It doesn't really matter, as long as it provides sensation: "Lestat understands that for him the essence of survival comes not from searching for the meaning of a vampiric existence but from discovering ways to feel intensely alive" (B. Roberts 56).

When the ancient vampire Marius comes to Lestat in a dream and accuses, "You act on impulse, you want to throw all the pieces in the air," Lestat shouts in return, "I want to affect things, to make something happen!" (*VL* 522). The actual deed is of no consequence; what matters is that it have an impact. The worst thing is contentment: "I think that to be this happy is to be miserable, to feel this much satisfaction is to burn" (*VL* 525), burning, of course, being the equivalent of death for a vampire. Lestat also admits to a very human "vanity of wanting to perform." Part of the excitement of his new career is "the eerie madness that had come over me when I saw myself on the television screen, saw my face on the album covers" (*VL* 528). For a creature whose existence depends on secrecy, Lestat finds his newfound fame a particularly delicious and forbidden thrill. He explains,

Louis, I mean for something and everything to happen. . . . I mean for all that we have been to change! What are we but leeches now— loathsome, secretive, without justification. The old romance is gone. So let us take on a new meaning. I crave the bright lights as I crave blood. I crave the divine visibility. I crave war. (*VL* 531)

Lestat and his maker, Rice, want to restore glamour and romance to vampirism, and between them, they have been very successful. In an age of AIDS and homophobia (*VL* was published in 1985), the vampires represent both the forbidden glamour of homoeroticism and the absolute taboo of sharing blood. Lestat's quest for "divine visibility" represents the quest of all outsiders to stand up and assert their presence boldly, a quest that draws readers to the book: "I will be the Vampire Lestat for all to see. A sqmbol, an outcast, a freak of nature—something loved, something despised, all those things. I tell you I can't give it up. I can't miss it. And quite frankly, I am not the least afraid" (*VL* 532). It is only afterward that he realizes "this little war of mine would put all those I loved in danger. What a fool I'd been to think I could draw the venom to myself" (*VL* 547). Rice can have it both ways for her readers. They can identify with Lestat's rebel outcast public assertion of self, but they can also identify with the dangers of public exposure. Lestat learns that there are consequences to his very public "coming out," just as he earlier learned there were consequences to his reckless creation of fledgling vampires. His impulsiveness is simultaneously a wellspring of destruction and the source of his appeal to readers. Like Napoleon, Lestat is "extreme in all things" (*Childe Harold* 3.36). The "fire / And motion of the soul" of the Byronic hero is "quenchless evermore" and "preys upon high adventure" (3.42).

Rice not only spurs a popular phenomenon in her creation of her Byronic vampires but also comments on the very phenomenon she creates. Even Louis' story, with all of its grief and self-pity, proves irresistible to the boy interviewer, who asks to be made a vampire himself, thus testifying "to the barrenness of his existence, which compels him to choose vampiric immortality over human life even after all that Louis has told him" (B. Roberts 32). As Ken Gelder observes, "the novel builds its own ideal reception—where the interviewer is thoroughly passified, standing as an image for the converted reader, the fan—into its structure" (110). The interviewer passionately explains why a vampire's existence would be preferable to ordinary human life:

> Don't you see how you made it sound? It was an adventure like I'll never know in my whole life! You talk about passion, you talk about longing! You talk about things that millions of us won't ever taste or come to understand. And then you tell me it ends like that. I tell

you . . . if you were to give me that power! The power to see and feel and live forever! (*IWTV* 339)

For the boy, an adventure filled with passion and longing is sufficient incentive to brave the griefs Louis describes. Louis is dismayed at the boy's request, saying "I have completely failed." As Jennifer Smith remarks, "this becomes Louis's last defeat. Not even when he tells all the horrors that have been his life can he destroy the lure of immortality" (21). The boy is insistent, declaring, "You don't know what human life is like!" (*IWTV* 340). Louis finds his vampire existence loathsome, but for the boy, human life is dull, lacking passion and adventure—hence the need for vicarious escape through fictions. The author's own comment is telling:

> He ends as a failure, angry that the boy's response is that he wants to be a vampire, and Louis does not seem to know, or take responsibility for, the fact that the reader's likely response is to want to be a vampire, too. He's definitely right when he says "I've failed." He's made it seem very glamorous and like a lot of fun, a lot better than ordinary life. (Qtd. in Riley 164)

It is Rice, more than any other vampire writer, who has made vampirism glamorous; she suggests that if offered the real thing, we might very well be inclined to take it. Doane and Hodges point out that "Rice's books . . . excite an appetite to consume them that is mirrored and elicited by her vampires, themselves in love with consumption as a way of achieving a radical self-sufficiency" (436). Like the boy interviewer, Rice's readers are irresistibly compelled to consume the novels, living off the fictional vampires the same way the vampires live off their victims, achieving a temporary feeling of power and completion. The boy's desire to become a vampire is Rice's own anticipation of the popularity of her novels. The one story will not suffice; The Vampire Chronicles now comprise an eight-book series, and Rice has embarked on a new series: New Tales of the Vampires, consisting of two books as of this writing.

In *The Vampire Lestat,* she self-consciously analyzes the phenomenon of the popularity of fictional vampires. Lestat describes the literary vampires of the nineteenth century as "feeding the insatiable appetite for 'gothic and fantastical tales'" (*VL* 500). Rice's readers similarly have such an appetite, and she creates characters who will feed it. Lestat explains, "We were the essence of that nineteenth-century conception—aristocratically aloof, unfailingly elegant, and invariably merciless" (*VL* 500). Rice's character Marius provides her analysis of the vampires' appeal:

> And in this world the vampire is only a Dark God. He is a Child of Darkness. He can't be anything else. And if he wields any lovely power upon the minds of men, it is only because the human imagination is a secret place of primitive memories and unconfessed desires. . . .
>
> Yet men love us when they come to know us. They love us even now. The Paris crowds love what they see on the stage of the Theatre of the Vampires. And those who have seen your like walk through the ballrooms of the world, the pale and deadly lord in the velvet cloak, have worshiped in their own way at your feet.
>
> They thrill at the possibility of immortality, at the possibility that a grand and beautiful being could be utterly evil, that he could feel and know all things yet choose willfully to feed his dark appetite. Maybe they wish they could be that lusciously evil creature. How simple it all seems. And it is the simplicity of it that they want.
>
> But give them the Dark Gift and only one in a multitude will not be as miserable as you are. (*VL* 465–66)

Marius expresses the very paradox of Romantic desire—desiring that which will make one miserable once attained. He explains that the vampires' power over men lies in the dark side of the human imagination, the side that wishes to fulfill all its impulses, no matter how destructive, without consequences. That is, of course, the key to the popularity of Rice's novels and Gothic themes in literature, film, and music. In the real world, such impulses must be condemned and disavowed. We cannot act on most of them, but the vampires can, and Marius explains why the "pale and deadly lord in the velvet cloak," the Byronic vampire, is such an appealing figure. It is both the vampires' immortality and their pure evil that the mortal desires, and Marius notes the "simplicity" of such an existence. Vampires have urges and fulfill those urges. Yet the vampire wannabes do not realize the paradox. If their desire for a vampire existence were attained, they would be miserable.

As readers of Rice's novels, we have the best of both worlds—we have the vicarious experience of the vampires' power to fulfill their impulses, but we don't have the miseries of immortality and meaninglessness that accompany that power. Rice thus includes performances within her novels, performances that reveal precisely why her novels are so popular. The nineteenth-century version of the commodification of vampires is her creation of the Theatre of the Vampires, where Parisian audiences attend performances in which actual vampires murder actual victims on stage, while the audience believes it is witnessing a very clever and convincing illusion. The audience's desire for a Gothic spectacle provides the vampires with the safest cover possible—open acknowledgment of their existence. The theater vampire Eleni recounts, "The crowd positively roars. I tell you we could feast on mortal victims on stage and the Parisians, thinking it all the most novel illusion, would only cheer" (*VL* 341). By the time Louis and Claudia arrive in Paris, that is precisely what happens. Lestat's rock performances are simply the contemporary version of the stylized nineteenth-century stage on which the vampires perform. He tells us that his "first album has sold 4 million copies" and his videos appear on MTV (*VL* 3). Like the theater vampires, he proclaims his existence on stage, giving a thrill to a rock audience who become instantly infatuated with his energy and glamour. As Lestat notes, it doesn't matter whether the rock singers "proclaim themselves angels or devils"—the audience will cheer either way (*VL* 5). He finds rock music itself to be "vampiric" with a supernatural sound (*VL* 6)—it is thus the ideal medium for him to express his Byronically grandiose self-image. In a typical rock concert, the singer's image is projected many times larger than life on giant screens, so that attendees at a large venue can actually see what is happening on stage. It is the perfect forum for Lestat and his overwhelming ego. And being a rock star gives him a chance to repudiate evil through his art—"in the roaring chants of the rock stars who dramatize the battles against evil that each mortal fights within himself" (*VL* 10).

Lestat shares with us a typical fan letter, asking him, "Please send us two tickets. We will be your victims. You can drink our blood" (*VL* 522). In his audience Lestat sees "pale mortal throats bared, boys and girls shoving their collars down and stretching their necks. And they were gesturing to me to come and take them" (*VL* 538). The image of the vampire is so seductive that even to serve as his victims has a glamorous appeal—the fans don't really expect Lestat to drain them, but they do wish they could be invited onstage to play the role. The fans at the concert dress in vampire clothes as well. Like the patrons at the Theatre of the Vampires, they want to participate in the larger-than-life theatricality of the vampire existence, a theatricality Lestat exploits to the fullest in consciously staged gestures: "Oh, this is too divine. What mortal could withstand this indulgence, this worship? I clasped the ends of my black cloak, which was the signal. I shook out my hair to its fullest. And these gestures sent a current of renewed screaming to the very back of the hall" (*VL* 536). The outlaw vampire becomes an irresistible focal point for the young rock fans' own feelings of alienation. Ironically, of course, their participation in the mass ritual of a rock concert confirms their insider status in a group composed of outsiders—the vampires and those who identify with them. Lestat demands of his audience, "HOW MANY OF YOU WOULD BE VAMPIRES?" (*VL* 536), sending the crowd into a frenzy as fans try to rush the stage. Of course, it is all an elaborately staged performance, the audience believes. It was "nothing but art! No one would be hurt. It was safe, this splendid hysteria" (*VL* 538). Rice's vampires, of course, also provide a safe experience of the dark side for her readers. Lestat's fans do not believe any of it is real: "When I screamed, they thought it was the sound system. When I leapt, they thought it was a trick. And why not, when magic was blaring at them from all sides and they could forsake our flesh and blood for the great glowing giants on the screens above us?" (*VL* 538). Even the live vampire on stage cannot compete with his projected image on-screen.

Lestat's popularity and his vampire-clad imitators in the crowd point to an inevitable consequence of his outlaw appeal—the institutionalization of outlawry. Rice presents several examples comparable to the Devil's Night greeting cards that so incense Top Dollar in *The Crow*. Even the rebels and outsiders cannot resist the comfort of rules and rituals and conventions, and the vampires begin to become as regulated as the human society they have supposedly transcended. We see the first example of this in Louis and Claudia's encounter with the Theatre des Vampires. Even the look is institutionalized. The female vampires have all dyed their hair black, and they suggest that Claudia should do the same. Louis remarks, "The realization was coming to me that I found them dull in some awful way" (*IWTV* 245). He is offended that they have deromanticized vampirism by making it dull, "this unnatural group who had made of immortality a conformist's club" (*IWTV* 246), or as he says a few pages later, "a club of fads and cheap conformity" (253). They are like teenagers who proclaim their uniqueness and rebellion by wearing the same

T-shirt and ufconventional hairstyle as all their friends do, thereby turning unconvention and rebellion into a new form of group identity and conformity.

To be a vampire is not rebellion enough—Lestat must define himself as different by violating the rules of vampires themselves. In *The Vampire Lestat,* we learn of the Children of Darkness who are entirely bound by rules and conventional religious beliefs:

> And on these were imposed the Rules of Darkness. To live among the dead, for we are dead things, returning always to one's grave or one very nearly like it. To shun the places of light, luring victims away from the company of others to suffer death in unholy and haunted places. And to honor forever the power of God, the crucifix about the neck, the Sacraments. And never never to enter the House of God, lest he strike you powerless, casting you into hell, ending your reign on earth in blazing torment. (*VL* 225)

Lestat learns that these rules are utterly arbitrary. His creator, Magnus, had crucifixes in his collection of jewelry, and Lestat enters a church, even hiding under the altar, with no ill effects. The Children of Darkness have made of vampirism an institution, and they are offended by Lestat because he doesn't follow the rules. They live by elaborate regulations and rituals, all of which contain and delimit their expression of their vampire nature, providing a sense of safety, what Armand describes as "our Eden" and "our faith and our purpose" (*VL* 507). They exist "by the will of God, to make mortals suffer for his Divine Glory," and they accuse Lestat of blasphemy. Promethean rebel that he is, he brings them enlightenment: "The whole philosophy—and the whole is founded upon a lie. And you cower like peasants, in hell already by your own choosing, enchained more surely than the lowest mortal" (*VL* 219). The Children of Darkness are all too willing to accept the authority of God and Satan, but Lestat, like Manfred, refuses to accept the authority of either. He tells them, "You waste your gifts! . . . And worse, you waste your immortality! Nothing in this world is so nonsensical and contradictory, save mortals, that is, who live in the grip of the superstitions of the past" (*VL* 222). He disrupts the security of their constrained lifestyles and creates the Theatre des Vampires for them. Yet, as we have previously learned in *Interview,* the theater vampires have created a conformists' regime as stultifying as their predecessors, the Children of Darkness.

Rice suggests that the temptation of conformity and safety in sameness doesn't change with modern times. While Lestat's autobiography was designed to shake up the vampire population, it instead institutes a new set of conventions. Louis tells him, "Dark Trick, Dark Gift, Devil's Road—they're all bantering those words about, the crudest fledglings who never even styled themselves vampires. They're imitating the book even though they condemn it utterly. They are loading themselves down with Egyptian jewelry. Black velvet is once again de rigueur." Louis describes vampire bars adorned with "posters of vampire films," where the films themselves are shown and where killing is prohibited. Further, "the mortals who come are a regular freak show of theatrical types—punk youngsters, artists, those done up in black capes and white plastic fangs. They scarcely notice *us*. We are often drab by comparison" (*VL* 529). Vampirism has been reduced to a style—"Black velvet is once again de rigueur"— and it is a style the mortals do better than the vampires themselves. The real vampires frequent bars with the trappings of fictional vampires in Rice's ironically self-referential universe, and they use phones and answering machines to leave threats for Lestat (*VL* 526). Lestat himself is delighted that the other vampires are imitating him, and he is offended by Louis's lack of style. "Those clothes. Impossible. I mean, tomorrow night, as they say in the twentieth century, you will *lose* that sweater and those pants" (*VL* 532). The paradox of the outlaw hero is that he becomes so appealing and draws so many imitators that his outlawry is reduced to yet another fashion statement. Precisely because Lestat's Byronic outsider status speaks to so many, the character becomes an overnight rock star and his creator a bestselling novelist. The rebel against the rules of the Children of Darkness becomes the leader of a fashion trend, embodying a style so glamorous that even the other vampires imitate it, albeit less successfully than Lestat's mortal fans, who see him as a particularly romantic and glamorous performer. If Lestat's rebelliousness is reduced to style, of course, it does nothing to promote any kind of social change or improvement. Lestat wants to shake things up but only because shaking things up will relieve his boredom. Like the heroes of the *Crow* films, he sports the veneer of an antiestablishment rebel (down to the obligatory motorcycle), but his rebellion consists more of dramatic gestures than of direct action.

Interview with the Vampire began as a short story about vampires told from their point of view, written partly to help Rice recover from the death of her daughter, Michelle, at a young age—a grief that, of course, makes its way into the story of Claudia. In interviews, she describes Louis' melancholic state of mind as similar to her own at that time. But the simple twist of telling a vampire story from the vampire's point of view makes all the difference and paved the way for the popularity of vampires in contemporary culture. McGinley argues that "in making her vampires more human than Dracula, capable of love and suffering under the weight of a guilty conscience, which Dracula did not possess, Rice has modernized the vampire legend even further, while simultaneously returning it to its Byronic roots" (86). Rice's humanization of her vampires is the key to their popularity. From vampire-themed novels, films, television series, and erotica to vampire role-playing games, people can find any number of ways to identify with these mythic creatures, who are, after all, mortals writ larger than life, mirrors of the angst, isolation, and outsiderhood of Rice's readers. In "A Message from Anne Rice," included with the videotape of *Interview with the Vampire,* Rice says, "This movie is not just about vampires; it's really about us." Rice's popularity is directly attributable to her ability to render the concerns of her readers in a way that they can completely identify with, but she does so by portraying them in a glamorous, exotic, erotic, and larger-than-life fashion, thereby lending an aura of significance and romance to her readers' own feelings that they share with the vampires. Rice also confesses her affinity for her hero, Lestat: "He's my devil, my dark lover, my alter-ego. Sometimes I think he's my conscience." She notes further, "If you know Lestat, you know he's just dying to get into the spotlight." Rice here describes the appeal of the Byronic hero: demonic, dark, erotically irresistible, and a voice of conscience, a conscience that may defy the rules of society but defines its own morality. Yet without his humanity, the Byronic hero would ultimately alienate his readers. We envy his power and autonomy, his ability simply to do what he wants without fear of authority, but we are drawn to his humanity. If such a powerful being suffers from feelings of isolation and confusion and makes terrible errors in his dealings with others, then our own feelings and errors are more acceptable, particularly when we see them glamorized and romanticized in the form of vampires or other similarly powerful entities.

Race's vampires are, of course, not the only Gothic and Byronic figures that draw a contemporary audience. In the world of comics, Neil Gaiman's

Sandman series has achieved a cult status similar to that of Rice's novels. I was, in fact, introduced to *The Sandman* by several of my students. Like the vampires, Gaiman's Dream (aka Lord Morpheus, Lord Shaper, and many other names) is the Byronic wish for immortality and power incarnate. He is one of the family of the seven Endless—Destiny, Death, Dream, Destruction, Desire, Despair, and Delirium—who are older and more enduring than the gods and whose existences span that of all life on all worlds. Morpheus, of course, is the Lord of Dreams, and he presides over a metaphorical space known as the Dreaming. In a sample script (the writer's directions to the artists) included at the end of *Dream Country,* Gaiman describes Dream to artist Kelley Jones thus (Gaiman's scripts being quite detailed, with the look of his characters determined as much by him as by the artists):

> Anyway, this is what he looks like. Facially, and hair-wise, nothing much has changed—still a shock mop of black hair, and a long, thin, slightly androgynous face with good cheekbones and no eyes—just black shadows where the eyes should be with, occasionally, lone and distant single stars glinting in the sockets. But instead of wearing a black coat, put him in a large black leather jacket, with a high collar in the back, thin black jeans, and a jet-black tee shirt. He dominates any room he's in: He's regal, aristocratic; although in a leather jacket he looks more like the skinny, undead king of the style biker punks from hell. ("Original Script of *Calliope*" 26)

A handwritten note at the bottom of the page appends "Sandman is night's face." Gaiman's description of his protagonist blends all the elements that would appeal to readers with Gothic tastes and a predilection for dark heroes. Dream is "aristocratic" and charismatic—"he dominates any room he's in"—like Rice's vampires and Byron's heroes. He has the rebel outlaw appeal of the "skinny, undead king of the style biker punks from hell," with his leather jacket, like the Terminator and Eric Draven. He is "slightly androgynous" like Rice's vampires and Eric Draven, and, of course, the color black predominates in his description. His shadowed eyes with their occasional "lone and distant single stars" convey mystery and inscrutability. Dream's voice bubbles are also black, bounded in a white, wavering outline with white lettering. Dream's appearance shifts according to era—he dresses in attire appropriate to the age, and his form shifts as well, according to the point of view of the person or other being seeing him. In one story he appears as a cat, in another as an African tribal god. Gaiman thus envisions his Lord Morpheus in terms that will appeal to his own time and his intended audience. He has the aristocratic charisma of the nineteenth-century Byronic hero with an overlay of 1990s Goth-rock chic, or as his creator puts it, the Sandman is "pale, tall, brooding, dark, relatively humorless, and Byronic in a late adolescent kind of way" (Bender 238). His sister Death (possibly more popular among Gaiman fans than Dream is) also dresses in Goth-rock style, with black pants, a black tank top with spaghetti straps, black boots, a black belt with a wide silver buckle, and an ankh on a chain around her neck. Dream and Death, in appearance, are the embodiment of cool. Dream, like Rice's vampires and the *Crow* films, appeals to our dark sides. Explaining the reason for his creation of the nightmare Corinthian, who has sharp-toothed mouths in place of eyes, Dream explicates his allure thus:

> A dark mirror. Imagine that you woke in the night and rose, and seemed to see before you another person, whom slowly you perceived to be yourself. Someone had entered in the night and placed a mirror in your sleeping place, made from a black metal. You had been frightened only of your reflection. But then the reflection slowly raised one hand, while your own hand stayed still . . . A dark mirror . . . (*Sandman: Kindly Ones,* pt. 1, 14)

Although Dream is specifically referring to the Corinthian, who "was not intended to be a reassuring dream" (15), the *Twilight Zone*–horror film scenario he describes also explains his own appeal as well. Dream is a dark mirror of our own desires for pgwer, autonomy, and the ability to exact revenge, but he is laden with very human vulnerabilities and flaws. Thus, as such dark mirrors, he and Rice's vampires provide readers with a safe outlet for their own dark urges and impulses.

Gaiman begins Dream's story by placing him in a position of vulnerability, in which he has lost his powers and must go on a quest to gain them back. He has been captured by a sorcerer, Roderick Burgess, and is held captive for seventy years. He eventually escapes, and his apotheosis is rendered by artists Sam Kieth and Mike Dringenberg as a burst of energy and power, reminiscent of Blake's style. Dream's body is flexed, his legs and arms jutting behind him, and he faces a whirling vortex. His initial reflections examine his paradoxical condition: "It feels so good to be back. . . . I left a monarch. Yet, I return naked, alone . . . Hungry" ("Sleep of the Just" 31). Gaiman will firmly establish his hero's power throughout the series, yet he must also humanize him to create a point of identification for his readers. A monarch who is now naked, alone, and hungry has the pathos of a powerful figure made vulnerable, as he wearily remarks, "Exhaustion *bites* at my soul. I have answers of a *sort.* This will be an *uphill* quest," and the readers can identify with Dream's quest to recover his lost powers, powers embodied in a set of tools: a helm, a pouch of sand, and a ruby ("Imperfect Hosts" 22). His quest for revenge against his captor, who is portrayed in entirely unsympathetic terms, is also understandable. He is the wronged hero, on a quest to regain his status and revenge himself upon those who wronged him. Like Manfred's quest for forgetfulness, Dream's quest is a solitary one, and he keenly feels his isolation: "Tonight I feel alone. I have always been solitary, but here on the nightward shores of dream, loneliness washes over me in waves, lapping and pulling at my spirit" ("A Hope in Hell" 1).

Dream successfully perseveres in his quest, defying the hosts of Hell and making an enemy of Lucifer in the process. Although he is made vulnerable by his captivity, we cannot forget that Dream is an immortal being with powers far surpassing our own. Typical of the Byronic hero, he serves not as a role model that his readers can emulate but rather as a figure of far-reaching influence and remoteness. Dream has all the arrogance and power of the Byronic hero, ruling the Dreaming with a conviction of aristocratic entitlement. He revels in his isolation and superiority, resenting any implication that he needs others, berating Hob Gadling, a man to whom he had granted immortality: "You *dare*? You dare imply that I might befriend a mortal? That one of my kind might *need* companionship? You dare to call me lonely?" ("Men of Good Fortune," n. pag.). His tone is similar in arrogance to that of Manfred when he tells the Chamois Hunter, "I am not of thine order" (2.1.38). Dream, however, is willing to learn from his experiences on occasion, and he later acknowledges his friendship with Gadling: "I have always heard it was impolite to keep one's friends waiting. Would you like a drink?" ("Men of Good Fortune," n. pag.). While he lavishes guests with all the exotic foods and drinks the imagination can conjure, his own tastes, like those of Byron's Conrad, are austere: "He ate in the dream of the head chef in the best hotel in Sri Lanka, a dream of a certain meal described to the chef by his grandfather. The meal consisted of almost fifty separate courses, and over two hundred dishes. The king of dreams tasted sparingly of a vegetable dish, and a little plain rice, and was contented by the perfection of each" (*Sandman: Kindly Ones,* pt. 8, 2).

Dream wields his authority with monarchial ease and confidence, even as he acknowledges that his and his siblings' power is only a function of those they serve, humans: "We of the endless are the servants of the living—we are not their masters. *We* exist because they know, deep in their hearts, that we exist" ("Lost Hearts" 23). Like the Romantic poets', Dream's power is the imagination, and he asserts its enduring dominion: "Things need not have happened to be true. Tales and dreams are the shadow-truths that will endure when mere facts are dust and ashes, and forgot" ("A Midsummer Night's Dream" 21). During the Enlightenment, he insists to his brother Destruction that "reason is a flawed tool at best" (*Sandman: Brief Lives,* ch. 4, 20). With arrogant confidence, he adds, "So they begin to reorganize their lives on principles of reason. Well, what of that? It does not affect my domain" (21). Dream's authority comes naturally to him because he knows that humans will always need him, and his domain has a more powerful influence than that of reason, a claim similar to those made by Wordsworth and Shelley about the imagination's superiority to reason.

For those mortals who encounter him, Dream's presence is overwhelming. Barbie (a recurring character who lives in New York after her breakup with Ken) describes it as "like meeting God, or someone like that." She describes him as "very tall, and very beautiful, and very distant" (*Sandman: Game of You,* ch. 5, 32). At the same time, despite this distance, she says, "He stood there in silence, looking very tired, very alone. I felt really sorry for him and I didn't know why" (36). Dream's power and influence are all-pervasive, but his isolation is rarely broken. As the author describes him, "Dream accumulates names to himself like others make friends; but he permits himself few friends" ("Prologue," *Season of Mists* 11). Gaiman further notes, "Of all the Endless, save perhaps Destiny, he is most conscious of his responsibilities, the most meticulous in their execution. Dream casts a human shadow, when it occurs to him to do." It is that human shadow, the loneliness, that makes Dream accessible to readers and creates his poignancy. At the same time, his Byronic self-definition and assertion of his own moral code renders him heroic. Faced with his greatest challenge, the vengeance of the Furies, Dream does not back down: "Rules and responsibilities: these are the ties that bind us. We do what we do because of who we are. If we did otherwise, we would not be ourselves. I will do what I have to do. And I will do what I must" (*Sandman: Kindly Ones*, pt. 11, 24). Like Manfred, Dream insists on full autonomy: "We make choices. No one else can live our lives for us. And we must confront and accept the consequences of our actions" (*Kindly Ones*, pt. 12, 21). His sister Despair eulogizes him thus: "He was so wise; he seemed so certain of the rightness of his actions, and I, who do nothing but doubt, admired that in him" (*Sandman: Wake* 76). Yet such unswerving autonomy has its dangers, as Mikal Gilmore argues: "Dream comes to understand how his obsessions with his powers and responsibilities, with the noble rules of authority, were simply an echo of his own emptiness" (10). As the raven Matthew explains to Destiny, "*Nobody* was close to your brother. Not unless you're talking about astronomical distances . . . y'know—the sun is close to Alpha Centauri . . . He . . . He wasn't very good at *close*" (*Wake* 64). Yet Matthew is still caught in Dream's spell, eulogizing him as "the most important person in the *world* to me" and "the coolest, strangest, most in*fur*iating boss . . . friend . . . boss . . . I ever had" (*Wake* 80).

Matthew's alternation between the labels "boss" and "friend" sums up Dream's ambivalence in dealing with those he considers inferiors, his employees in the Dreaming and mortals in general. Most of the time, he asserts a Byronically haughty superiority and contempt, coldly rebuking those who question his authority and position. He *is* capable of moments of gentle respect and friendship with others, but such moments are rare. Dream wields his authority with severity and is quick to punish transgressors. Once freed from his captivity, Dream scolds Alex Burgess, the son of his original captor (Roderick Burgess having died during the seventy-year interim) and judges him for his deeds:

> There are offenses that are *unpardonable*. Can *you* have any idea what it was *like*? Can you have *any idea*? *Confined* in a glass box for three score years and ten. A human *lifetime*. *Time* moves no *faster* for my kind than it does for humanity, and in *prison* it *crawled* at a snail's pace. . . . I was . . . I am . . . the *lord* of this *realm* of *dream* and *nightmare*. You barred me from my realm with your foolish circle. . . . You threatened, cajoled and pleaded for gifts that are neither mankind's to receive nor mine to give. You had no thought for the

harm you must have brought to your world. . . . Lord what fools these mortals be. ("Sleep of the Just" 36)

On the one hand, Dream forces Burgess to imagine what his confinement was like, emphasizing the crawling pace of time. He then declares his authority and pronounces sentence: *Eternal waking.* Burgess will live a lifetime in a permanent nightmare. Although Dream derives his dominion from humans, he consistently perceives them as insignificant, describing the object of one quest as, "after all, just a human, just one human" ("Imperfect Hosts" 23). Like Manfred, who disdains the "mass" of people, Dream finds most humans beneath his notice, treating them, as Bender notes, "like mayflies whose most notable characteristic is a relatively brief life" (47), and he "almost never demonstrates warmth, compassion, or humor" (Bender 31). He casually anforms Shakespeare of Marlowe's death, and when the Bard is upset, Dream remarks, "I did not realize it would hurt you so." Shakespeare incredulously retorts, "You did not *realize*? No, your kind care not for human lives" ("A Midsummer Night's Dream" 16). His clueless ineptitude about human behavior is much like the Terminator's. In his self-centeredness and pomposity, Dream is frequently a "dork" and needs periodic nudges to point him in the direction of appropriate behavior: "The Sandman therefore comes across as someone who is very conscientious, capable, and even self-sacrificing when performing his job; but he's remarkably deficient when it comes to handling people and relationships" (Bender 32).

He is also capable of finding in humanity a source of amusement. When a young man who has died has been trapped in an alternate dream world, imagining that *he* is the Sandman, Dream patronizingly addresses him as "little ghost" and allows himself a rare burst of uproarious laughter, exclaiming, "*Ohhh, humanity, I love you.* You never cease to amaze me" ("Playing House," n. pag.). He is amused by the mortal's pretensions to his own exalted state, but he is moved as well. There is a naïveté in the young man's imagined role as a superhero, and Dream regards such naïveté in the same manner that the narrator of *Don Juan* views Juan's innocence—amused but also with a wistful longing for a state he will never attain again himself. Moments later, however, he unfeelingly tells the young man's widow, Hippolyta "Lyta" Hall, that her son (gestated for two years in a dream state) belongs to him: "Take good care of it. One day I will come for it. I have a prior engagement, I am afraid. I can discuss this no further" ("Playing House," n. pag.). Had Dream taken the time to explain to Lyta the exalted role her son would play as Dream's successor, he might have saved himself and his realm a great deal of anguish. But it never occurs to him that the child's mother deserves an explanation. Human lives become a form of experiment for his amusement; he grants Hob Gadling immortality on a mere whim, because "it might be interesting" ("Men of Good Fortune," n. pag.). Hob, now a guinea pig in Dream's experiment about how an ordinary human being will deal with immortality, is to meet his benefactor every hundred years to tell him what it's like. It is only very reluctantly that Dream eventually concedes that he may have been looking for a friend and that he values Gadling's company.

Human beings also serve as tools for Dream's own purposes. Overhearing William Shakespeare lament to his contemporary, Christopher Marlowe, "I would give *anything* to have your gifts. Or more than anything to give men dreams that would live on long after I am dead," Dream makes a bargain with the Bard ("Men of Good Fortune," n. pag.). He will grant him the ability to write "great plays" if Shakespeare will pay him with two plays about dreams. The first, *A Midsummer Night's Dream,* is to be a tribute to Dream's old friend (and possible former lover) Titania, the Queen of Faerie, and the second, *The Tempest,* will be a fantasy of escape for himself. He explains, "I wanted a tale of graceful ends. I wanted a play about a king who drowns his books, and breaks his staff, and leaves his kingdom. About a magician who becomes a man. About a man who turns his back on magic." When asked why, he says, "Because I will never leave my island" (*Sandman: Wake* 181–82). He elaborates, "I am . . . in my fashion . . . an island" and "I am Prince of stories, Will, but I have no story of my own. Nor shall I ever." Dream, of course, is mistaken, as he has a story of his own, the story in which he appears, but he presents himself to Shakespeare as one apart: "I am not a man. And I do not change." Dream is the Byronic outsider, isolated by his role and his abilities, and in his request that Shakespeare write a play about a king who leaves his kingdom and abandons his magic, he reveals his own longing to escape his responsibilities and powers and become an ordinary man. At the same time, he is largely indifferent to the consequences of his bargain on the playwright, insisting that Shakespeare would not have been satisfied with the life of an ordinary actor and playwright.

Shakespeare, however, laments that he has neglected his family and used all events in his life as fodder for his plays, just as Dream uses human dreams for his own purposes:

> Whatever *happened* to me in my life, happened to me *as* a writer of plays. I'd fall in love, or fall in lust, and at the height of my passion, I would think "so *this* is how it feels," and I would tie it up in pretty words. I *watched* my life as if it were happening to someone else. My son died, and I was hurt, but I *watched* my hurt, and even *relished* it, a little, for now I could write a *real* death, a *true* loss. My heart was broken by my dark lady, and I wept, in my room, alone; but while I wept, somewhere inside I smiled. For I knew I could take my broken heart and place it on the stage of the Globe, and make the pit cry tears of their own. And now . . . I am no longer young, my health is not good, and my daughter consorts with a lecherous ape, which her fancy amends to a gallant prince. My wife sleeps in her father's bed, far from me; and she treats me like a foolish child. And Prospero and Miranda, Caliban and Gonzalo, aethereal Ariel and silent Antonio, all of *them* are more real to me than silly, wise Ben Jonson, Susanna and Judith; the good citizens of Stratford; the whores and oyster-women of London town. (*Sandman: Wake* 180)

Shakespeare regrets his own lofty ambitions, deriding his own vanity in concealing his name in a psalm he rewrote and worrying that he has struck a Faustian bargain with the devil, although Dream reassures him, "There is no witchcraft, Will, no magic. I opened a door within you, that was all" (181). The Bard describes his artistic life as that of a parasite, feeding off actual human experiences to transmute them into mediated experiences. His own griefs, even the death of `is son, become a vehicle for creating staged events that will produce tears in his audience, and his characters are more alive to him than his family and friends. Shakespeare, in Gaiman's conception, is Dream's human double, mediated through the figure of Prospero, the magician-artist-king. Both are observers. Gaiman's Shakespeare distances himself from his own life and feelings, turning them into the means of furthering his ambitions, and Dream moves through the dreams of mortals, picking and choosing the materials he needs or wants for his own inscrutable goals, just as he takes the child Daniel as his property without any consideration for his mother or for the ordeals that Daniel himself will have to endure. When Hob Gadling asks Dream whether he struck a deal with Shakespeare for his soul, Dream dismissively answers, "Nothing so crude" ("Men of Good Fortune," n. pag.), but as we learn in *The Wake*, it is perhaps his soul that the Bard has given up after all.

Like a true Romantic, Dream must frequently confront the unattainability of his ideals and the gap between desire and actuality. Like Shelley in *A Defense of Poetry*, who notes that "when composition begins, inspiration is already on the decline" (504), Dream, when forced to unmake his flawed creation, the Corinthian, realizes that "the gulf between conception and execution is wide, and many things can happen on the way" (*Sandman: Kindly Ones*, pt. 1, 14). The gulf between conception and execution is particularly wide in Dream's love life, which consists of a series of disastrously failed relationships. When Dream apologizes to a former lover, saying, "I did not intend to hurt you," she retorts, "And what if you did *not*? Intent and outcome are so *rarely* coincident" (pt. 9, 21). Like the speaker of Shelley's *Epipsychidion*, Dream searches for his perfect likeness, discarding lovers when they prove imperfect or alienating them with his off-putting autonomy, egotism, and lack of empathy. The three love affairs that Gaiman details are with the muse Calliope (the mother of Dream's son Orpheus), the African queen Nada, and millennia-old witch Thessaly-Larissa. Dream's self-centeredness, manifest in his neglect of his own son, eventually leads to his destruction, but his continual pursuit of romantic love and his overreactions to failed relationships particularly delineate his Romantic heritage. Dream's brother Destruction says of Orpheus, "He *reminded* me of you. A romantic fool. Self-pitying. But with a certain amount of personal charm" (*Sandman: Brief Lives*, ch. 8, 10). Throughout the series, Dream is revealed to be a self-pitying and romantic fool, too self-absorbed to imagine that his lovers might exist separately from himself. When she leaves Dream, Calliope explains to Orpheus, "It's been coming for a long time. He cannot share anything; any part of himself. *I* thought I could *change* him. But *he* does not change. He *will* not. Perhaps he *can* not" ("Song of Orpheus" 91). Yet she remembers him as initially being "the most gallant of lovers," adding, "When we made love it was like a *flame*: I felt utterly engulfed, utterly loved, *treasured*" (*Sandman: Wake* 45). For all his ineptitude in love, Dream is a vision of the perfect lover, as long as his lovers allow themselves to be "engulfed" and consumed. When Calliope insists on living separately from him, they begin to drift apart.

Dream's response to the failure of a love affair consists of a cold-hearted pursuit of revenge or a protracted wallowing in self-pity, complete with rainstorms all over the Dreaming. Yet he is unable to empathize with his son Orpheus's reaction to the death of his young wife Eurydice. He advises his son to go on with his life, saying bluntly, "She is dead. You are alive. So live" ("Song of Orpheus" 165). These words will come back to haunt him later. He disapproves of Orpheus's quest to retrieve his wife from the Underworld and of his acceptance of the immortality needed to make the journey. After Orpheus is torn apart by the Bacchante, Dream finds a safe refuge for what's left of him (a disembodied head) but addresses him unsympathetically: "You were unwise to seek favors of Death. But you have made your own errors. It was your own life" (47). He leaves his son, telling him, "I will not see you again," insisting, "Your life is your own, Orpheus. Your death, likewise. Always, and forever, your own" (48). He walks away, refusing to turn back as Orpheus pleads for him to return. Dream here advocates a ruthless code of self-sufficiency. Orpheus has made errors, in Dream's estimation, and he must take responsibility for them. Dream eventually takes responsibility for his own errors in love, but he cuts a wide swath of destruction in the process, committing sins that all his self-responsibility will not heal.

His most egregious behavior occurs in his love affair with the mortal Nada. He recklessly pursues her, despite knowing that such a relationship will prove destructive. She tells him, "I hunted you because I love you more than mortal man has ever been loved by woman. And I fled you because it is not given to mortals to love the Endless" ("Tales in the Sand," n. pag.). Gaiman sets up a Romantic tale of unattainable love. Nada cannot help but love Dream, but she is aware of the danger he represents and the disaster that will result if she agrees to his offer to become his queen forever. As we learn from Byron, Maturin, and Brontë, the Byronic hero may be a passionate lover, but he will destroy his beloved in the process. As the narrator of Nada's legend relates, "Love is no part of the Dreamworld. Love belongs to Desire, and Desire is always cruel" ("Tales in the Sand," n. pag.). Dream's predatory nature is revealed when Nada takes the form of a gazelle, and he takes the form of a hunter who kills her. She tears her own maidenhood, hoping this will make her undesirable to Dream, but he insists, "I am no mortal man, and I love you as no mortal man could love. . . . What matters your body to me?" His statement here evokes the arrogance of the Byronic hero—Heathcliff also insists that his love for Catherine transcends the love of mere mortals—as well as the Shelleyan contempt for the body, a contempt that Gaiman immediately belies, for their lovemaking makes "every living thing" dream "of her face, and of her body, and of the warm, salt taste of her sweat and her skin." Nada's predictions turn out to be correct, and the morning after their union, her city is destroyed by a fireball, and she kills herself to prevent more damage. When she rejects him, he condemns her to Hell: "You hurt me. You could have been my Queen, but instead you chose the realm of Grandmother Death. Once more I will offer my love to you, once more, and that is all. If you refuse me a third time, I will condemn your soul to eternal pain." When he encounters her in Hell after ten thousand years, he tells her, "I still love you. But I have not yet forgiven you" ("A Hope in Hell" 7). Dream here behaves in a thoroughly irrational and reckless manner. Nada reciprocates his love, but she is not willing to pay the price of violating the taboo on relationships between mortals and the Endless. Yet he takes her refusal as a personal rejection, and as a being with supernatural powers, he has the means to act on his most vindictive impulses.

Throughout the tale of his love for Nada, Dream shows no indication of being able to empathize with her feelings or situation. He thinks entirely of himself, oblivious to the destruction of Nada's city and people. As Desire puts it, "Because she *hurt* your petty pride, you've had *her hurt* and *tortured* for *ten thousand years*," and Dream's response is a haughty dismissal: "I do not . . . care for the . . . company here" ("Prologue" 18, 19). Still clueless as to the significance of his actions, he justifies himself to his sister, Death: "Sister—you *know* how I felt for Nada once. What I feel for her *still*. But she *defied* me. I gave her due warning, and *still* she spurned me" (21). He is shocked when his favorite sister, as he puts it, *turns* on him, and when he whines, "I would have made her a goddess," Death snaps, "Maybe she didn't *want* to be a goddess, little brother. Did you ever consider *that*?" She finally pronounces, "Anyway, condemning her to an *eternity* in Hell, *just* because she *turned you down* . . . That's a *really* shitty thing to do" (22). This has never occurred to him before, and he responds, dismayed, "Is this how you feel? Truly? That I have not behaved fittingly? That I have been unjust?" Dream is still incapable of sympathy for Nada; what horrifies him is that his own behavior may have been unfit and unjust, that he may have violated his own moral code. It is on this basis—his sense of and image of himself—that he resolves to free Nada from her torments, regardless of the risk to himself: "If I have committed a wrong, then I have but one course. It must be made right" (23). His decision rests on an impersonal code of morality, not on any regret for pain he has caused to his former lover. As he leaves, Death mutters "Idiot," while wiping a tear from her eye.

Dream's pomposity and his continued lack of understanding are revealed in the speech he makes to his subordinates before embarking on his mission:

> Some time ago, I entered into a brief relationship with a mortal woman. For a number of reasons, the relationship did not terminate in a satisfactory manner, and, against my wishes, the lady . . . killed herself. I . . . condemned her to Hell. I sentenced her to torment and imprisonment, never to end unless one day I stood before her, and told her she was forgiven, that she was free. She has been there now ten thousand years. Her name is Nada. It has been pointed out to me . . . that I may have acted hastily. Mistakenly. Wrongly. That what I did was not honorable. So I intend to go to Hades and set her free. (*Sandman: Season of Mists,* ch. 1, 5)

Dream's rhetoric here serves to distance him from the events he describes. He understates—"the relationship did not terminate in a satisfactory manner"—and his use of the passive voice—"it has been pointed out to me"—is formal and off-putting. He asserts his responsibility for his actions, for self-responsibility is crucial to his moral code, but he relates the facts in a dry, flat manner that ignores the utter horror of Nada's suffering, with only the ellipses and pauses revealing that Dream is feeling anything. Only later does he begin to understand it. As he traverses the landscape of Hell, he notes that Nada is held "in a barred cell carved from rock, lined with needle-sharp shards of volcanic glass" without food or water and it occurs to him to "suppose that she must be hungry. She must have been hungry for a long time" (ch. 2, 4). After railing to Alex Burgess about the torments of his own seventy-year confinement, it takes him ten thousand years and some blunt talk from his sister for Dream to begin to comprehend the suffering he has inflicted on his former lover. But he only begins to understand it, and the awkwardness and reluctance of his apology indicate his continued obtuseness and self-absorption: "Ten thousand years ago, I . . . I condemned you to Hell. I now think . . .

I think I might have acted wrongly. I think perhaps I should apologize. I should tell you that I am sorry" (epilogue, 5). Nada reacts accordingly:

> You think you *may* have acted wrongly? You think *perhaps* you'll apologize? You *think*? And *now* what? You expect me to accept that, and say no more. One half-hearted apology, and you've somehow kissed it all better? I spent ten thousand *years* in hell. I could scarcely stand in that oubliette. I burned by day and froze by night. Glass shards cut my flesh. I starved, and hurt, and wept, and waited. All that because of you. And you "think perhaps you should apologize"? You . . . *you* . . . you make me *sick*. (6)

Dream's distance and remoteness make it almost impossible for him to empathize with human suffering, although he wallows in his own griefs. Nada strikes him in the face, and he is furious, beginning to threaten her, and she exclaims, "Yes? What will you do to me, Dreamlord? Send me *back* to Hell?" It is only then that he truly realizes his culpability: "I . . . I am sorry, Nada. You are right. What I did was foolish, and heartless, and . . . unfair; you hurt my pride, and I hurt you. I was wrong. There is nothing else I can say" (7). When Dream can be shaken out of his complacency and formality, he becomes an appealing character; Nada accepts his apology and his offer of reincarnation in a new body. They reach an understanding of the impossibility of a relationship, as she will not become his queen and he will not abandon his responsibilities to be with her, but he promises, "I will always care for you, Nada" (15). Nada is desirable in that she is unattainable; it is possible that Dream alienates his lovers precisely so he can indulge himself in a Shelleyan unfulfilled desire. One character suggests, "You really don't *like* women, do you?," and Dream's behavior indicates that like the poets in Shelley's *Alastor* and *Epipsychidion,* he far prefers an imaginary and ideal lover, who is a reflection of his own yearnings, to one who has her own thoughts, needs, and desires (*Sandman: Brief Lives,* ch. 5, 18).

Dream's propensity for self-indulgent romantic angst is particularly evident in his reaction to his breakup with Thessaly. Once again he imagines a perfect companion, and once again he is disillusioned to learn that she does not conform to the image he painted of her. After she leaves him, his emotions create rainstorms all over his realm, and he orders her rooms erased and forbids any mention of her name. We see him, in chapter 2 of

Brief Lives, leaning on a balcony in a quintessentially Romantic pose, barefoot, rain streaming around him, and his dark cloak flapping in the wind (fig. 2). His face is set and grim, and the drops running down it could be either rain or tears, or both. Dream's melancholy is countered by the ever-practical Mervyn, a handyman with a jack-o'-lantern head who does odd jobs around the Dreaming. When the faerie girl Nuala sympathizes with Dream, remarking that he must be "very *sad,*" Mervyn retorts,

> Nah. He en*joys* it. I mean, hell, it's a *pose,* y'know? He spends a coupla months hanging out with a new broad. Then one day the magic's worn off, and *he* goes back to work, and *she* takes a hike. Phhhht. Now, guys like *me,* ordinary joes, *we* just shrug our shoulders, say, hey, that's *life,* flick it if you can't take a joke. Not *him.* Oh no. *He's* gotta be the tragic figure standing out in the rain, mournin' the loss of his beloved. So *down* comes the rain, right on cue. In the meantime everybody gets dreams fulla existential angst and wakes up feeling like *hell.* And *we* all get wet. (*Sandman: Brief Lives,* ch. 2, 4–5)

Gaiman creates a protagonist who embodies existential angst, and he clothes him with all the attributes of the Romantic hero: black garb, black hair, pale skin, and a hopeless love life. But he also includes the voice of an anti-Romantic, who dismisses it all as a pose, and the artist's drawings of Dream corroborate Mervyn's suspicions. Dream is a cliché of Romantic melancholy; he strikes theatrical and melodramatic poses as he leans on his balcony in the rain, too distracted even to put on a pair of shoes, although he has donned the requisite black cape. We must concur with Mervyn that Dream does in fact enjoy it, that he cultivates the pose of "the tragic figure standing out in the rain." Meanwhile, the Dreamlord, in his self-absorption, is oblivious to his effect on others, the angst-filled dreams that haunt everyone's sleep and the persistent rain that drenches his subordinates. While the other inhabitants of the Dreaming cope with floods, Dream reflects, "This is foolish . . . Why do I hurt so? I scarcely knew her. A handful of months, little more . . . I would have given her worlds of her own, strung like sapphires on a silken cord" (ch. 2, 9). One frame shows a close-up view of his face, mouth turned down, eyes entirely shadowed, and long strands of hair washing over his forehead, along with the streams of raindrops and tears. Mervyn concludes that his boss is a "flake" and charitably concedes, "It's not *his* fault, y'*know?* It's like, you hang out with poets and those guys, you're *bound* ta go a little flaky" (ch. 6, 16). Gaiman gets the readers to sympathize with Dream but does not allow them ever to take him entirely seriously. He explains, "Whenever I felt the Sandman was going overboard, I'd bring Merv on; he's the little voice in the back of my head that says, 'Somebody really ought to tell Dream that he's acting like a flake'" (Bender 167).

Dream travels through the waking world, hoping to find Thessaly again, but he is forced to face harsh truths. His brother Destiny tells him, "She does *not* love you, and, truly, she never *did*. She will not change her mind, no matter how long nor how deeply you wish this were the case" (*Sandman: Brief Lives*, ch. 7, 9). As Thessaly relates her version of her failed affair with Dream, Gaiman constructs a scenario remarkably similar to the poet's love for the Moon in Shelley's *Epipsychidion*. The poet imagines a perfect love, a soul of his soul, then hopes to find her in the real world: "In many mortal forms, I rashly sought / The shadow of that idol of my thought" (267–68). He meets Mary Shelley, "who seemed / As like the glorious shape which I had dreamed / As is the Moon" (277–79), but "the cold, chaste Moon" (281) proves a disappointment. She ceases to reflect his imaginary ideal conception of love back to him but instead begins to exert *her* influence over *him*. The poet describes himself as lying "within a chaste cold bed" (299), where he can only be a reflection of her: "And all my being became bright or dim / As the Moon's image in a summer sea / According as she smiled or frowned on me" (296–98). Thessaly initially resists any involvement with the Dream-King, seeing him only as "a rather brooding and self-absorbed young man . . . and too *thin*." Thessaly imagines herself immune to the stereotypically Romantic demeanor that Dream presents, and against her better judgment, she lets him court her, explaining, "He *loved* me. I do not *doubt* that. In hindsight, I do *not* believe that *I* loved him: I simply felt his love for me, burning and all-consuming, and reflected it back, as the cold light of the moon reflects the sun. I did not *know* that, at the time. I thought I loved him" (*Sandman: Wake* 60). Thessaly, a witch, is associated with the moon, using ritual to draw down the moon in one episode, and is delineated by her perfectly round, moon-shaped glasses and the moon pendant she wears. She explains Dream's irresistible appeal—the "burning and all-consuming" love with which he surrounds his lovers. And, like a Romantic, he loses interest in her once the courtship is over: "Gradually, his interest in me waned, although I doubt he realized it. He *had* me, after all; he had installed me in his world, in his castle. He no *longer* needed to woo me; and and [*sic*] he returned to work. To his duties" (61). When she wants to talk about the relationship, Dream merely shrugs, avoiding her questions. Once attained and installed in his world, Thessaly is no longer as desirable, but her departure, of course, rekindles the flame, leaving Dream in the state of romantic angst described above. Yet Thessaly continues to care for him. She relates this story at his wake, concluding by saying, "I swore I would never shed another tear for him," as the frame shows her face and the tears running from her eyes. That is the paradox of Gaiman's protagonist. As Gilmore observes, "Morpheus is, at times, a plain and simple pill or prick. He is haughty, cold, and callous. He woos then abandons lovers, or worse" (n. pag.). But he also takes responsibility for his actions and has a vulnerable streak a mile wide. His very cluelessness about people and lovers is endearing, for it 'umanizes him in the eyes of his readers. And his capacity for passion makes him an irresistible lover, even to Thessaly, who was aware of his flaws from the start.

Dream's appeal to women sets up another Shelleyan situation. In *Alastor,* while the young poet fruitlessly pursues his ideal dream lover, even to the point of death, he remains entirely oblivious to the Arab maiden who pines for him. Just as he pursues an unattainable love, he becomes a similarly unattainable love object to the Arab maiden, "Enamoured, yet not daring for deep awe / To speak her love" (133–34). In a similar fashion, the faerie girl Nuala pines for Dream, devoting herself to cleaning duties around his castle, much as the Arab maiden brings the young poet food. Both engage in serving a remote love object who remains largely indifferent to their existence. When Nuala's brother returns to bring her back to the land of Faerie, Nuala is heartbroken, saying, "H-He didn't even *try* to fight for me, brother. He didn't care if I stayed or went" (*Sandman: Kindly Ones,* pt. 2, 24). When she confesses to Dream, "I wanted you to *love* me," he rebukes her: "And do you think that love is a gift? Like a bauble, or a trinket? Something I can reach into a pouch and present to you?" He offers her a dream of his love as a consolation prize, but she points out, "I already have that, my lord" (*Kindly Ones,* pt. 11, 8). To her, he represents a dream of perfect, unattainable love: "I loved him as deeply and as well as any man was loved by a woman," and she holds herself responsible for his destruction (*Sandman: Wake* 51).

Of course, it is actually Dream who is responsible for his own destruction. Like Manfred's heroes and Rice's vampires, he embodies the downside of superhuman power and immortality, as well as its irresistible charisma. Dream is simultaneously very human and not human enough in his self-absorption, his lofty and pompous self-conception, and his inflexibility. Gaiman constructs a moving story arc of Dream's epic self-destruction, but he also undermines his protagonist's pretensions. Unity Kincaid tells him, "You're obviously not very bright, but I shouldn't let it bother you" ("Lost Hearts," n. pag.). Mervyn accurately, if cynically, observes that Dream's problem is that he never has to deal with "real life": "He's a *good* guy, but he, y'know, *overreacts*. One *little* thing goes wrong, and he acts like the *sky* is falling" (*Sandman: Brief Lives,* ch. 9, 17). Mervyn's sarcastic epithet for his boss is "tall, pale and interestin'," and, contemptuous of Dream's moodiness, he asks, "So what *I* want to know is, what crawled up *his* butt and died?" (*Sandman: Kindly Ones,* pt. 4, 22). The backtalking dog Barnabas is similarly dismissive, describing Dream as "tall, officious, rather stuffy? Looks like he doesn't get *out* enough?" (*Kindly Ones,* pt. 13, 15). Pale, thin, and androgynous, Dream indeed looks and acts as if he is allergic to sunlight, and the voice of anti-Romantic practicality, Mervyn, is so inured to his employer's tendency toward overreaction that he doesn't recognize a serious crisis. What crawled up the Dreamlord's butt and died on this particular occasion was the necessity of killing his own son, an act that sets in motion Dream's destruction. In *The Kindly Ones,* Gaiman frames Dream's undoing on a scale reminiscent of classical tragedy, but the sarcastic digs by the anti-Romantic voices in his tale are meant to remind us that Dream's tragic end is the result of his own character flaws, including a tunnel vision that limits his possibilities: "Dream, my brother, you forget *nothing* you have an interest in; you forget *instantly,* those things you do *not* care to know," Destruction informs him (*Sandman: Brief Lives,* ch. 8, 18).

The first story arc Gaiman gives us establishes his protagonist as hopelessly self-indulgent and obtuse. By stripping Dream of his powers, Gaiman sets up a Byronic quest to transcend one's limitations. Dream must search and fight to restore his position, but when he achieves all of his goals, he finds them curiously unsatisfying. Like Manfred, who never achieved what he wanted despite his command of supernatural forces and his acquisition of knowledge forbidden to humankind, Dream discovers that the success of his quest leaves him feeling empty. In the story that established Death as one of Gaiman's supreme achievements, "The Sound of Her Wings," Dream gets some advice from his older sister. He sits in a park, dispiritedly feeding pigeons, and confesses that his revenge on his captors "felt . . . fine, I suppose. But it didn't feel as satisfying—as I had expected" ("Sound of Her Wings," n. pag.). He relates his adventures in regaining the tools that embody his power, then explains,

> I was more powerful than I had been in eons. . . . You see, until then I'd been driven. I'd had a true quest, a purpose beyond my function—and then, suddenly, the quest was over. I felt . . . drained. Disappointed. Let down. Does that make sense? I had been sure that as soon as I had everything back I'd feel good. But inside I felt worse than when I started. I feel like nothing. (n. pag.)

Dream's realization is akin to that of Wordsworth, in book 6 of *The Prelude*, who is disappointed at his experience of crossing the Alps, and discovers that

> Our destiny, our being's heart and home,
> Is with infinitude, and only there;
> With hope it is, hope that can never die,
> Effort, and expectation, and desire,
> And something evermore about to be.
>
> (book 6, lines 604–8)

Thus it is that Wordsworth's imagined image of Mont Blanc is far more compelling than the real thing, which causes him to grieve, "To have a soulless image on the eye / That had usurped upon a living thought / That never more could be" (526–28). Romantic desire is infinite, always pursuing that which is "evermore about to be."

A desire once attained becomes contained, finite, and bounded, and it ceases to hold the allure of the infinitely unattainable. That is why Manfred's powers can never satisfy him, and Astarte holds mgre sway over his heart when she is dead than when she was alive. That is why Victor Frankenstein sacrifices everything in his ardent pursuit to create artificial life, yet is crushed when he first sees the results. That is why poetic inspiration inevitably overshadows the "feeble" results, as Shelley tells us. And as Dream learns from Thessaly, "intent and outcome are so *rarely* coincident" (*Sandman: Kindly Ones*, pt. 9, 21). Dream's quest to regain his powers gives him a purpose and goal, as he says, "beyond [his] function." But, of course, the Romantic pursuit of the unattainable serves as an excuse for self-indulgent melancholy and brooding. As Mervyn notes, Dream *enjoys* his rain-generating moods. For a Romantic, the gloom induced by the pursuit of unattainable desires is an indication of a superior state of being. Those who aspire and fall are more alive than those "meaner spirits" who are "morally dead" and never attempt to stretch beyond the limits of their being, Shelley tells us in the preface to *Alastor* (69). But Death will have none of Dream's wallowing in his own misery. She yells,

> You are *utterly* the stupidest, most *self-centered,* appallingest *excuse* for an *anthropomorphic personification* on *this* or any *other* plane! An *in*fantile, ado*lescent,* pa*thetic* specimen! Feeling all *sorry* for yourself because your little *game* is *over,* and you haven't got the— the *balls* to go and find a *new* one! ("Sound of Her Wings," n. pag.)

Death demolishes Dream's Romantic self-indulgence in two incisive frames, bonking her brother on the head with a loaf of bread in her frustration. Death is Gaiman's answer to the Romantic yearning for unfulfilled desires that Dream represents. As Tom Peyer puts it, Gaiman and the artists "twisted reader expectations by casting dream-weaver Morpheus as the grim, pale, gaunt one and Death as his cheerful foil" (102). Byron, Shelley, and Keats romanticized and glamorized death, as do Rice's vampires, but Death goes about her business in a compassionate, practical, and *un*romantic manner. She knows her visits are rarely welcome, but she has a job to do and does it. When she comes for an infant who asks, "Is that all there *was*? Is that all I get?", she answers simply, "Yes, I'm afraid so" ("Sound of Her Wings," n. pag.). When Bernie Capax, who lived for fifteen thousand years, asks, "That's pretty good, *isn't* it? I lived a pretty long time," Death refuses to distinguish him on the basis of his longevity, answering, "You lived what anybody gets, Bernie. You got a lifetime. No more. No less" (*Sandman: Brief Lives,* ch. 3, 5). If all anyone gets, from the infant to the long-lived Bernie to Dream himself, is a lifetime, then it would behoove us, Death suggests, to stop sulking, as she tells her brother, and get on with life. As Peter Straub puts it, "What is of brief duration (and any duration is brief) is to be embraced, valued, reluctantly surrendered. Only the mad and stupid throw their lives away" (n. pag.). While Death is a vision of Goth-rock nightclub chic, her signature ankh is a persistent reminder of her creed—that one must make the most of life, as one never knows when it will be cut off, and she has no patience for Dream's whiny, "*in*fantile, ado*lescent*" emotional immaturity. Her presence is what gives life its meaning, and she is appalled by Dream's *in*ability to find his very existence a cause for celebration. She refuses to romanticize herself, delighting in life's simple pleasures, like watching *Mary Poppins* and other movies with happy endings, and we learn in Gaiman and colleagues' *Death: The High Cost of Living* that she must spend one day as a mortal every hundred years, "better to comprehend what the lives she takes must feel like, to taste the bitter tang of mortality" (ch. 3, 3).

For all his obtuseness and tendency toward self-pity, one of Dream's endearing qualities is his ability to learn a lesson, and he is instructed by accompanying his sister on her routine: "Permitting him to tag along as she casually and graciously collects the dead, she cheers him up by s`eer example: if she can find satisfaction in her everyday routine, so can he" (Peyer 102). Dream realizes, "My sister has a function to perform, even as I do. The Endless have their responsibilities. I have responsibilities" ("Sound of Her Wings," n. pag.). He relates, "I walk by her side, and the darkness lifts from my soul. I walk with her, and I hear the gentle beating of mighty wings." Death exercises her power with gentle compassion, a trait that Dream frequently lacks, and she lacks Dream's pretension, pomposity, and self-aggrandizement. Now he feeds the pigeons with joy instead of morose self-pity, his face graced by a rare smile: "I have found the solace I sought, though not in the way I imagined. From dreams I conjure a handful of yellow grain . . . I throw the grain into the air. And I hear it. The sound of wings" ("Sound of Her Wings," n. pag.). This time he learns his lesson, humbly thanking his sister, but Gaiman will continue to humble his protagonist throughout the series.

Dream is frequently hampered by his inflexibility and resistance to change, as well as his disinclination to admit that he can change. When his long-missing brother Destruction notes a new compassion in Dream's attitude toward mortals' lives, Dream observes, "I doubt I have changed that much" (*Sandman: Brief Lives*, ch. 8, 8). Yet as Straub notes, "The concept of change, of drastic change to come and unalterable changes that have already occurred haunts *Brief Lives*" and, I would add, the subsequent books in the series (n. pag.). Like Rice's Armand, Dream learns that inflexibility is the bane of an immortal existence. The vampires Armand describes, who can't adapt to changing times, eventually destroy themselves, and Dream apparently does the same. Contrasting himself to the inflexible and rule-bound Dream, Lucifer remarks, "I told him that there was *always* freedom, even the ultimate freedom, the freedom to *leave.* You don't have to stay *anywhere* forever" (*Sandman: Kindly Ones,* pt. 12, 14). When Matthew asks the Dreaming's librarian, "Lucien? Why did it *happen*? Why did he *let* it happen?" Lucien counters, "Let it, Matthew? I think he did a little more than *let* it happen . . . Charitably . . . I think . . . sometimes, perhaps, one must change or die. And in the end, there were, perhaps, limits to how much he could let himself change" (*Sandman: Wake* 59). Desire, the sibling with whom Dream has the most contentious relationship, eulogizes him thus: "He *never* had sense enough to come in out of the rain" (74).

In many ways, Gaiman has set up Dream as an unsympathetic character. In his arrogance, inflexibility, and dismissive or exploitive attitude toward mortals, Dream could well alienate his readers. Gaiman sets up an ending for his story that simultaneously humanizes Dream—making him sympathetic by making him vulnerable—and emphasizes his heroism and conviction. Some plot summary is necessary here. In Gaiman's mythology, Orpheus is the son of Dream and Calliope. After Orpheus's disastrous attempt to free Eurydice from the Underworld, he is left immortal, and after being ripped apart by the Bacchante, he now exists as a disembodied head. Dream provides for him a resting place on a Greek island, to be tended by a family of caretakers for perpetuity, and when Orpheus's head is stolen and taken to France during the French Revolution, Dream arranged for its rescue and return to his island. Otherwise, he neglects his son entirely, vowing never to see him again. He finally breaks his vow to request Orpheus's assistance in locating his older brother, Destruction, and in turn, he has promised his son a boon—his long-desired death. Setting in motion the chain of events that will lead to his destruction, Dream announces, "I have to kill my son" (*Sandman: Brief Lives,* ch 8, 24). He accomplishes the deed in a dramatic frame in which both figures appear as black silhouettes in profile, Orpheus's tangled hair mirroring his father's. Dream then emerges with his arms covered in blood, which drips onto the ground, forming red flowers. Returning to the Dreaming, he allows himself the rest of the day in privacy, intending to return to his duties the following day, noting, "I have many responsibilities" (ch. 9, 15). When he reflects on the responsibilities he had been neglecting in his melancholic reaction to his breakup with Thessaly, he may also be referring to his son. Washing the blood from his hands, Dream conjures an image of the young Orpheus in the bowl of bloody water, recalling his own callous response to the death of Orpheus's new bride: "She is dead. You are alive. So live" (ch. 9, 19). His face almost entirely shadowed, he repeats "So live" and despairingly takes himself to a chair in an arched chamber, sitting with his head in his hands.

By spilling the blood of a member of the family, Dream is now vulnerable to the persecution of the Furies. They are aided by Lyta Hall, the mother of Daniel, who has disappeared. She holds Dream responsible for her son's kidnapping; her anger literally fuels the Furies in their quest to destroy Dream. Dream is, in fact, responsible for Daniel's disappearance and bodily death, for he has chosen Daniel (a child gestated for two years in dreams) as his successor. Essentially, Dream has staged an elaborate suicide, which not only serves the author's purpose of humanizing his protagonist but also humanizes the anthropomorphic personification of Dream itself. Frank McConnell suggests that Dream's captivity in the first book was the impetus for the later events. Dream "has been taught painfully that he is not only a transcendent projection of human consciousness, but that he is, after all, dependent upon human consciousness for his existence." He thus "accepts—or engineers?—his death and transfiguration into a *new* Dream, into a version of himself more human—the new Dream is the exaltation of the child, Daniel—than he thinks he could be" (n. pag.). McConnell observes that the plot of the series has been "Dream's dawning realizatign of the poignancy of mortal life, and of his own inescapable implication in that poignancy," for in killing his son, Dream "has entered time, choice, guilt, and regret—has entered the sphere of the human." As McConnell notes, *Sandman* "is a magnificent parable about the humanization of myth." Power and immortality do not constitute heroism—for Dream, those are givens of his existence. His heroism lies in his humanity: his flaws, his ability to learn from his mistakes, his understanding of his own limitations, his defiance of a superior power, and his graceful relinquishing of his own power and position. *The Kindly Ones* and *The Wake* spark the reader's identification with Dream, impelling the reader to mourn Dream's loss along with the other mourners at his funeral. At the same time, Gaiman refuses to take his myth entirely seriously. He offsets the intensity of *The Kindly Ones* in his afterword, saying,

> I still do not know how successful *The Kindly Ones* was, how close I got or how far I came from what I set out to say. Still, it's the heavi-

est of all of these volumes, and thus, in hardback at least, could undoubtedly be used to stun a burglar; which has always been my definition of real art. (n. pag.)

Just as Manfred accepts his impending death yet defies the spirit that comes to claim him, Dream steadfastly accepts his fate but defies the authority of the Furies, wishing to die on his own terms. Like Manfred, he is his "own destroyer." At first his arrogance is misguided; he tells the Furies, "This is my world, ladies. I control it; I am responsible for it. You will neither destroy it nor will you destroy me" (*Sandman: Kindly Ones,* pt. 8, 19). He stands defiantly, the triple shadow of the Furies (which Gaiman conflates with the three Fates) projected on the wall behind him. But the next frame shows a wider-angle view, which shrinks Dream's figure considerably. In fact, he gets smaller as we progress down the page, from the zoom in on his large eyes that fill the first frame, to the view of his head that fills the second, to the view of his head and torso in the third frame, to the small and vulnerable looking figure in the final frame of the page. But it is not only his arrogance that dooms him; as Thessaly tells him, "I think you care about other people too much. It'll get you into *trouble* one day" (pt. 9, 20). And, in fact, it is his promised boon to the faerie Nuala that allows the Furies to attack him, for his departure from the locus of his power makes him and the place itself vulnerable. Nuala summons him to try to warn and protect him, but her act, in fact, has the opposite effect. We see Dream accept responsibility for his own actions: "I killed my son. I killed him twice. Once, long ago, when I would not help him; and once . . . more recently . . . when I did." He explains, "In my pride I abandoned him for several thousand years; and then, at the last I killed him" (pt. 11, 6). He accepts that he must abide by the rules; although Orpheus requested to be killed, Dream must still take responsibility for the deed, both for abandoning his son and for leaving no other option for his son but to request his own death. Nuala asks, "You *want* them to punish you, *don't* you? You *want* to be punished for Orpheus's death." "Dream's response is simply a wordless, tight close-up of his tortured face" (McConnell, n. pag.). He also acknowledges that his long imprisonment has changed him, but he knows that he does not have sufficient humanity or adaptability to survive. Earlier in the story, Odin asks Dream, "Are you a spider, who's spun a web of cunning and deceit and now waits patiently for his prey to come to him; or are you a deer, frozen by the light of a hunter's flame, as disaster comes toward you?" (pt. 7, 8). The answer to both questions is, of course, *yes*. To use McConnell's words, Dream has both engineered and accepted his own demise.

Although he knows that the Furies "will not leave until [he] is destroyed, by [his] own hand or another's," he continues to defy them (pt. 10, 17). When he orders them to leave, he is punished with a lash to the face with a barbed chain. Typically, he chooses to keep the scar as a means of self-punishment. When Lucien the librarian asks what he is going to do, Dream answers with the laconic terseness of an Eastwood hero: "Do? I am going to do whatever I can do. I will do what I must" (23). Thus he announces, "I have decided to confront the Ladies of the Fury, though it could mean my doom," explaining, "I will do what I need to do to make them leave the Dreaming, and to cease to trouble its inhabitants," and what he needs to do, of course, is acquiesce in his own destruction (pt. 12, 1, 3). He bids good-bye to the raven Matthew, his form silhouetted against a burst of light, resembling a halo. For all his ironic gestures of dismissal, Gaiman is apotheosizing his hero in transcendent fashion. And at the same time, he reminds us of just why it is that Dream must go. Even at the end, he fails to understand relationships with others. When Matthew tells him, "It was good being your friend," Dream questions, "Friend?" as if the concept bewilders him. Frustrated, Matthew responds, "Yeah. Friend. Shit. *I* don't know. What-*ever*" (pt. 12, 12). Dream attempts to dissuade the Furies from destroying his realm, and they remind him that he has no power to fight them: "You cannot even *touch* us" (pt. 12, 18). As Matthew flies away, Dream rids himself of his gloves and his shirt, standing, bare-chested against a background of gray thunderclouds. The next frame provides a close-up of his set, determined, and shadowed face as he awaits the arrival of his sister Death. He will not allow the Furies to kill him but instead will choose the manner of his own destruction, as if he were saying, as Manfred does, "The hand of death is on me—but not yours" (3.4.141).

When his sister joins him, he confesses, "I am tired, my sister. I am very tired" (pt. 13, 2). Death accuses her brother of planning a complicated form of suicide: "I dgn't know anyone who can be so completely straightforward and so utterly devious at the same time." She adds, "The *only* reason you've got yourself into this mess is because this is where you *wanted* to be" (pt. 13, 5). Dream's world is ultimately an utterly self-centered one—he is his own first and last cause, and he explains that the

Dreaming was not the same for him since he killed his son. For him, "even the freedom of the Dreaming can be a cage" (pt. 13, 6). She suggests that he could have simply left, in the manner of their brother Destruction, but still true to his own code of personal responsibility, Dream insists, "No. I could not," and Death reluctantly agrees, "No. You couldn't. Could you?" (pt. 13, 6). When Dream notes that he has made all the necessary preparations, Death insists, "Hmph. You've been making them for *ages*. You just didn't let yourself know that was what you were doing" (pt. 13, 10). They touch each other's hands, and Dream vanishes in a star-shaped burst of light that fills a vertical frame that takes up a third of a page. Dream has fulfilled his purpose to the extent of his abilities; realizing his own limitations, he passes the position on to one more suited for it. Gilmore suggests, "It's Morpheus's flaws that, I think, make him truly worthy of the mythic dimension that Gaiman has placed him in, and it's Dream's recognition of his shortcomings that finally allows him to win whatever redemption he pulls off—that makes him, finally, a real hero" (11). In these flaws and their recognition, Dream attains both his mythic quality and the humanity that makes him accessible to readers. As Gilmore notes, "It isn't just a god or an endless being who dies. Far worse (and far better), it is a man, who has finally delivered his own troubled heart, and saved others in the process" (11).

Even in dying, Dream does not abandon his responsibilities. His attention to the child Daniel reveals that he has, however unconsciously or consciously, been planning his demise almost since his recovery from his seventy-year captivity. It is hinted that Dream arranges Daniel's kidnapping by the team of Loki and Robin Goodfellow. As Dream instructed, apparently, they begin a ritual of purification by fire, burning Daniel's mortality away. But Dream sends one of his creations, the nightmare Corinthian, to rescue Daniel before the process is completed. Robin Goodfellow explains, "We burned away *most* of his mortality, you know. Not *all* of it. But another few days, another few fires, and we would have had it all" (*Sandman: Kindly Ones,* pt. 10, 2). Daniel is being transformed into one of the Endless, but Dream apparently realizes that his own lack of humanity is a flaw that must be avoided in his successor. So Daniel is left with a portion of his former mortality, enough to humanize him sufficiently to make him a more flexible and empathetic Lord of Dreams. He is transfigured from a toddler to a tall, thin young man, completely white, whereas Dream was defined by his black hair and black clothes. The new Dream speaks in white voice bubbles, and everything is white except for his black eyes.

In *The Sandman: The Wake,* Daniel begins to take on his new responsibilities, and Gaiman hints to the reader that he has qualities his predecessor was lacking. As Daniel starts to recreate the Dreaming, rectifying the damage done by the Furies, he brings back from the dead the affable Fiddler's Green, who does not want to return to life: "It *hurt.* It was deeply upsetting and painful. However, it *happened.* I am *dead.* If you bring me back to life, my death will have no *meaning.* I had a *fine* existence. . . . I lived a good life and it *ended.* Would you take that away from me?" (33–34). The next frame shows the new Dreamlord looking puzzled, running his fingers through his hair. But he learns his first lesson. The beings who inhabit the Dreaming have their own existences and their own desires, independent of his own, and Daniel grants Fiddler's Green's wish not to be brought back to life. He learns also that the desire for immortality is hardly universal. The life of Fiddler's Green had meaning in that it had a clear line of demarcation—his death. Those moments he cherished would cease to have significance in an eternal existence. Daniel also willingly admits his vulnerability to the raven, Matthew, who would just as soon have his old boss back: "This is very new to me, Matthew. This place. This world. I have existed since the beginning of time. This is a true thing. I am older than worlds and suns and gods. But tomorrow I will meet my brother and sisters for the first time. And I am afraid" (49). When Matthew asks whether he can be sent on to the next stage of his existence, Daniel readily agrees, having learned from his encounter with Fiddler's Green.

Daniel also does not maintain his predecessor's haughty aloofness. He touches the hippogriff who guards the gate of his castle, and the mythical beast says, "Our lord would not have done as you are doing. In the thousands of years that I served him, he did not touch me" (72). He explains that Morpheus fed him slices of apple and "was always *most* pleasant and gentle-mannered," but adds, "*save* when he was displeased." The original Dream is remembered as courteous but aloof, and Daniel's touch reveals that he will not maintain the same distance between himself and his retainers that his predecessor did. He will be a more human and more humane Dreamlord, with a humility and a flexibility that enable him to learn from others and from his previous incarnation's mistakes. The reader can safely assume that the new Dream, with part of his mortality remaining, will succeed where his predecessor erred. Yet, it is his predecessor who is the protagonist of this ten-volume series. It is Morpheus who captures the reader's attention with his power and arrogance, combined with a self-indulgent egotism that renders him utterly inept in his relationships with others. As Steve Erickson points out, Dream "is pompous and morose, harsh and utterly self-absorbed. . . . His conduct tends to the extreme" (14). He suggests that Dream "may be the most morally neutral comic book hero ever" and that the *Sandman* has been a story about "one loss after another: loss of faith, loss of friendship, loss of love, loss of innocence, loss of certainty, loss of identity, loss of the past, loss of the soul, loss of our dreams every time we wake, with Dream the agent of all our life's losses, until Death transacts the last and greatest loss of all." It is what Erickson calls "the melancholy that pervades the book" that creates sympathy for an otherwise unsympathetic and inhuman being. If Dream were immortal *and* infallible, he would bore his readers. He suffers and learns and knocks his head against the wall of his own obtuseness, finally realizing that those qualities by which he defined himself—his adherence to rules, his resistance to change, his unquestioned sense of his own superiority, his creed of self-sufficiency—have brought him low. His humanization and his process of self-discovery reach their culmination in Daniel—the product of Morpheus's understanding of his own failings.

As both Rice and Gaiman realize, the Romantic hero is an icon with continuing appeal. He combines superhuman abilities with a very human vulnerability. Lestat and Dream have both attained that ultimate of human yearnings—immortality and power—and they both learn that immortality and power bring with them their own burdens. Disillusioned, they wallow in Shelleyan self-absorption and self-pity, but eventually take steps toward self-knowledge. Lestat remakes himself as a rock star, choosing a guise that will allow his vampire self fullest expression in the modern world, and Dream remakes himself into a new and more human incarnation. Ultimately, Lestat and Dream's immortality reminds us that, in our circumscribed human existences, we may not be so bad off. Another Byronic hero, *Star Trek*'s Q, serves a similar function but with a twist. Q combines the egoism and self-absorption of the heroes described in this chapter with the roles of leader and moral guide that we saw in the heroes discussed in chapter 2. Q is an outlaw who despises the very humanism that defines the *Star Trek* universe, but he undertakes a complex transformation over the course of his appearances on the various *Star Trek* series, becoming a type of Carlylean hero-leader who knows better than we do, and whom we must follow.

4

Star Trek's Q
A Byronic Hero for *The Next Generation*

Seeking forgiveness from the Phantom of Astarte, Byron's Manfred agonizes, "I have so much endured—so much endure" (2.4.118). In the year 2369, a much more powerful but equally self-absorbed being, bearing an uncanny resemblance to Byron himself, laments, "Heavy is the burden of being me."[1] The character of "Q," from the television series *Star Trek: The Next Generation (TNG), Star Trek: Deep Space Nine,* and *Star Trek: Voyager,* is one of the most explicit reincarnations of the Byronic hero our contemporary culture has produced. Q was a recurring and popular character on *Star Trek: TNG,* appearing in both the series premiere as well as its finale seven years later, and he has also been the subject of several *Star Trek: TNG* novels. The actor who plays Q, John de Lancie, looks remarkably like Byron; and his performances effectively evoke the character's Byronic dimensions in a self-consciously campy and flamboyant fashion (figs. 3, 4). His evocation of Byron was deliberate, as the actor consciously conceived of Q as a character who was "mad, bad, and dangerous to know." Like Byron's Lucifer, Q has superhuman abilities, and he frequently functions in the role of satanic tempter. *Star Trek: TNG* centers on the adventures of the crew of the Starship *Enterprise,* commanded by Captain Jean-Luc Picard (Patrick Stewart). Q, as we learn in his visits to the *Enterprise,* is a representative of a vastly superior civilization, the Q Continuum; he can transport himself throughout the universe instantaneously; and he has quasi-godlike powers to alter or create environments, suspend the laws of physics, manipulate space and time, and influence human destinies. At the same time, he is world-weary—or, more appropriately, universe-weary—bored and cynical, deems himself immeasurably superior to human beings, and yet is unable to resist meddling in their affairs as a means of stimulation.

This chapter explores the extensive parallels between the role of Q and Byron's heroes by examining the *Star Trek* episodes in which Q appears and Q's evolution as a character.[2] In many ways, his character has evolved from the defiant Prometheanism and misanthropy of Manfred and Lucifer to the somewhat wistful and longing cynicism of the narrator of *Don Juan.* Q, in fact, embodies aspects of the hero-leader described in chapter 2 and the self-absorbed, disillusioned immortal being described in chapter 3. Although he is often played for laughs, Q is not simply and exclusively a parody of the Byronic hero. Like another contemporary Byronic hero, the Terminator, Q initially appears on *Star Trek: TNG* as the callous agent of oppressive authority; he terrorizes the crew of the Starship *Enterprise* on the mandate of his superiors in the Q Continuum. As in the case of the Terminator, however, Q's popularity caused him to be recast as an increasingly heroic figure. Over the seven years of this series, Q develops more of an appreciation for human beings and human values. Like the Terminator, Eric Draven, Rice's vampires, and Gaiman's Dream, Q is increasingly humanized. At first he embodies our own desires for power and autonomy, yet to gain his viewers' sympathies, he sheds some of his arrogance and acknowledges the value of human life, in spite of its limitations. Ultimately, Q comes to intercede between humans and the Q Continuum, defining his own moral code and fulfilling the myth of the powerful individual, the heroic leader who serves as protector and guide. The ethos of *Star Trek: TNG* seems to be a faith in human progress, and whether he is tormenting humans or assisting them, Q's function in the universe of this series is to question but ultimately to confirm that faith. In that function, his Byronic qualities are modified specifically to satisfy the devoted audience of the entire *Star Trek* canon.

Q's character follows a clear evolution over the course of the series. He appeared in one or two episodes a year, and as the series progressed, Q became more likable, more ethical, more aware of his own limitations as an omnipotent being, and more appreciative of humans. Initially he is portrayed as an omnipotent prankster, sadistically tormenting weaker species. At the same time, from the onset of the series, despite his own transgressions, Q presents himself as a moral arbiter. In *Star Trek: TNG's* premiere, Q appears as a powerful and sadistically playful villain in the tradition of the spoiled, powerful, and pesky Trelane from the original *Star Trek* episode, "The Squire of Gothos." Q delights in experimenting with the crew of the *Enterprise* through elaborate games and scenarios of his own devising. His aim in these encounters is to "test" humankind and to demonstrate, to his own satisfaction, their utter inferiority. In the pilot for the series *Star Trek: TNG,* an episode titled "Encounter at Farpoint," Q entraps the *Enterprise* in a gridlike force field. He compels the crew to stand trial for the crimes of humanity in a twenty-first-century court of horrors, with himself as judge, jury, and prosecutor. In his over-the-top performance, de Lancie makes Q into the quintessential antithesis of all that *Star Trek* stands for, a representative of a species Captain Picard eloquently condemns as "self-righteous life forms who are eager not to learn but to prosecute, to judge anything they don't understand or can't tolerate." Despite Q's threats, we know, of course, that the *Enterprise* is going to continue its "trek through the stars" and that Q is going to be soundly trounced by Captain Picard, a liberal humanist who confidently extols humankind's progress. Nevertheless, Q is already proving himself the questioner; his condemnation of humankind's past behavior is accurate, as he describes the slaughter of "millions in silly arguments about how to divide the resources of your little world" and humans' "murdering each other in quarrels over tribal god images." He is, however, no match for Picard; Picard must acknowledge humankind's past brutality, yet he reaches a fair and nonviolent solution to the puzzle of Farpoint Station. Q, muttering "lucky guess" in a display of sour grapes, is forced to let the *Enterprise* continue on her way.

In his second appearance, also in the first seasgn, an episode titled "Hide and Q," Q forces the crew to prove themselves in an elaborate game with arbitrary rules. Once again Q kidnaps several crew members, interrupting a mission in which lives are at stake. Q has no concern for the consequences, snapping derisively, "Your species is always suffering and dying." Despite some heated exchanges with Picard, Q's interest here is in the first officer of the *Enterprise,* Riker (Jonathan Frakes), whom he correctly surmises to be an easier target, someone far more likely than Picard to succumb to the satanic temptations he offers—knowledge and power. With an alluring voice, Q offers "the realization of your most impossible dreams." Successfully seduced, Riker makes a pact with the devil he soon regrets. Q sets up a "completely unfair" and completely rigged test, in which the crew is forced to try to prove itself against heavily armed "soldier things" in, appropriately enough, Napoleonic-era uniforms. As the test is in fact unfair, the only way Riker can save his companions is by using the powers Q has lent him. Riker then makes an utter fool of himself, trying to force gifts on his friends that they do not desire and naively buying Q's line that the Q "think very highly of us." Although Riker is, on the surface, the focus of the episode, Q's visit to the *Enterprise* really serves to present *Star Trek* creator Gene Roddenberry's vision in the form of Picard's humanism. Picard quotes Hamlet's speech "What a piece of work is man, how noble in reason, how infinite in faculties, in form and moving how express and admirable, in action how like an angel, in apprehension how like a god." Q incredulously responds, "Surely you don't see your species like that, do you?" to which Picard replies, "I see us one day becoming that, Q." Q's function here is purely to provide an occasion for Picard to express an optimistic faith in human progress that is inextricable from a belief in the concept of gradual evolution. Picard insists that Q's power "is too great a temptation for us at our present stage of development."

Although Q almost succeeds in tempting Riker to allow himself to be the Continuum's guinea pig, whereby they can study the "human compulsion" to "learn" and "explore," it is Picard who triumphs at the end of the episode, thoroughly humiliating both Riker and Q. Picard defeats Q with mockery and with his sound knowledge of human nature. When Q appears on the bridge in a monk's robe, intoning, "Let us pray for understanding," Picard snaps, "Let us do no such *damn* thing." But he allows Riker to go through the ritual of presenting his friends with parting gifts, for Picard knows precisely what the result will be. As the crew members begin to reject the benefits Riker tries to confer upon them, the camera occasionally pans toward Picard, sitting in his captain's chair with a studied confidence and a slight smile, as events transpire exactly as he anticipated. When Riker finally realizes the folly of having signed his soul over to Q, the first officer turns to his captain in shame, admitting, "I feel like such an idiot." Picard replies briskly, "Quite right. So you should." Picard's scorn withers both Riker and Q, rendering both of them the objects of the viewers' laughter. Q is unceremoniously whisked off the bridge by his superiors, protesting, "No! No! If I could just do one more thing!" and howling melodramatically as he disappears. The episode concludes with a moral tag so explicit it should be engraved on a plaque. The android Lieutenant Data (Brent Spiner) asks, "Sir, how is it that the Q can handle time and space so well and us so badly?" Picard replies aphoristically, "Perhaps someday we will discover that space and time are simpler than the human equation."

Like Manfred and Lucifer, Q is completely contemptuous of humankind, deeming them inferior and puny in all respects. Manfred, unable to accept his own humanity, describes his species as an unstable compound of "Half dust, half deity, alike unfit / To sink or soar" (1.2.40–41). For Manfred, humankind's "low wants" must inevitably impede their "lofty wills" (1.2.44). While Manfred bitterly mocks his own condition, Lucifer mocks Cain with a similar discrepancy between the power of humankind's capacity for "high thought" and the inferiority of humans' physical condition, which he describes in terms of "a servile mass of matter" and "gross and petty paltry wants, / All foul and fulsome" (2.1.50–55). Lucifer fuels Cain's already existing discontent with his mortality by showing him wrecked worlds of beings far superior to humans, beings who existed before humans were created. According to Lucifer, humans are but "Reptiles engendered out of the subsiding / Slime of a mighty universe" (2.2.97–98). At the same time that Lucifer has tempted Cain with increased knowledge, he mocks Cain's attempts to learn more than he is capable of absorbing, to see the thrones of both God and Lucifer:

> Thy human mind hath scarcely grasp to gather
> The little I have shown thee into calm
> And clear thought: and *thou* wouldst go on aspiring
> To the great double Mysteries! the *two Principles*!
> And gaze upon them on their secret thrones!
> Dust! limit thy ambition; for to see
> Either of these would be for thee to perish!
>
> (2.2.401–407)

Lucifer's final suggestion to Cain is delivered with a patronizing flourish, drumming in the message of human inferiority, ironically, as a means to prevent human sorrow.

> And this should be the human sum
> Of knowledge, to know mortal nature's nothingness;
> Bequeath that science to thy children, and
> 'Twill spare them many tortures.

(2.2.418–424)

Both *Manfred* and *Cain* eloquently express the Romantic condition, the aspiration beyond "the fitting medium of desire" to a higher, limitless state and the consequent frustration that this aspiration can never be fully realized (*Childe Harold* 3.42). His inability to maintain his capacity for imaginative flight forever similarly hampers the speaker of *Childe Harold,* for "this clay will sink / Its spark immortal" (3.14).

Q shares Manfred and Lucifer's distaste for human limitations and "low wants." In "Encounter at Farpoint," he accuses humans of being "a dangerous, savage child-race"; in *Star Trek: TNG*'s series finale, "All Good Things . . . ," he returns Jean-Luc Picard to the courtroom to convict humans of "being inferior." While Q acknowledges humankind's potential to evolve into a much higher species, he repeatedly refers to humans with such epithets as "a grievously savage race," "a pitiful species," "foolish, fragile nonentities," "weak and . . . incompetent," "commonplace little creatures," "a minor species in the grand scheme," and "an ape-like race." Q mocks humans' ventures into space as "wasted effort, considering human intelligence." When a crew member challenges Q's credentials as "an expert in humanity," he responds, "Not a very challenging field of study, I grant you." Q's need to disparage humankind is almost desperate; however, the crew never takes Q terribly seriously. They are all aware that Q feels threatened by human potential, and at the same time, Q is much too fascinated by humans to do them serious damage in spite of his capacity to do so. While Q makes threats and occasionally temporarily immobilizes various members of the crew, he never *directly* harms any of them.

Q's misanthropy is most thoroughly developed in the third-season episode "Deja Q," in which he has been stripped of his omnipotence and his immortality by his superiors for spreading "chaos through the universe." This episode has the closest parallels to *Manfred* in its depiction of an individual whose reality cannot match his self-conception. Both Q and Manfred urgently desire to transcend the constraints of their human condition. Thoroughly humiliated at his "significant career change," Q announces to the crew, "I stand before you defrocked, condemned to be a member of this lowest of species, a normal, imperfect, *lumpen* human being." He does not make a good adjustment, strenuously objecting to the clothes that have been provided for him ("These aren't my colors!"), panicking the first time he falls asleep ("How terrifying. How can you stand it day after day?"), and complaining,

> It was a mistake. I never should have picked human. I knew it the moment I said it. To think of a future in this shell. Forced to cover myself with a fabric because of some outdated human morality. To say nothing of being too hot or too cold. Growing feeble with age. Losing my hair. Catching a disease. Being ticklish. Sneezing. Having an itch. A pimple. Bad breath. Having to bathe?

Childe Harold despises his own "human frailties" (3.14), condemns himself as "A link reluctant in a fleshly chain" (3.72), "Spurning the clay-cold bonds which round our being cling" (3.73), and anticipates "when at length the mind shall be all free / From what it hates in this degraded form, / Reft of its carnal life" (3.74). *Don Juan's* narrator regrets his gray hair (1.213) and his diminished capacity for indulging in women and claret (1.216). Likewise, Q abhors the limitations and discomforts to which a physical existence condemns him. As he remarks, "I can now stub my toe with the best of them." The contrast between his previously omnipotent state and his human vulnerability is particularly displayed when he is in the brig and carelessly runs into the force field that is holding him in. He complains, "*This* is getting on my nerves, now that I have them." Later he experiences severe back pains and demands, "What's the right thing to say? Ow?" In addition to the new physical discomforts he suffers, Q dreads having to engage in "human interpersonal relationships." Just as Manfred explains to the Abbot that he could not use his abilities to guide mankind because "I disdained to mingle with / A herd, though to be a leader" (3.1.121–122), Q anticipates not being able to fit in with the rest of the crew, remarking, "I'm not good in groups. It's difficult to work in a group when you're omnipotent." Despite his humiliation, Q retains all of his arrogance until he is made aware of just how `elpless he has become. He tries to boss around the crew members by flaunting his superior knowledge, and when an old enemy mocks him as "Just one of the boys, eh," Q snaps, "One of the boys with an IQ of two thousand and five!"

Stripped of his powers, Q is utterly incompetent in spite of his arrogance. The comic incongruity of his melodramatic responses to natural human functions makes him a repeated butt of humor, as in the following two exchanges:

> Q. I've been entirely preoccupied by a most frightening experience of my own. A couple of hours ago I realized that my body was no longer functioning properly. I felt weak. I could no longer stand. The life was oozing out of me. I lost consciousness.
> PICARD. You fell asleep.
> Q. How terrifying. How can you stand it day after day?
> PICARD. You get used to it.
> . . . .
> Q. Ow! I think.
> DR. CRUSHER. Now what?
> Q. There's something wrong with my stomach.
> DR. CRUSHER. It hurts?
> Q. It's making noises.
> DR. CRUSHER. Maybe you're hungry.

Neither Picard nor Crusher (nor the viewers) can muster much sympathy. Without his powers, Q is a joke. De Lancie brings out Q's physical vulnerability in the markedly different way he holds himself and moves in "Deja Q." With his powers *intact*, Q is hyperkinetic, restlessly emitting energy from an apparently unlimited source. He is in constant motion, as if unable to be contained in the confined spaces in which he finds himself, pacing, gesturing flamboyantly, circling like a vulture, sitting down only to jump up immediately, and punctuating displays of his power with a superfluous and hyperbolic snap of the finger. In the second-season episode "Q Who," for instance, he vanishes out of a chair with his trademark burst of light, and the chair rocks back and forth, testifying to the energy that has been released. Even when sitting, he doesn't relax but strikes calculated poses, putting his arms behind his head and crossing one leg over another in an exaggerated simulation of relaxation or leaning back coyly, one leg stretched out, his hands wrapped around one knee in a seductive manner. *Without* his powers, however, in "Deja Q," he is awkward and subdued, his posture revealing his lack of energy and confidence. He stands listlessly with his shoulders slumped and arms folded, or stoops, or leans forward, his hands on a table, instead of making the most of his height. His movements lose their usual sharpness and quickness, and his uniform makes him look almost fat. As soon as his powers are restored, energy floods his being. He sits up straight, his eyes gleam demonically, and he snaps his fingers purposefully in order to restore his favorite Starfleet uniform and his carefully constructed image. Back on the bridge, he looks slimmer and draws himself up to his full height. Blowing a kiss to Picard with two hands, he has restored his usual campy flamboyance.

Early in "Deja Q," frustrated that no one believes he is human, Q demands, "What must I do to convince you people?" and Worf (Michael Dorn) replies succinctly and devastatingly, "Die." To be human is to be defined by mortality (as the film *Star Trek: Generations* repeatedly emphasizes). As he apparently learns by the time of the sixth-season episode "Tapestry," mortality gives life focus and purpose, but his first experience of the possibility of dying devastates him. His newfound vulnerability makes him a target for a species he had earlier tormented, the Calamarain, and after being attacked and nearly killed, he becomes acutely aware of mortality for the first time. Q echoes Manfred's assessment that humans are ultimately defined by the fact that "mortality predominates" (1.2.45). As we see in the play, for all of his supernatural abilities, Manfred does not have power of choice over his own death; the day is appointed, and he can neither hasten it by suicide or put it off. Q tells Picard, "Don't be so hard on me, Jean-Luc. You've been a mortal all your life. You know all about dying. I've never given it a second thought. Or a first one for that matter. I could have been killed. If it hadn't been for Data and that one brief delay he created, I would have been gone. No more me. And no one would have missed me, would they?" As with Manfred, this unbearable internal conflict between his image of what he wants to be and the actuality of his condition impels him to attempt suicide, because "as a human, I would have died of boredom." While bemoaning his own mortality, Q is initially incapable of empathizing with the fate of others. His utter self-absorption is revealed in his complete lack of concern for the android, Data, who is injured while saving Q's life. This inability to put himself in the place of others is reminiscent of Manfred's accusing complaint to the Phantom of Astarte: "Look on me! the grave hath not changed thee more / Than I am changed for thee" (2.4.119–120). Observing no celebration at his narrow escape, Q mutters, "The cheers are over-whelming." Q simply cannot function as a human being; he cannot imagine himself endangering his own life to save another's as Data does for him; he confesses his own selfishness, although noting, "it has served me so well in the past"; and he is terrified of dying. Q notes, "As I learn more and more what it is to be human, I am more and more convinced that I would never make a good one. I don't have what it takes. Without my powers I'm frightened of everything. I'm a coward, and I'm miserable, and I can't go on this way."

His attempted suicide, however, leaving in a shuttle craft and exposing himself to the attacking Calamarain, is also at least partially a self-sacrifice intended to save the ship and its crew. Q's own utter incompetence as a human leads him to a new appreciation of humanity; he can't help but be impressed with how well they cope with their limitations and vulnerabilities once he has experienced them for himself. He still doesn't understand Data's desire to be human, saying, "There are creatures in the universe who would consider you the ultimate achievement, android. No feelings, no emotions, no pain. And yet you covet those qualities of humanity. Believe me, you're missing nothing." But he admires the android nevertheless, telling him, with a self-deprecating smile, "If it means anything to you, you're a better human than I." Q seems to realize more and more over the course of the series that humans have made the most of what he sees as very meager endowments. Although he becomes increasingly human himself, he never loses his conviction of his own superiority. At the end of "Deja Q," Picard is about to chalk up yet another triumph for liberal humanism, remarking, "Perhaps there's a residue of humanity in Q after all." In the middle of issuing his command, "Engage," with his traditional gesture of pointing to the stars, Picard is nonplussed to discover a cigar appear in his hand, with Q's disembodied head wreathed in the smoke, replying "Don't bet on it, Picard." Omnipotent and immortal again, Q gets the last word.

Like many other superheroes of the late twentieth century, Q combines superhuman abilities with very undeveloped social skills. Although he is subject to the authority of the Q Continuum, Q provides viewers with a vicarious experience of power, limitlessness, and autonomy: like Lucifer, he is "exempt from time" (1.1.535); if another being irritates him, he can simply wipe it out of existence; if a being dear to him is killed, as

Picard is in one episode, he can restore its life; if he is bored where he is, he can transport himself instantaneously across the galaxy. For his own diversion, Q can construct elaborate scenarios and games and force inferior beings to participate, or he can hurl the *Enterprise* into a life-threatening situation as a test. He announces to Picard in "Q Who," "The hall is rented, the orchestra engaged; it's now time to see if you can *dance*." He delights in tormenting species less powerful than he. At the same time, he reveals the limitations of omnapotence and immortality, just as Manfred learns that all of his power and knowledge "avail'd not" to bring him any peace of mind. Manfred can never be satisfied with what he has attained, for with his "knowledge grew / The thirst of knowledge" (2.2.94–95), and all he has learned is that "Sorrow is Knowledge" (1.1.10) and "The Tree of Knowledge is not that of Life" (1.1.12). Q similarly suffers from a surfeit of knowledge. He is so bored with his own existence, that he develops a fascination with humans and desires their companionship, in spite of their inferiority; yet he is so arrogant, egotistical, irritating, and overbearing that he alienates humans even when he is trying to assist them or gain their assistance. In "Deja Q," at his moment of greatest vulnerability, he casts aspersions on the very human qualities upon which he must rely. Confident that Picard will offer him protection from his enemies, Q sneers, "I know human beings. They're all sopping over with compassion and forgiveness. They can't wait to absolve almost any offense. It's an inherent weakness of the breed." Matching, if not exceeding, Manfred's histrionic self-absorption in his dealings with others, Q throws temper tantrums when he doesn't get his own way and continually laments that he is misunderstood: "I add a little excitement, a little spice to your lives, and all you do is complain" ("Q Who").

Q is the quintessential isolated Byronic outsider, unable to fit into either of the two societies with whom he interacts. Within his own species, his rebelliousness makes him an outlaw; he is exiled by them in one episode ("Q Who") and stripped of his powers by them in another ("Deja Q"). In an appearance on *Star Trek: Voyager* ("The Q and the Grey"), he is the leader of the rebel side in a civil war within the Continuum against the conservative faction. As we have herein seen, he cannot adapt himself to humans either. Q's greatest frustration seems to arise from the fact that despite his power, he never earns the respect or awe of the crew of the *Enterprise*. He cannot understand their complete lack of interest in emulating him. The series' creators developed a comic incongruity between

Q's awesome abilities and the utter disrespect with which he is received. There is a similar comic undercurrent in Manfred's encounter with the Chamois Hunter. When Manfred loftily and arrogantly proclaims, "I am not of thine order," the Chamois Hunter replies, "Thanks to Heaven! / I would not be of thine for the free fame / Of William Tell" (2.1.38–40). Q's insistent assertions of his superiority are repeatedly dismissed in a similar fashion. In the sixth-season episode "Tapestry," for instance, Picard skeptically rejects Q's self-designation as God, remarking, "I refuse to believe that the afterlife is run by you. The universe is not so badly designed."

Q's arrogant demeanor is revealed most prominently in his relationship with Picard, to whom he is romantically attracted.[3] His attitude is inevitably superior and overbearing, and Q succeeds only in alienating the object of his desires. Jealous of Picard's romantic attachment to the unscrupulous archaeologist Vash, Q derides him: "I had high hopes for you, Picard; I thought you were a bit more evolved than the rest of your species, but now I realize you're just as weak as all the others. Still it pains me to see the great Jean-Luc Picard brought down by a woman." He then confesses, in an explicit acknowledgment of his attraction to the Captain, "This human emotion, love, it's a dangerous thing, Picard, and obviously you're ill-equipped to handle it. She's found a vulnerability in you, a vulnerability I've been looking for for years. If I'd known sooner, I would have appeared as a female." Unable to alienate Picard's affections from Vash, Q does the next best thing and lures Vash away from Picard.

De Lancie manages to portray Q as wickedly subversive and tyrannically authoritarian at the same time, as Q claims the viewers' allegiances by repeatedly deflating Picard's pompous demeanor. When Picard worries, in "Tapestry," that changing his own past will irrevocably alter history, Q, in a fit of pique, snaps, "Please! Spare me your egotistical musings on your pivotal role in history. Nothing you do here will cause the Federation to collapse or galaxies to explode. To be blunt, *you're not that important.*" In his performances, de Lancie engages the viewers into a type of complicity with Q. In his first two appearances, where he is clearly the villain, Q is often the object of the viewers' laughter as he is defeated by Picard's liberal and humanistic demonstrations of his species' progress. In Q's subsequent appearances, however, the audience laughs *at* him less and *with* him more. De Lancie seems to offer a challenge to his audience, as if to say, "Look, I'm going to make very clear to you that this guy is arrogant, egotistical, tyrannical, and sadistic, but at the same time, I'm going to make you like him, and you're not going to be able to help taking his side." Illustrating the central confusion Q provokes, one of my students commented, "Q is so cool—I've never liked a 'bad guy' so much." Thus, when Q sadistically teases and humiliates Picard, the viewers share in Q's derision, rather than condemning him as a bully. In "All Good Things . . . ," during an early courtroom scene, Picard demands information from Q, who taunts him, "Oh, you'd like me to connect the dots for you, lead you from A to B to C, so that your *puny* mind could comprehend. How *boring.*" The jeering spectators in the courtroom become a stand-in for the viewers as they laugh at Picard's obtuseness and discomfiture and relish Q's clear intellectual superiority and command of the situation. The two episodes I've cited are those in which Q is clearly operating on Picard's behalf. The viewers are thus drawn into a type of sadistic, vicarious identification with an all-powerful and cruel, but charismatic and witty, authority figure. The viewers enjoy Q's triumphs over Picard because de Lancie has made the character impossible to dislike and because they have been convinced that Q actually "knows better" than the Captain and thus deserves to be obeyed.

Q essentially embodies two of the most ambivalent manifestations of the Byronic hero: the tempter and the imperialist.[4] The tempter offers knowledge, and the imperialist offers leadership; but both almost inevitably harm their intended "beneficiaries." Byron's Lucifer essentially plays both roles, demanding Cain's worship in exchange for knowledge. Mocking Cain's fear of death, Lucifer remarks, "And I, who know all things, fear nothing; see / What is true knowledge" (1.1.300–301). When Cain declines the bargain, Lucifer insists, "Thou art my worshipper; not worshipping / Him makes thee mine the same" (1.1.319–320). Like Lucifer, Q tempts humankind with knowledge that they cannot attain on their own, *and* he repeatedly demands their submission. In his sadistic playfulness, Q often resembles a trickster figure such as Loki, but de Lancie's performance evokes Milton's Satan as well. In "Hide and Q," Q's most explicitly satanic appearance, Q, as detailed above, temporarily succeeds in seducing Riker, the first officer, into accepting the grant of the Q's power, offering him "a gift beyond any human dream" and "the greatest adventure ever offered a human." In "Q Who," the following season, Q is still the satanic tempter, whispering in a sinister fashion, his lips touching Picard's ear as he tries to compel the captain to eat from the tree of knowledge he offers. He remains as autocratic and interfering as ever, kidnapping Picard in a shuttle craft and threatening to keep him there, for decades if necessary, until the captain concedes to Q's demands. His demeanor is far more threatening and menacing than in his earlier appearances; he bites off his words with ferocity, as he declares with a hiss, "We have bus*i*ness, Picard." When Picard staunchly insists, "Keeping me a prisoner here will not compel me to discuss anything with you," Q whips around behind the captain's shoulder, places his lips immediately next to Picard's ear, and threatens, "It will in *time*." That move, to appear immediately behind the person whom he is addressing and speaking directly into that person's ear, in a satanic manner that is both seductive and menacing, becomes a part of Q's repertoire in subsequent appearances. Byron's Lucifer tells Cain he will satiate his thirst for knowledge, yet the knowledge Lucifer provides is a terrible conviction for Cain of human inferiority and future sorrow, a knowledge that leads to fatal results. In "Q Who," Q offers Picard knowledge of a similar kind:

> You judge yourselves against the pitiful adversaries you've encountered so far. The Romulans, the Klingons. They're nothing compared to what's waiting. Picard, you are about to move into areas of the galaxy containing wonders more incredible than you can possibly imagine and terrors to freeze your soul. I offer myself as guide only to be rejected out of hand.

Angered at what he sees as Picard's arrogance in his conviction that the *Enterprise* is perfectly capable of exploring the galaxy without his help, Q throws a tantrum and hurls the ship across the galaxy to expose it to the depredations of a much more powerful and utterly ruthless species, the Borg. Much to Q's delight, Picard is forced to confess his own helplessness and beg for Q's help in order to escape. When the captain later berates Q for indirectly causing the loss of eighteen lives, Q snaps, "If you can't take a little bloody nose, maybe you ought to go back home and crawl under your bed. It's not safe out here. It's wondrous, with treasures to satiate desires both subtle and gross. But it's not for the timid."

Q also plays the role of tempter in "True Q," a sixth-season episode in which a young woman, Amanda Rogers, unbeknownst to herself, is found to be a member of Q's species. When she is unwilling to abandon her previous human life to join the Q Continuum, Q successfully seduces her with knowledge and power, showing her the wonders of the galaxy from outside the ship: "What do humans have to offer you that even begins to compare with that? Your future contains wonders that you can't even imagine. The universe could be your playground." Q's success as a seducer increases as the series progresses, and Q's character is presented in a more heroic light. Despite Picard's early rejection of Q in "Encounter at Farpoint" and "Hide and Q," Q's satanic charm eventually works on the usually steadfast captain, when Q persuades Picard to violate one of his most cherished principles in both "Tapestry" and "All Good Things . . . ," Q's final two appearances on *Star Trek: TNG.* Picard willingly interferes with the continuity of time, changing his own past in the former episode and describing their potential future to the crew in the latter episode, with a view toward *modifying* that future. He is beginning to accept Q's conception of the arbitrariness of human notions of time, allowing himself to be seduced by Q's superior knowledge and ability, just as Cain is transformed by the sights Lucifer reveals to him. The results for Picard are not fatal, however; Picard uses the knowledge Q offers him to become reconciled with his own past in "Tapestry" and to improve relations among his crew in "All Good Things . . . ." Although Q operates with a satanic allure, he serves as Picard's guardian angel in "All Good Things . . . " and takes on the role of God in "Tapestry." Q has come a long way from his humiliating failure in "Hide and Q."

Along with his role as tempter, Q embodies the authoritarian and imperialist potential of the Byronic hero, most clearly revealed by Byron in his ambivalent characterization of Napoleon in "Ode to Napoleon Buonaparte" and in *Childe Harold,* canto 3. Byron's fascination with energetic and powerful leaders is, of course, tempered by his acknowledgment of the loss of life and destruction such leaders can incur. *Star Trek: TNG*'s creators reveal less ambivalence, however. While Q is portrayed as a kind of despotic bully and an autocratic tyrant and does indeed indirectly cause loss of life through his actions, his character is depicted increasingly as a force for good. The lionization of the heroic and powerful individual contains an antidemocratic impulse, which is exhibited in Q's recurring visits to the *Enterprise.* The *Enterprise* is the flagship of Starfleet of the United Federation of Planets, whose Prime Directive forbids interference in the internal affairs and development of other cultures even if their values contradict those of the Federation. Q, by contrast, is a despot and an imperialist, however enlightened and however benevolent his intentions eventually turn out to be. Interference is his way of life, and he forces the crew of the *Enterprise* into a dangerous first contact with the overwhelmingly powerful and hostile Borg to prove to them that their own methods of diplomacy and respect for other cultures are doomed to fail. Q delights in forcing Picard to humble himself and ask for help; enlightened despot that he is, he takes his powerless people under his protection and single-handedly, with a snap of the finger, rescues the ship. Q abounds in regal gestures like the arrogant snap of the finger, and he frequently attires himself in costumes of figures with absolute authority: the all-powerful judge in the postatomic horror courtroom in "Encounter at Farpoint" and "All Good Things . . . ," the Napoleonic marshal in "Hide and Q," the high sheriff of Nottingham in "Qpid," and, most explicitly, God in "Tapestry." After Picard had just died on an operating table due to the failure of his artificial heart, Q intones, "You're dead. This is the afterlife. And I'm God." Half-jokingly incensed at Picard's skeptical response, Q snaps, "Blasphemy! You're lucky I don't cast you out or smite you or something." He explains, as well, "I can take your life and give it back to you again with a snap of a finger." Q is no democrat, and he has no respect for the autonomy of what he sees as inferior cultures; he exults in exerting his omnipotence and absolute authority (putting the crew of the *Enterprise* into elaborate games and scenarios with arbitrary rules that only he knows, as in "Hide and Q" and "Qpid"). While he inevitably rescues them (even if the crew members do prove themselves, they cannot return to the ship without Q's assistance), it is only upon their submission to his despotic authority. As Thomas Richards remarks, "despite his tricks he almost always acts as the protector of Starfleet. Q blends comedy with the essence of a supreme being" (44). The creators of the show make very clear that this is a hierarchically structured universe, with a clearly designated chain of being. Amanda, once her Q nature is revealed, cannot remain among humans unless she gives up her powers; she poses too great a danger and must join others sharing her superior nature. Riker, on the other hand, cannot adopt the powers of the Q because he is not capable of handling them. Each would be punished (with death in Amanda's case) for violating his or her appointed place.

Despite his ultimately benevolent intentions, Q takes a sadistic satisfaction in humiliating Picard. Realizing he is completely outmatched by the Borg in "Q Who," Picard willingly abases himself to save the lives of the crew. He demands, "Q, end this," and Q, in his usual flippant tone, replies, "Moi? What makes you think I'm either inclined or capable to terminate this encounter?" Picard then appeals directly to his tormenter's sadistic streak: "If we all die here, now, you will not be able to gloat. You wanted to frighten us, we're frightened. You wanted to show us that we're inadequate for the moment, I grant that. You wanted me to say I need you, *I need you*!" After rescuing the ship, Q tells Picard, "That was a difficult admission. Another man would have been humiliated to say those words. Another man would have rather died than ask for help." He is both gratified and moved by Picard's willingness to submit to him. Surprisingly, in spite of his satanic demeanor in "Q Who" and Picard's firm insistence that Q's "help is not required," Q is proven right in the end: "In this episode, Q comes to the *Enterprise* like a god coming to earth to warn humanity that it has overreached its bounds" (Richards 48). Picard and his crew do *not* have the capacity to handle every challenge they meet; and Picard comments ruefully, "Maybe Q did the right thing for the wrong reason. . . . Perhaps what we most needed was a kick in our complacency to prepare us for what lies ahead." Richards argues that "the crew of the *Enterprise* is a little too perfect, a little too supremely confident in its own manifest destiny to explore the final frontier. Q has come to cut human beings and their allies down to size, and as we have seen, he has good reason to do so" (47).

In spite of his own questionable behavior and ethics, Q presents himself as both judge and enforcer of human morality, lecturing humans on their militaristic past in the series premiere, "Encounter at Farpoint"; claiming "superior morality" and preventing Amanda from using her power in a potentially destructive fashion in "True Q"; and in "Q-Less," helping prevent Vash from "setting Federation ethics back two hundred years" with her unscrupulous dealing in rare artifacts, including what turns out to be an embryonic life form. His apparent inconsistency leads him to be blamed frequently for wrongs he did not commit; just as Byron's narrator protests in *Don Juan,* "Why do they call me Misanthrope? Because / They hate me, not I them" (9.21), Q, in a parody of the isolated and misunderstood Byronic hero, complains, "I suppose it's my fate to be the galaxy's whipping boy. Heavy is the burden of being me" ("Q-Less"). While he never loses his arrogant demeanor, he reveals himself as working for humans' interests, and even incurs Picard's gratitude in the last two *TNG* episodes in which he appears. In his earlier manifestations, Q is apparently amoral, with a callous disregard for human life, despite his judgmental stance, but in his later incarnations, he appears to have developed a degree of ethical sensibility: in "Deja Q," he commits a "selfless act" by offering to sacrifice himself for the lives of the starship's crew and, after his powers have been restored, grants the android, Data, the gift of laughter and rescues a threatened planet; in "Qpid" he tries to warn Picard that the woman he loves will inevitably hurt him; in "Tapestry," he gives Picard another chance at life; and in "All Good Things . . . ," he assists Picard in solving the life-or-extermination puzzle his superiors in the Q Continuum have established. While he may echo the Continuum's continuing condemnation of humankind, Q has developed a concern for the value of human life. Although he remains the outsider, he seems to have found his niche in mediating between the two cultures he can never fully be a part of.

"True Q" and "Q-Less" (an episode of *Star Trek: Deep Space Nine*) are notable for the ways in which they turn our expectations of Q on their heads. Both episodes lead us to believe that Q is once again reprising his satanic role, in each case trying to lure a woman to join him, and apparently displaying an utterly callous lack of concern for human life. In "True Q," Q investigates a young woman, Amanda Rogers (Olivia d'Abo), who is serving as an intern on board the *Enterprise*. We learn that although she believes herself to be human, she is actually the daughter of two members of the Q Continuum who had taken on human form and decided to live on Earth. When they refused to give up their Q powers, they were executed by order of the Continuum, and Amanda was adopted by human parents. Q's mission is to evaluate Amanda's powers and persuade her to join the Continuum if she is in fact completely Q . . . or execute her if she isn't. Q positions himself as the rebel once again, obeying the orders of his superiors with a palpable reluctance. He manages to offend just about everyone, treating Amanda in a patronizing manner (almost every word he uses to describe her is prefaced by the adjective "little"), and repeatedly uttering such misanthropic remarks as, "Do you think she will want to remain an enfeebled mortal?" Q has nothing but contempt for Amanda's human side; and he tempts her in his traditional satanic manner, standing seductively at her shoulder, speaking in her ear, and offering her power and knowledge. We, the viewers, are even more inclined to distrust Q when we eventually learn that he has come as a potential assassin and will kill Amanda if she is some kind of hybrid, remarking in a classic case of the pot calling the kettle black, "Do you think it's reasonable for us to allow omnipotent beings to roam free through the universe?"

If he had actually assassinated her, Q would have been presented as a tyrant who should be rebelled against and resisted at all costs, an autocratic, malevolent, and despotic dictator who opposes everything the democratic, noninterfering, and life-respecting Federation stands for. The interesting thing is that Q *is* presented as an autocratic, malevolent, and despotic dictator, *but*—and here's the crux of the matter—the episode slams our expectations into reverse by having Q turn out to be *right* in the end. By the end of the episode, we are convinced not only that he is entitled to decide whether Amanda lives or dies but also that he is a merciful judge, who generously grants her the boon of deciding her own future. Not only that, but the decision she makes violates our expectations even further. To put it another way, this episode does everything possible to lead us to *condemn* Q as a type of fascist dictator or unfair judge, but it concludes by forcing us to *respect* him as such. It's as if the series' creators want to present Q in his leadership role in as unfavorable a light as possible so as to reinforce the message that we need and should respect powerful and autocratic leaders even if their methods and demeanor are both arbitrary and brutal. And we will be presented with the identical message in "All Good Things . . . ." So much for Picard's liberal humanism.

"True Q" initially sets us up to perceive Q as the villain. Amanda's initial reaction to Q is revulsion; she wants nothing to do with him and gets the viewers firmly on her side by telekinetically hurling Q across the room. Q is made to look even worse when Amanda begins to query him about what it means to be a Q:

AMANDA. And what do you do with this power?

Q. Anything we want.

AMANDA. Do you use it to help others?

Q. I think you've missed the point, my dear. Clearly you've spent far too much time with humans. As a Q, you can have your heart's desire, instantly, whatever that may be.

Of course, that is precisely Q's appeal. Q is wish fulfillment incarnate; who among us wouldn't want to be able to "have [our] heart's desire, instantly, whatever that may be"? We probably also suspect that our initial impulse, were we granted this boon, would be to benefit ourselves, not help others.

Once Amanda begins to learn the possibilities of her Q nature, she begins to act in a characteristically selfish and Q-like fashion. She kidnaps Riker, who is in the middle of a date, transports him to a type of Victorian garden with a gazebo, and tries to force him to fall in love with her. The scene is excruciatingly embarrassing as Amanda momentarily commits the equivalent of emotional rape but quickly realizes her error. Given Amanda's initial negative response to Q, her dismay that the Q do not use their powers for good, and the painful lesson she learns about misusing her powers herself, we have every expectation that she will reject her Q heritage and choose to remain human.

"True Q" also sets up an expectation that Picard's humanism will triumph over Q's misanthropy. Lambasting Q's self-designation as Amanda's "judge, and jury, and, if necessary, executioner," and demanding "by what right have you appointed yourself to this position?" Picard is infuriated at Q's calm reply of "superior morality." The captain launches into an impassioned speech that would *seem* to embody the ethos of the *Star Trek* canon:

> Your arrogant pretense at being the moral guardians of the universe strikes me as being hollow, Q. I see no evidence that you are guided by a superior moral code or any code whatsoever. You may be nearly omnipotent, and I don't deny that your parlor tricks are very impressive, but morality, I don't see it! I don't acknowledge it, Q! I would put human morality against the Q's any day. And perhaps that's the reason that we fascinate you so. Because our puny behavior shows you a glimmer of the one thing that evades your omnipotence. A moral center. And if so, I can think of no crueler irony than that you should destroy this young woman, whose only crime is that she's too human.

This magnificent peroration, with its eloquent and ardent sincerity, a discourse that could serve as the rallying point for just about any oppressed group rising up against their oppressors, Picard's own Declaration of Independence against the Continuum, his "Civil Disobedience," his "I Have a Dream" speech, is immediately punctured and deflated by Q's cool remark: "Jean-Luc, sometimes I think the only reason I come here is to listen to these *wonderful* speeches of yours." In an instant Picard has gone from being the eloquent defier of tyrannical and immoral authority to being a pompous and inflated windbag. Q turns out to have a moral center after all, as he offers Amanda the choice between joining the Continuum or becoming fully human, without powers. We also learn that he made this decision *before* hearing Picard's apparently superfluous speech, as he tells Picard *immediately* afterward, "This time your concern is unwarranted. We've decided *not* to harm her. And we are prepared to offer her a choice." Yet the humanistic ethos that Picard embodies might still be redeemed, Q might be humiliated in defeat . . . *if* Amanda decides to become fully human. But she doesn't. Amanda cannot resist using her power, albeit as a force for good, as she takes action to save lives on the planet below. She then announces, "I am Q," and agrees to depart with her almost-assassin to join the Q Continuum, moral center or lack thereof notwithstanding. Instead of rebelling against the Continuum's tyranny and opting for her human side, Amanda willingly joins the Continuum, thereby implicitly condoning their actions in killing her parents. Unlike *Cain,* in which Byron effectively undermines Lucifer's claims to authority, "True Q" reinforces Q's. As William D. Brewer suggests, "Lucifer's worldview is negative and counterproductive: it leads to Cain's frustration and his murder of Abel" (104). "True Q," by contrast, validates Q's worldview and his leadership, and he wins this round. He may be brutal, autocratic, sadistic, and callous, but he has compelled our allegiance; we want to see him offer guidance and leadership, and, not incidentally, cut our noble and inhumanly perfect Captain down to size. We want an all-powerful and all-knowing guide who will allow us to feel subversive by defying the captain's authority *and* that of the Continuum; but who will assert dominion over us in such a flamboyant, entertaining, irresistible, and enticing manner that we don't notice that he's deprived us of our human rights. Q's creators are not as careful as Byron is to temper our admiration of his outlaw heroes.

Like "True Q," the *Deep Space Nine* episode "Q-Less" similarly allows de Lancie to inject some malevolence into his performance, but once again Q turns out to be the hero in a villain's disguise. The episode contains two parallel plots that converge at the end, both of which serve to set Q up as the *apparent* villain. One plot involves a mysterious and life-threatening power drain on the space station that will eventually suck the entire station into a nearby wormhole to be torn apart if not stopped in time. The other plot involves Q's attempt to resume his relationship with his former girlfriend, Vash (Jennifer Hetrick). Although Q vehemently protests being held responsible for the energy drain, he remains the most likely suspect. O'Brien (Colm Meaney) remarks, "A blasted menace, is what he is." The crew is unable to locate the source, and Q only "helps" with taunts and jibes from the sidelines. It turns out, however, that he is actually trying to guide Commander Sisko (Avery Brooks) and his crew to the truth, but Q is doing so with his usual technique of indirection, the same technique he will use the following year in "All Good Things . . . ." Q drops hints and makes sarcastic remarks, but he expects the crew to do the rest. Eventually Q does provide Sisko with some useful information: "I'll tell you what's going on. While you're here conducting futile experiments, Vash is below engaged in base commerce and setting Federation ethics back two hundred years. Believe me, gang, she's far more dangerous to you than I am." And he's right. The power drain is being caused by an embryonic life form Vash brought back from the Gamma quadrant to auction off as a rare artifact. Despite his apparently callous demeanor ("I'm going just to sit right here and watch. I've never seen a space station torn apart by a wormhole before"), Q actually serves as a moral force. He is disgusted by Vash's brand of capitalism, remarking, during the auction, "I hate to interrupt such a thrilling display of naked avarice, but I thought it was only right of me to warn you that this station is hurtling toward its doom, and it's very unlikely that any of you will survive to enjoy your purchases. I just thought I'd mention it. Please carry on."

Within the other plotline, Q offers to take Vash on a "grand tour of the universe," but she demurs, insisting, "It's over, Q; I want you out of my life. You are arrogant, you're overbearing, and you think you know everything." Exhibiting his typical lack of interpersonal skills, he replies, "But I do know everything," to which Vash counters, "That makes it worse." As he discovers, threats don't work either; he snaps, "Really, Vash, this playing hard to get is growing tedious. Let's not forget that I'm the Q and you the lowly human. I'll decide when this partnership is over, understand?" Q's demeanor toward Vash is clearly coded as that of a potential rapist. He pushes her onto a bed and shows no compunction about threatening and brutalizing her. The misogyny of "Q-Less"'s treatment of Vash is veiled by the *apparent* feminism of her declaration of independence from Q. Yet, ultimately, it is Q who is given sympathetic treatment by the end of the episode. While he does not succeed in reclaiming Vash, his displays of his powers make clear that he could have won Vash if he wanted to. Thus, when Q regretfully opts to release her, he is seen as all the more magnanimous. Suddenly Q is sensitive and vulnerable, and Vash seems cold-hearted by comparison. Although she acknowledges, "In some ways I'm going to miss you too," she's already planning her next archaeological expedition, this time in partnership with the Ferengi businessman Quark (Armin Shimerman), the embodiment of unfettered and unprincipled capitalism. As Q's star rises during the course of "Q-Less," Vash's falls; and she is made to look worse and worse. Vash prostitutes and degrades herself to Quark, willingly performing oo-mox, a Ferengi ear-rubbing sexual ritual, in order to bargain him down, and her proficiency during this act clearly indicates that this is not the first time she has done so. Q's disgusted reaction, "How perfectly vile," is right on. Vash accuses Q of being "evil," of being willing to "kill all these people to get even with me," and he responds, "I must admit the thought had occurred to me, but this station is in enough trouble without me. Although I'd be glad to save you. All you have to do is ask." It turns out, however, that Vash is ultimately responsible for the life-threatening power drain. She will violate any ethical principle in her pursuit of monetary gain. Presumably, she thus "deserves" any abuse Q chooses to inflict upon her. In both "True Q" and "Q-Less," Q's misogyny, callousness, and brutality are ultimately irrelevant; he represents pure power, and therein lies his appeal. He doesn't have to kill Amanda or rape Vash to prove his point; it is enough that he could do so without any fear of repercussions. When Q allows Amanda and Vash to choose their own fates, it is as if he is granting them a *privilege*. As far as Q is concerned, humans have no inalienable *rights*.

Despite his authoritarianism toward humans, Q is hardly a model citizen among his own species. In his fascination with individual humans (particularly Picard) and his desire to render them assistance, Q violates the spirit of the institutional authority of the Q Continuum, who have imperialistically designated themselves as the judges of humankind's evolution. In the finale of the *Next Generation* series, "All Good Things . . . ," Q's superiors set up an elaborate test of Picard's ability to expand his mind and unravel an elaborate time-travel paradox. Q viciously lays into Picard, laughing derisively at the human's inept attempts to solve the puzzle. When Picard (understandably) asks, "Did you create the anomaly?" Q responds, with a malicious laugh, "No no no. You're going to be *so* surprised when you realize where it came from," then adds in a much harder tone, "If you ever figure it out." Q's misanthropy is in full force as he taunts Picard, "You're such a limited creature—perfect example of why we made our decision. The trial never ended, Captain. We never reached a verdict. But now we have. You're guilty." Q is completely in control. Picard's humanism will not help him here:

> PICARD. We've journeyed to countless new worlds, we've contacted new species, we have expanded our understanding of the universe.
> Q. In your own paltry limited way. You have no idea how far you still have to go. But instead of using the last seven years to change and to grow, you have squandered them.
> PICARD. We are what we are, and we're doing the best we can. It is not for you to set the standards by which we should be judged.
> Q. Oh, but it is, and we have. Time may be eternal, Captain, but our patience is not. It's time to put an end to your trek through the stars, make room for other, more worthy species.
> PICARD. You're going to deny us travel through space?
> Q. You obtuse piece of *flotsam*! You are to be denied *existence*!

We seem to be in the same situation as "Encounter at Farpoint," where Picard the humanist defeated Q the misanthrope, except that it turns out that Q is really on Picard's side. Picard murmurs, "Q, I do not believe even you are capable of such an act"; but as in "Q-Less," Q is incensed at the accusation: "I? There you go again always blaming me for everything. Well, this time I'm not your enemy, I'm not the one who causes the annihilation of mankind. You are." Despite Picard's ultimate success, the Q continue to appoint themselves both judge and jury; as Q explains, "You just don't get it, do you, Jean-Luc? The trial never ends." The members of the Q Continuum are described much like a faceless, impersonal bureaucracy; it was their *collective* decision to put humankind on trial in the series pilot and its finale, to execute Amanda's parents for leaving the fold (and to consider executing her), and to strip Q himself (temporarily) of his powers. While Q must act as their representative, he assimilates more human values, and he acts as much as possible on his own, particularly in the assistance he renders Picard in the ultimate test in "All Good Things . . . ." Like a parent who will not define a word for his child but tells him to look it up in the dictionary, Q will not give Picard the answers but does provide indispensable hints, without which Picard would not have succeeded in saving humankind from destruction. De Lancie, himself, saw the significance of his final scene with Picard as revealing that "Q has a vested interest in this man making it." Describing the attitude he wanted to project, he commented, "I have become ifterested enough and attached enough to his struggle that I'm willing, even though I'm compelled to play the game dictated to me by my higher ups. . . . I'm willing to give him clues" (qtd. in Stein, "Minding"). When Picard thanks Q for his help, Q says, "I was the one who got you into it. A directive from the Continuum. The part about the helping hand, though, was *my* idea." He sees his role as helping humankind realize their full evolutionary potential in charting "the unknown possibilities of existence" (he really has, as he responded in "Deja Q" to a character who was listing his transgressions, taken up missionary work). Anticipating his future involvement in overseeing humankind's development, Q says "I'll be watching. And if you're very lucky I'll drop by to say hello from time to time. See you *out there.*"

Like so many popular culture heroes, Q defines his own moral code, independent of institutional authority. His appeal to his audience lies in his simultaneously godlike and irreverent pose. He has the power to solve all of his protégé Picard's problems, yet at the same time he subverts both Picard's authority and that of the Continuum. He is the heroic individual who takes the law in his own hands (even suspending the laws of nature when it suits his purposes). He intercedes between the humans he wishes to protect and the impersonal bureaucracy that oppresses them, and he is seen as an ultimately beneficial force to humans despite his imperious demeanor and brutal methods. While Picard continues to rail against the Q Continuum's "arrogant pretense at being the moral guardians of the universe," objecting that they don't have the right "to set the standards by which we should be judged," he nevertheless reacts with gratitude to Q's benevolently intended, if autocratically administered, guidance. Q is the heroic leader–guardian angel who, despite his exasperation at his protégés' ineptitude, defends them against the evils of institutional authority (in "All Good Things . . . "), their own greed (in "Q-Less"), and their own self-doubt (in "Tapestry"). He is ultimately a kind of benevolent despot.[5] Surprisingly, given the usual humanistic ethos of *Star Trek,* the series' creators thus presume that Q is *entitled* to evaluate humans' worthiness! In their development of a hero for a contemporary audience that seeks out the fantasy of powerful leaders, Q's creators seem to suggest that people are actually better off submitting to the despotic and arbitrary authority of a powerful individual and that the elaborate tests Q designs, however rigged they are, are somehow beneficial to his "subjects." As a leader, Q proves extremely tempting; the pure power that he wields offers the promise of solving all our problems for us . . . as long as we submit to his authority. He has no respect for humans' civil rights or democratic traditions; like any imperialist he feels entitled to impose his dominion on an inferior species. He wins the viewers over completely, however, with his wicked and subversive sense of humor, with his charisma, and with his promise to cut through the crap and get right to the truth. The audience excuses his brutality because, after all, Q has good intentions and he is right.

The series' creators, in the Q episodes, seem to concur with Mill's notion that "the initiation of all wise or noble things, comes and must come from individuals; generally at first from some one individual. The honour and glory of the average man is that he is capable of following that initiative" (66). Although a powerful and sometimes autocratic leader himself, Picard becomes, *in his interactions with Q,* that "average man" who derives his "honor and glory" from following Q's initiative.[6] Although Picard is usually portrayed as competent, intelligent, confident, resourceful, ethical, and otherwise deserving of respect, in the Q episodes he is uncharacteristically fallible, almost inevitably walking right into whatever trap Q sets for him and making the wrong decisions& One of the things that distinguishes starship captains (at least those who anchor the *Star Trek* series) is their ability to solve apparently insurmountable problems, to overcome apparently impossible odds with their quick thinking, resourcefulness, and decisiveness. Often it is not only action on the captain's part that saves the day but also his or her humanitarianism or diplomatic ability that disarms an apparently overwhelming enemy. Picard, like his colleagues Kirk, Sisko, and Janeway, does this kind of thing all the time—*except* when he encounters Q. Picard *does* overcome Q in "Encounter at Farpoint" and "Hide and Q." From then on, however, he is clearly out of his league. Although in "The Best of Both Worlds," part 2, Picard defeats the Borg both through his strength of will and presence of mind, in "Q Who," the captain is compdetely helpless. Although Picard and his crew have solved any number of apparently unsolvable technological difficulties, they are unable to make any real progress with the falling Bre'el moon in "Deja Q." The potentially workable solutions result from Q's superior knowledge and the suggestions he offers La Forge and Data, and it is Q who ultimately restores the moon's orbit. Although Picard has dealt with any number of temporal anomalies successfully, in "All Good Things . . . ," he clearly required Q's assistance. Starship captains typically either defeat or win over "superior" beings with their intelligence and humanistic morality; that Q so consistently either tricks Picard or provides him with assistance he cannot live without seems to me an uncharacteristic violation of *Star Trek*'s usual vision of human progress and ability. The Captain, after all, is simultaneously the representative of the human species and a superior human being, the embodiment of human evolution and potential. While he may be vulnerable to overwhelming physical and psychological pressure, as in "Best of Both Worlds" and "Chain of Command" (in which Picard is tortured by a Cardassian inquisitor), the types of head games Q plays with Picard, *if Q were a typical antagonist,* really would not transcend Picard's intellectual, moral, and diplomatic ability.

But Q is not a typical antagonist; he is extremely funny, dynamic, and popular with fans; and part of his popularity results from his ability to knock the almost "inhumanly" perfect Picard off his pedestal. It is as if the writers can't help giving Q the upper hand, even though by doing so they are contradicting *Star Trek*'s usual humanistic message. This contradiction actually points to a much larger conflict within the *Star Trek* series. The Roddenberry vision of human progress keeps coming in conflict with the necessity for drama and action that fans want in a science fiction series. The *Star Trek* writers' solution has been to create consistently powerful opponents, opponents whose bloodthirstiness and ruthlessness repeatedly remind us of human moral superiority. Yet these opponents keep being softened and humanized. The Klingons, the Ferengi, the Cardassians, and the Borg all become more and more "human." However, while Picard and his crew eventually humanize their worst enemies, Q's function is to humanize *Picard.* The implication is that even the heroic Jean-Luc Picard requires the guidance of a more powerful and knowledgeable authority figure. Ronald D. Moore, writer of "Tapestry" and cowriter of "All Good Things . . .," defines Q's role as specifically to test Picard, while also noting that Q serves to puncture Picard's demeanor, to bring him down to a more human level. Adapting the Byronic hero for contemporary viewers who are largely powerless against institutional authority themselves, Q's creators seem to suggest that people are actually better off submitting to the despotic and arbitrary authority of a powerful individual: the elaborate tests Q designs, however rigged they are, are somehow beneficial to his "subjects." While Q continues to mock what he sees as the banality of human concerns, Q nevertheless concerns himself with Picard's individual peace of mind in "Qpid" and "Tapestry," although practicing a kind of guerrilla psychotherapy. When Riker, reflecting on Picard's experience in "Tapestry," says, "It sounds like he put you through hell," Picard insists, instead, that he owes Q "a debt of gratitude" for his "compassion" in helping him become reconciled to his own past. And Riker further confirms the validity of Q's lesson with his overt admiration of Picard's youthful recklessness, saying, "I wish I'd had the chance to know *that* Jean-Luc Picard." In "All Good Things . . . ," Picard uses his knowledge of how the crew drift apart in the future to urge them to strengthen their relationships with him and with one another in the present, even joining them in a game of poker for the first time. Presumably they will forge stronger bonds because of Q's interference.

The question arises as to whether we should welcome Q's leadership or view him as a potential threat, a charismatic but dangerous fascist-to-be. In his first two appearances on the series, Q clearly reveals the dangers of aggressive individualism. He is irresponsible and callous and is soundly trounced by Picard, the spokesperson for liberal humanism. Subsequent to those appearances, however, there is an interesting shift. Q's appearances from the second season onward follow a similar pattern. There is a setup whereby it *appears* as though Q is the villain and is going to be defeated, but a reversal occurs, and Q is shown to be both in the right and actually on humans' side. This is particularly the case in "True Q," "Q-Less," "Tapestry," and "All Good Things . . . ." In "Q Who," for instance, Q sadistically demands, "Where's your stubbornness now, Picard, your arrogance? Do you still profess to be prepared for what awaits you?" But Q is, in fact, in the right. Picard's arrogance leads him foolishly to underestimate the dangers awaiting in the galaxy. I suggest that the pattern of reversal that Q's episodes employ emphasizes even more forcefully that Q is being portrayed as a leader who deserves our allegiance and respect.

Q's leadership potential is nevertheless always allied explicitly to his outlaw stance; like Lestat shaking up the Children of Darkness, Q is a rebel who challenges the status quo. Again like Lestat, Q promotes change not out of any lofty ideals but rather as a means to pursue sensation, whatever the cost. His initial desire to join the *Enterprise*'s crew in "Q Who," for instance, was simply the result of boredom. Exiled from the Continuum as a result of his failure to tempt Riker (in "Hide and Q"), he describes himself as having "been wandering vaguely, bored really, my existence without purpose." Lestat's rock concert makes a statement, and he hopes it will provoke a war, but Lestat's motives are more to stir things up and create some excitement than for any noble cause. Q is similar. As a fellow Q describes him in the *Voyager* episode "Death Wish," "Q rebelled against this existence by refusing to behave himself. He was out of control. He used his powers irresponsibly and all for his own amusement, and he desperately needed amusement because he could find none here." Q's colleague praises Q for defying the stultifying authority and stagnation of the Q Continuum, noting that he came close to serving as a catalyst for change: "For a moment there you really had our attention, my attention. You gave us something to talk about." He describes Q as "irrepressible" and as someone who "forced [him] to think." Ultimately, Q's rebellion against his own kind highlights the disadvantages of transcending the human condition and reaffirms western, individualistic values against the bureaucratic, authoritarian, and corporate values reflected in the Continuum.

Rejecting the Continuum's continuing derision of human potential, Q learns that, in their ignorance and innocence, humans have advantages he lacks; and he begins to seek them out as romantic partners to fill the gaps he perceives in himself& Just as Manfred learns that knowledge cannot satisfy him, Q learns that in many ways knowledge is boredom. With his omnipotence he has, like Childe Harold, "felt the fulness of satiety" and remains cynical and isolated (3.4). He is portrayed more frequently in a serious mode, trying to forge a genuine connection with Picard while realizing what he himself is missing. Q might say, as does the narrator of *Don Juan,*

> Now my sere fancy "falls into the yellow
> Leaf," and Imagination droops her pinion
> And the sad truth which hovers o'er my desk
> Turns what was once romantic to burlesque.
>
> And if I laugh at any mortal thing,
> 'Tis that I may not weep.

(4.3–4)

At the same time, Q acquires a more mature perspective on his own jaded condition. He is aware, as *Don Juan's* narrator puts it, that "never more on me / The freshness of the heart can fall like dew" (1.214), but he develops an appreciation of an innocence of perspective that he can never recover. Just as *Don Juan's* narrator "deem[s] not, what I deemed, my soul invincible" (1.213), Q, despite his physical invincibility, learns the limitations of his own soul as well, for he cannot help taking the wonders of the universe for granted. In "Q-Less," Q gains the viewers' sympathy by admitting his own fallibility and pleading to Vash, "It's not going to be the same without you. When I look at a gas nebula, all I see is a cloud of dust. Seeing the universe through your eyes I was able to experience wonder. I'm going to miss that."

In his romantic endeavors, Q's ego demands that he find a lover who is a mirror of himself, yet his growing appreciation of humanity encourages him to value those he loves in their human fallibility. He wants a lover who will complete him, provide him with the human qualities he has grown to value, but at the same time reproduce him or herself in his image, to reflect his glory back to him. This paradoxical tension is similar to Manfred's feelings for Astarte. On the one hand, he desires her for her "gentler powers" and "virtues" (2.2.112, 116), for she completes him by providing qualities he "never had" (2.2.115); on the other hand, he wishes to perceive her as a mirror of himself, for to acknowledge her more human qualities would undermine his own dilated self-image. In his romantic attraction to Picard, Q admires the Captain for having the human qualities he himself lacks; however it is his narcissism that compels Q to perceive Picard as a reflection of himself. To Q, Picard embodies all of humankind's potential concentrated in one person; at the same time, in failing to achieve that potential in the time Q `ad allotted him, Picard is a continuous source of frustration for Q. Ronald Moore explains that the writers of *TNG* thought of Q as being in love with Picard, although Q himself would never admit to being in love with a human (Stein, "Minding").[7] John de Lancie describes Q and Picard as alter egos. I take this idea further, however, and look at the particular way Q is in love with Picard, his alter ego. Q thinks he sees a great deal of himself in Picard, and he likes what he sees. Nevertheless, he would like to see even more of himself reflected in the mirror he has selected.

In his egotism and self-absorption, Q can only love someone who reflects his glory back to him. At the same time, he has begun to learn the limits of his omnipotence, the purposelessness of his long existence. Thus Picard not only can serve as a mirror for Q but can complete him as well, provide him with the human qualities he lacks, the ambition and drive and determination and "passion and imagination" that are fundamental to Picard's character. Q's adoption of Picard's Starfleet uniform continuously emphasizes the way these characters serve as doubles for each other. Q has three goals, then, in his pursuit of Picard: 1) to prove to Picard how similar the two of them really are; 2) to show Picard that the way in which he resembles Q, his dark side, as it were, is an essential part of him and cannot be separated from the whole; and 3) to bring Picard up to his own level of knowledge and awareness in order to make him an appropriate object of desire to such an exalted being. Just as Manfred and Astarte share "the same lone thoughts and wanderings" (2.2.109), and Maturin's Melmoth the Wanderer tries to infect Immalee with his misanthropy and gloom, Q wishes to remake Picard into his own image, and is constantly frustrated when the object of his affections doesn't live up to expectations. In language reminiscent of Victor Frankenstein's comment in regard to Elizabeth in the first edition of *Frankenstein*, "I loved to tend on her, as I should on a favourite animal" (65–66), a crew member describes Q's interest in Picard as "very similar to that of a master and his beloved pet" ("All Good Things . . ."). Q's ambivalent attraction to Picard manifests itself in the rapid fluctuations of his demeanor; one moment he sincerely regards the Captain with affection and benevolence, the next he sarcastically condemns Picard for his human limitations. Q seems to want Picard somehow to rise to his level of understanding and to join him in his misanthropy. Q is always unduly infuriated by Picard's strenuous defense of humankind; and he seems outraged that the Captain doesn't share his conviction of human inferiority, since he so strongly desires to see Picard as transcending human limitations. In "Qpid," for instance, Q is jealous of Picard's love for Vash but is even more disappointed when he realizes he erred in thinking Picard "a bit more evolved than the rest of your species." Q can only justify his own attraction to a mere human by convincing himself of Picard's superiority.

"Tapestry" is another episode that implies Q's romantic interest in Picard and reveals Q's effort to remake Picard in his own image. Picard has been mortally wounded, and Q grants him an opportunity to relive his own past differently, the idea being that if he avoids a bar brawl in which he was stabbed in the `eart as a young man, he can avoid getting the artificial heart that kills him years later. In one scene Picard awakes in bed after an amorous encounter with an old girlfriend, feels a finger stroking his ear, and rolls over to find Q lying next to him and greeting him with a sultry "Morning, Darling."[8] Despite Q's apparent compassion and charity in allowing Picard to relive his past in this episode, there is more to this exercise. The subtext is Q's narcissistic desire to prove to Picard how similar the two of them really are. When Picard relates some of his romantic misdemeanors, Q responds in an unmistakably affectionate tone, "I had no idea you were such a cad. I'm impressed." Describing himself in his youth, Picard remarks, "I was a different person in those days. Arrogant, undisciplined, with far too much ego and far too little wisdom. I was more like you," to which Q replies, "Then you must have been far more interesting. Pity you had to change." When Picard avoids the altercation in his youth in which he was stabbed in the heart, thereby assuring his safety years later, Q returns him to an alternative present where he finds himself in a much less desirable position; Picard is a dull, plodding, junior lieutenant of astrophysics, not a starship captain. He insists to Q, "I can't live out my days as that person. That man is bereft of passion and imagination. That is not who I am!" Q replies: "Au contraire. He's the person you wanted to be. One who was less arrogant and undisciplined in his youth, one who was less like *me.*" Picard confesses, "You're right, Q. You gave me the chance to change, and I took the opportunity. But I admit now it was a mistake." Q thus triumphantly proves to the Captain that it was Picard's very resemblance to Q himself that made him the person he is, that Picard's arrogant, undisciplined, and Q-like qualities were essential to his development. Q teaches Picard to accept and value his own "low wants" because they cannot be extricated from his "lofty will." A flawless Picard would be a passionless junior officer with no imagination; however, a flawed Picard contains the seeds of future greatness. In this episode in particular, de Lancie and Stewart use body language, physical proximity, and tone of voice to convey an intangible sense of intimacy, shared understanding, and ease that the two characters evince in each other's company. Despite Picard's frequent irritation with his capricious mentor and guide, the dialogue shows Picard willingly confiding in Q, almost boasting, about his youthful misadventures. Picard tells Riker, "There's still part of me that cannot accept that Q would give me a second chance. Or that he would demonstrate so much compassion. And if it was Q, I owe him a debt of gratitude." He explains further, "There are many parts of my youth that I'm not proud of. There were loose threads, untidy parts of me that I would like to remove. But when I pulled on one of those threads it unravelled the tapestry of my life." That loose thread he pulled, of course, was his resemblance to Q, the egotism and arrogance they both share but that Picard tries to deny. Interestingly, Picard can be most himself with Q, can act on those impulses his disciplined exterior usually represses. In "Tapestry," Q holds up a mirror to Picard, and that mirror is Q himself. Picard learns his lesson, learns to accept and embrace that mirror image as an inextricable part of who he is.

Q renews his efforts at reshaping the Captain in "All Good Things. . . ." His principal concern is that Picard live up to the image he (Q) has of him, to conform to his expectations; he tells the Captain, "I believed in you. I thought you had potential." Thus, Q continues to prod Picard with a combination of helpful hints and sarcastic derision. Once Picard succeeds in collapsing the spatial anomaly that would have destroyed humankind, Q fairly beams with pride in his protégé: "The Continuum didn't think you had it in you, Jean-Luc. But I knew you did." But when Picard asks Q, "Are qou saying that it worked? We collapsed the anomaly?" Q responds irritably with the petulance of an unappreciated lover, "Is that all this meant to you, just another spatial anomaly, just another day at the office?" Mocking his recalcitrant pupil's limited ability to comprehend what was at stake, Q sighs, "The anomaly. My ship. My crew. I suppose you're worried about your fish, too. Well, if it puts your mind at ease you've saved humanity. Once again." Q's tone during this final scene is one of both indulgence and irritation. On the one hand, he is proud that Picard is able to make a leap in understanding, but on the other hand, he seems overly frustrated at Picard's lack of comprehension. The two seem to achieve a moment of genuine communication that is reinforced by their physical proximity; however, it is quickly obvious that Picard is not ready to understand what he is being offered. He demands, "Q, what is it that you're trying to tell me?" Q, about to whisper a reply in the captain's ear, changes his mind and says only "You'll find out." Q's frustration seems to lie in the fact that Picard remains almost exclusively focused on the salvation of humankind, which for Q is a minor concern. His priority has been an effort to jump-start Picard's development, to bring the Captain up to his own level of knowledge and awareness. I believe that is why Q insists on helping Picard solve the puzzle his superiors had mandated. For Q, the entire significance of the test was whether Picard "had the ability to expand [his] mind and [his] horizons," in other words, to share Q's "same lone thoughts and wanderings," to become the mirror of himself that he desires. Throughout his appearances on the series, John de Lancie effectively captures Q's half-mocking, half-affectionate but invariably proprietary demeanor toward Picard in the inflection with which he delivers his repeated epithet, "mon Capitaine."

In portraying powerful and dominating characters, de Lancie and Stewart both show great skill in bringing out those characters' vulnerabilities, thereby making them more human and giving them a greater capacity to connect with the audience. One of the lessons of the series, particularly in the Q episodes, is that humans are worthy because of their mortality and their limitations; in striving to overcome these limitations and to expand their knowledge and in the ambition and drive these limitations provoke, humans might, as Q reflects, have the potential to advance even beyond his own species ("Hide and Q"). Riker's misuse of the powers Q has granted him and his ultimate rejection of those powers reinforce the message even more strongly that humans should be content with their natures and their *gradual* evolution. Despite all of his power and despite having all of the wonders of the universe at his disposal, Q involves himself repeatedly in human concerns, moderating some of his arrogance with a genuine if peremptory affection for at least one of his charges. Like Manfred, who eventually reaches for the Abbot's hand and remarks, "'tis not so difficult to die" (3.4.151), thereby revealing his acceptance of his own humanity, Q must moderate the misanthropic stance of the Byronic hero to connect with his audience.

The creator of a popular "text" has to contend with an ambivalence on the part of his or her audience; on the one hand, the audience wants a hero who is larger than life, one who will provide them with a vicarious experience of self-sufficiency and power; on the other hand, they want that hero to be human after all, to share their values and emotions. In movies, this progression from superhero to quasi human being takes place over the course of a couple of hours, as in *Terminator 2* or *The Crow*. In *Star Trek: TNG*, Q is gradually humanized over the course of a television series, but the effect is the same. In their particular reincarnation of the Byronic hero, the creators of this series serve a specific ideological purpose, reinforcing the idea of the heroic individual, the well-intentioned and powerful leader who must be followed, however uncomfortable his edicts may make one. At the same time, the writers affirm the worth of all of those who are followers by having the hero champion the value of human frailties and limitations. The viewers are encouraged, not to *imitate* Q in his subversion of institutional authority, but rather to offer their allegiance to a strong leader who will solve all their problems for them. Q's discontent with his omnipotent and immortal state tells us plainly that humans are really better off in their relative powerlessness.

Q is a very appealing character and is extremely popular among fans of *Star Trek: TNG.* This affection is no doubt due, in large part, to de Lancie's witty, energetic, and flamboyant performances as well as his on-screen chemistry with Patrick Stewart. Q is wickedly funny, sexy, and charismatic; and he has evolved into a hero who clearly has humans' best interests at heart. The occasional vulnerability Q evinces makes his character even more likable. At the same time, Q as a character is both reactionary and misogynistic, having no compunction about trampling on humans' civil liberties in the process of providing them with leadership. He flaunts conventions, defines his own moral code, defies authority, and asserts an incarnate individualism. In all these ways, Q is the Byronic hero par excellence. But if that were all he is, he would lose much of his audience appeal. Q is a Byronic hero for *our* generation in his gradual repudiation of his own Byronism. He pays us the ultimate compliment of revealing that he would rather be like us, with our capacity for wonder and our awareness of "how important each moment must be" ("Tapestry"). We should be grateful that Q is willing to serve as our protector and guide and be even more grateful that we do *not* share his powers and immortality. Q ironically serves to teach us to appreciate our own flawed humanity, showing us, in effect, that omnipotence isn't everything it's cracked up to be.

5

"She Moves in Mysterious Ways"
The Byronic Heroine

Emily Brontë's Catherine Earnshaw and Thomas Hardy's Eustacia Vye, though created thirty years apart, represent a frequently occurring type in Victorian fiction: the nontraditional, nonconforming female. While these women fail to conform to the expected roles imposed by their society, their authors, in creating them, rely on conventional literary models, in part to illustrate just how greatly these women deviate from their traditional female roles. Anne Mellor places *Wuthering Heights* within a tradition of "specifically masculine Romanticism," labeling this process "ideological cross-dressing" on Brontë's part (186). Judi Osborn specifically uses the term *Byronic heroine* to characterize Catherine (45–51).[1] Likewise, Penny Boumelha, in her discussion of *The Return of the Native*, places Eustacia Vye within the literary tradition of the Byronic hero. Boumelha notes that Eustacia shares some of the characteristics of the "Romantic hero—a solitary status in opposition to the group, a sense of the validity of individual experience and of self-generated ethical values" (54). In their rebellion against a conventional society that stifles individuality, both Catherine Earnshaw and Eustacia Vye can thus be seen as Byronic heroines. In reacting against a male-dominated society, these Byronic heroines take on the characteristics of the rebellious, ambitious, narcissistic, individualistic, and ultimately self-destructive Byronic male.

The Byronic heroine, like her male counterpart, is not just a nineteenth-century phenomenon. There are many heroines of recent action-adventure and science fiction films and television series who similarly adopt the violence, rugged individualism, and creed of vengeance of the Byronic hero of their times.[2] This discussion will be limited to two quintessentially popular and influential Byronic heroines: Sarah Connor (Linda Hamilton) of the two *Terminator* films (*The Terminator* [1984] and *Terminator 2: Judgment Day* [1991]) and Ellen Ripley (Sigourney Weaver) of the *Alien* film series (*Alien* [1979], *Aliens* [1986], *Alien³* [1992], and *Alien Resurrection* [1997]). Despite the surface feminism of their portrayals, the heroines' adoption of stereotypically exaggerated masculine qualities leaves both Sarah and Ripley disempowered. Like Catherine and Eustacia, they fulfill the Victorian angel-monster dichotomy, graphically demonstrating the monstrousness of women who violate their "proper" gender role. I am interested in examining why Brontë and Hardy, as well as the makers of the *Terminator* and *Alien* films, cast their heroines' rebelliousness in masculine terms, why they have their heroines become what they themselves are rebelling against. It is not simply that these women adopt stereotypically masculine traits as a means of rebelling against a restrictive society. All four of these women rebel in specifically Byronic terms. Brontë and Hardy consciously and deliberately place their heroines within the Romantic tradition. The authors do not simply show the danger of involvement with a Byronic male, such as Heathcliff or Damon Wildeve; they emphasize the peril of identifying with the Byronic male and attempting to appropriate *his* character traits. While, on the one hand, Brontë and Hardy present their heroines in a fairly sympathetic light, on the other hand, they must negate the threat these women pose to a conventional and male-dominated society. The traditional and adaptable women, young Catherine (Catherine's daughter) and Thomasin Yeobright, are allowed to survive and flourish, while the rebellious Catherine and Eustacia meet early deaths. Neither Brontë nor Hardy can allow their Byronic heroines to succeed in their aspirations. While one might expect that the situation of this type of fictional heroine would have improved considerably by the latter part of the twentieth century, such is not the case. The contemporary Byronic heroine must similarly be contained to negate the threat she poses. Along these lines, it is interesting to consider, in particular, the ways in which nineteenth-century authors such as Brontë and Hardy compare with male filmmakers of the late twentieth century in developing strong female characters.

The four *Alien* films and the two *Terminator* films portray active, aggressive, heroic female characters; however, whether suc` fidms can be considered feminist is a matter of some critical dispute. Films of this type would have a certain appeal to the filmgoing audience, regardless of the gender of the protagonist. Filmgoers have an intuitive attraction toward the underdog outlaw who must define his or her own moral code and battle society's impersonal and corrupt institutions. Such films usually involve the heroines engaging in explosive violence to accomplish their goals. And because of the ineptitude or corruption of the institutionalized powers that be, the heroines must take matters into their own hands. Like male protagonists in action-adventure or science fiction films, Ellen Ripley and Sarah Connor allow their audience, most of whom probably feel that institutions (the government, the IRS, credit bureaus, multinational corporations, the police) have an undue influence over their lives, a vicarious opportunity to feel empowered. When Ripley must fight not only the aliens but also the corrupt, profit-hungry Company, with its indifference to human life, the audience intuitively sympathizes with her. Likewise, the audience is behind Sarah Connor's attempt to escape from the impersonal and exploitive mental institution and to stop the construction of the destructive Skynet computer.

In another way, the gender of the protagonists is significant. First, such powerful heroines were relatively rare in film in the 1980s and early to mid 1990s, although their presence is increasing contemporaneously with the writing of this book, with such female action heroes as Michelle Yeoh's martial arts heroes (in *Tomorrow Never Dies* [1997] and *Crouching Tiger, Hidden Dragon* [2000], for example), Carrie Ann Moss's Trinity (*The Matrix* [1999], *Matrix Reloaded* [2003], and *Matrix Revolutions* [2003]), and Angelina Jolie's Lara Croft (*Lara Croft: Tomb Raider* [2001] and *Lara Croft Tomb Raider: The Cradle of Life* [2003]). Female action heroes are becoming more prevalent on television, as well, including such heroes as Xena *(Xena: Warrior Princess)$* Buffy Summers *(Buffy the Vampire Slayer)*, Sara Pezzini *(Witchblade)*, and Max *(Dark Angel)*. In the *Terminator* and *Alien* films, however, despite the surface feminism, there is a distinctly misogynist undercurrent. These films were made at a time when audiences were less familiar with (and perhaps less comfortable with) female action heroes. For a female audience, an audience particularly oppressed by lower wages, the glass ceiling, objectification by men, and sexual harassment, it is certainly satisfying to watch Sarah Connor use a broken-off mop handle to knock out the lascivious male attendant at the mental hospital; to see Ripley defeat Ash, the android who tried to shove a rolled-up girlie magazine down her throat. Just as in the movies discussed in chapter 2, the villains and the institutions they represent are portrayed as so irredeemably evil that the heroines' violence is justified. It is not surprising that women would be drawn to texts, whether nineteenth-century novels or contemporary films, in which victimized women lash out at and rebel against their oppressors. Ultimately, however, emulating stereotypically masculine traits does not serve these women well. Their acts of violence provide only a momentary escapist gratification to viewers.

Ellen Ripley and Sarah Connor are direct descendants of what I call the Byronic heroine, just as the male heroes discussed in chapters 2 and 3 derive their lineage from the Romantic hero. Significantly, while both of these heroines appropriate a Byronically masculine sense of power and autonomy, they are not permitted to retain it. The two film series, as Elayne Rapping suggests in regard to the film *Thelma and Louise,* embody "the ultimately containing and conservative strategy of allowing audiences to vicariously rebel against constricting norms and then accept their 'just' and inevitable punishment (31)." In the world depicted by nineteenth-century fiction and late-twentieth-century mainstream film, it is unusual for an aggressive, autonomous woman to fit in. She must be disempowered or destroyed, lest she become the monster she opposes. Emulating the most stereotypical and extreme version of masculinity does not offer women a genuine solution to female oppression.

Dissatisfied with the constricted roles expected of them, both Catherine and Eustacia attempt to define themselves by identifying with and emulating the Byronic male, in some ways even outdoing Heathcliff and Damon Wildeve in their Promethean aspirations and narcissism. Paradoxically, however, their adoption of exaggeratedly male characteristics culminates in a renewed dependence on men. Catherine and Eustacia are both ambitious, yet they cannot realize their ambitions with their own exertions and must rely on men to help them achieve their goals. Ultimately, their rebellion fails; both Brontë and Hardy imply that despite a woman's dissatisfaction with her traditional role, the solution is *not* to adopt Byronic traits. The Byronic heroine is an anomaly: a rebel and an individualist in a society that thwarts, stifles, and punishes rebellion and individuality on the part of women. Unable to accommodate themselves to the expectations of their societies, Catherine Earnshaw and Eustacia Vye self-destruct, both having run out of options, leaving death as the only way out. Similarly, the film heroine is not allowed to retain her heroic stance. Sarah Connor is reduced to passivity toward the end of *Terminator 2,* leaving the heroic action up to the male hero. Ellen Ripley self-destructs altogether before being reincarnated as a monstrous amalgam of human and alien in the fourth film of the series.

Catherine Earnshaw and Eustacia Vye, in their appropriation of the rebelliousness, isolation, ambition, and narcissism of the Byronic hero have incurred the incomprehension of critics as well as their own society. Both women have drawn critical fire, getting blamed for the downfall of the male protagonists and being condemned as self-centered and immature. Catherine is labeled "self-centred" and "loveless" (Leavis 94); the sole cause of "her own and Heathcliff's great miseries" (Craik 10); and self-indulgent (Spacks 141). In making Heathcliff out to be the sole victim and Catherine the victimizer, these critics vastly oversimplify, failing to account for the sexism of Catherine's society and, more specifically, for Heathcliff's violence and dysfunction. Eustacia is similarly victimized by her critics. She is characterized as "selfish," "self-deceiving," "arrogant," "willful," and "prey to unhealthy melancholy, self-pity and caprice" (Evans 251); "a vain, naïve, arrogant daydreamer" (Eggenschwiler 445); and a "romantic heroine" prone to "an essential passivity and destructiveness" (Hyman 59); and characterized by "egocentricity" and "blindness to the suffering of others" (Hyman 61). To understand Eustacia's longings and behavior, however, it is essential to realize that she is specifically rebelling against conventional female roles. As Morgan remarks, "Eustacia is suffocated in a man-made world" and "is prevented from coming into being in a world that denies autonomy, identity, purpose and power to women" (82). Like Morgan, Mickelson offers an instructive feminist reading of Eustacia's position, but she also notes that "like some women today, Eustacia, having no pattern to follow but the masculine one, often imitates some of the less attractive traits found in men" (68). Mickelson thus provides a more complex account, noting both her "selfishness" (81) and the fact that "Hardy is compassionate toward Eustacia for wanting a life richer and more interesting than the Heath offers" (82).

The account, in this study, of Catherine and Eustacia as Byronic heroines mediates between seeing them as utterly self-centered on the one hand or passive victims on the other. This perspective considers, instead, that in reaction to a society which stifles and denies identity to women, Catherine and Eustacia fight back by emulating the destructive qualities of their society's icon of masculinity, the Byronic male. In response to male and institutional oppression, Catherine and Eustacia, as well as Sarah and Ripley, attempt to go one better, to outdo the men in their lives by adopting their own rebelliousness, ambition, and narcissism. Like Hardy and Brontë, Sarah and Ripley's creators portray the Byronic heroine as a freakish anomaly.

Catherine and Eustacia are outsiders in their families and societies, rebelling "in high Promethean fashion" against and refusing to conform to their expected feminine roles (Hardy 259). I believe that Brontë is ultimately pessimistic about the possibilities for happiness of an independent, rebellious woman at her time. The author, in spite of her own sympathy for (and temperamental similarities to) her heroine, renders her unlikable because she sees no other options in portraying the condition of an energetic, nonconforming woman. Catherine, though a victim, is unlikable because she responds to her victimization by emulating the methods of her oppressors, just as Heathcliff is unlikable because he so effectively uses money and class as a weapon against the innocent descendants of those who used money and class to oppress him. Catherine essentially responds to the expectations and demands of others by adopting Heathcliff's bad temper and self-absorption. Catherine takes on a domineering role, demanding always to have her way and losing her temper when she doesn't. She urges Nelly, for instance, to warn Edgar about her temper, insisting that he allow her to have her own way: "To this point he has been discreet in dreading to provoke me; you must represent the peril of quitting that policy, and remind him of my passionate temper, verging, when kindled, on frenzy" (101). Here she uses her potential for violent temper as a threat, a type of emotional blackmail designed to keep Edgar compliant. In a similar fashion, Heathcliff inspires fear with his use of violence to get others to serve his interests. Far from fulfilling the traditional role of the Victorian wife, Catherine expects her husband to tolerate her relationship with Heathcliff and bullies him into complying with her desires.

Just as Catherine refuses to play the role of the dutiful daughter or wife, Eustacia Vye rebels against her society's expectations of the behavior of a single woman. In her isolation from her community, she is reminiscent of a Manfred or a Victor Frankenstein. Like Manfred, Eustacia provokes speculation and wonder among her neighbors, who think that "she is very strange in her ways, living up there by herself" (33). Her behavior seems so eccentric to the inhabitants of Egdon, that she is accused of being a witch and is attacked by Susan Nunsuch with a stocking needle. In a further attempt to combat Eustacia's "witchcraft," Susan models a wax figure resembling her, punctures it repeatedly with needles, and melts it on the fire. Eustacia's creator thus has it both ways; he generates sympathy for his heroine at the same time that he warns his female readers against nonconformity and rebellion by making Eustacia suffer the consequences—ostracism and worse. At the same time, like Manfred, Eustacia isolates herself voluntarily, deeming herself superior to her neighbors: "I have not much love for my fellow-creatures. Sometimes I quite hate them" (192). According to Boumelha, "her physical isolation from the community is reinforced by a mutual awareness of her difference. She regards the local girls with something like contempt. Her alienness, in turn, is perceived by the Egdon inhabitants as a threat." Thus "her individualism leaves her on the feared and misunderstood margins of society" (53).

Hardy characterizes Eustacia specifically as a nonconformist: "Thus she was a girl of some forwardness of mind, indeed, weighed in relation to her situation among the very rearward of thinkers, very original. Her instincts toward social nonconformity were at the root of this" (76). At one point, she actually resorts to cross-dressing in an attempt to secure some of the power, the possibility for adventure, and the potential for self-expression unavailable to her as a woman. Deen argues that "Eustacia in the mumming assumes the heroic masculine role to which she is always aspiring. She wants to alter her essential human condition, to change her sex. A dissatisfaction so thoroughgoing amounts to a denial of life itself" (211). I believe that Deen is misconstruing the nature of Eustacia's dissatisfaction. Eustacia's cross-dressing reveals a Byronic discontent, but the nature of her discontent is gender-specific, and this episode "constitutes . . . an exploration of the limits of her gender" (Boumelha 55). She does not deny her "essential human condition" or "life itself" so much as the socially prescribed gender restrictions that bind her. Her motivation for cross-dressing is specific to her frustrations with her social position; the form of rebellion she adopts is modeled, however unsatisfactorily, on the Byronic hero. Her role as the Turkish Knight in the mummers' performance is reminiscent of the exoticism of Byron's heroes in his eastern tales, but it is a mockery as well. Eustacia knows full well that she has no real opportunities for independent adventure; she dresses as the Turkish Knight to secure the only adventure available to her—a love affair. Even her selection of the role is constrained by Victorian notions. After slaying the Valiant Soldier and sword fighting with Saint George, the Turkish Knight dies slowly:

> This gradual sinking to earth was, in fact, why Eustacia had thought that the part of the Turkish Knight, though not the shortest, would suit her best. A direct fall from upright to horizontal, which was the end of the other fighting characters, was not an elegant or decorous part for a girl. But it was easy to die like a Turk, by a dogged decline. (141)

Even in taking on a male role, Eustacia must concern herself with what is "elegant or decorous." Although dressed as a man and wielding a sword, she is not allowed to achieve any real power, for the success of her performance depends upon the chivalrousness of the other mummers, with the Valiant Soldier dying histrionically despite a "preternaturally inadequate thrust from Eustacia" and Saint George taking "especial care to use his sword as gently as possible" (140).

Hardy couches Eustacia's rebellion specifically in Romantic terms; her rebellion "in high Promethean fashion, against the gods and fate" (259) is reminiscent of Byron and Shelley's fascination with the figure of Prometheus. As Deen argues, "She is emblematic of the feeling and infinite desire which rebel against inevitable limitation, and thus is the supremely tragic figure of the novel" (210). What Eustacia sees as fate and Deen sees as "inevitable" are social constructs of female roles that are so rigid that Eustacia can perceive them only as the works of the gods and fate. This rigidity is why she must rebel in *Byronic* fashion; while the restrictions of her gender role are societally imposed, they appear so overwhelming and so resistant to any attempt to transcend them that Eustacia may just as well be rebelling against fate and with equal chance of success.

In evoking the Romantic Prometheanism of Byron and Shelley in the creation of his heroine, Hardy consciously sets Eustacia up for failure and, ultimately, self-destruction. Given her own socially imposed paralysis, she reveals her frustration at Clym's acceptance of his social condition by exclaiming, "God! if I were a man in such a position I would curse rather than sing" (259).

Just as Catherine and Eustacia adopt the rebelliousness and violent temper of the Byronic male, the heroines of the *Terminator* and *Alien* films emulate the violence and aggression of the male action-adventure hero to rebel against the conformity and restrictive roles imposed on them by their society. Despite the advances of feminism since the nineteenth century, these films nonetheless reveal very restrictive expectations of female behavior. When a woman violates those expectations, she becomes subject to male harassment and coercion and must react in as destructive a fashion as do Catherine and Eustacia.

Typically, the contemporary Byronic heroine employs verbal, as well as physical, aggression to get her way. Like Catherine Earnshaw with her violent temper, the contemporary Byronic heroine resorts to sarcasm and outbursts of temper simply to make herself heard in a society that doesn't take her seriously. Sarah Connor's furious temper in *Terminator 2* thus results from a situation of powerlessness and oppression. Her attempts to forestall the coming takeover by the Skynet computer and the ensuing nuclear war are met with utter skepticism. For her pains, she is locked up in a mental institution and her son is taken away from her with no visitation privileges. Silberman (Earl Boen), the director of the institution, views Sarah as a curiosity, a freak to show off to visiting medical students. When he, naturally enough, refuses to believe her scenario of mass nuclear destruction, Sarah retaliates in the only way allowed to her, sarcasm: "On August 29th, 1997, it's going to feel pretty fucking real to you too! Anybody not wearing two million sunblock is gonna have a real bad day!" Ellen Ripley in the *Alien* series must also operate in a conformist and repressive society. The future she inhabits is largely controlled by the otherwise unnamed "Company," which seems to have replaced all governmental functions. Like the Skynet computer in *Terminator 2,* the Company of the *Alien* films is an inhuman, faceless, impersonal bureaucratic mechanism, with no concern for human life. On the one hand, the directors of the Company pretend not to take Ripley's account of the aliens seriously; on the other hand, through the first three films, the

Company maneuvers secretly to bring an alien back for their bioweapons division, although this process must necessarily entail the loss of many lives. In *Alien,* Ash, the android representative of the Company, tries to shove a rolled up girlie magazine down Ripley's throat as a means of re-asserting the Company's patriarchal control over her. His action is symptomatic of the repressive and violent tactics of the male antagonists throughout the series. Thus, in all four films, Ripley must display the violent temper of the male action-adventure hero simply to make herself heard. Sherrie A. Inness points out

> Toughness for Ripley is not some new feminist ideal, where she takes the best parts of femininity and masculinity and forges them into a type of toughness that has not yet been seen. Instead, Ripley can be perceived as a man in a woman's body, reason enough for critics to complain about her being just another Rambo figure. (107)

Furthermore, in all four films, Ripley must take on an aggressive leadership role to combat both the aliens and the institutional powers (in *Alien Resurrection,* the Company is replaced by the equally impersonal and ruthless United Systems Military; to emphasize its patriarchal nature, the computer, dubbed "Mother" in *Alien,* is now "Father").[3]

In a hostile and dangerous environment, Sarah Connor and Ellen Ripley cannot afford to be passive and compliant; the only way to be taken seriously and to ensure their survival is to act masculine. Just as Catherine orders people around in an attempt to gain a modicum of power and Eustacia mocks Damon Wildeve in an attempt to thwart her own powerlessness, Ripley must act aggressive, overbearing, and unfeminine to survive. As Inness argues, "Ultimately, Ripley's lack of emotion will save her. Only by moving away from the displays of emotion that are usually considered 'normal' for women will she be able to become a tough hero, because our culture considers toughness and displays of emotion to be antithetical" (106). *Alien³* places Ripley in a particularly hostile environment, a penal colony of particularly aggressive criminals, those with double-Y chromosomes; in this environment, she is the only woman. The men resent her presence, most having taken vows of celibacy in what turns out to be part of a rather tenuous religious conversion. Dillon (Charles S. Dutton), the leader of the sect, tells Ripley, "You don't want to know me, lady. I'm a murderer and rapist of women," to which she coolly replies, "Well, I guess I must make you nervous," before sitting down at a table with him and the others. During the attack by the aliens, Ripley must again take on a leadership role and persuade this group of misogynist prisoners to follow her.

Ripley's status is even more tenuous in *Alien Resurrection.* She is considered merely a "meat by-product" by her creators, who cloned her from a drop of blood for the sake of extracting an alien queen larva from her. If anything, she is more callous than in the previous films, demanding, "Who do I have to fuck to get off this ship?" When another character asks her how she dealt with the alien before, she casually returns, "I died." And when Ripley encounters Purvis (Leland Orser), who has been used as a host, she is ruthlessly and unsympathetically direct: "There's a monster in your chest. . . . It's a really nasty one. And in a few hours it's going to burst its way through your ribcage, and you're gonna die. [Pause] Any questions?" Ripley takes a sadistic delight in Purvis's state of panic, and the audience laughs, enjoying her callous detachment in the same way they enjoy the Terminator's casually ruthless demeanor. When Purvis asks who she is, she coolly responds, "I'm the monster's mother." Ripley, in fact, mocks Call's concern for others. When Call (Winona Ryder), an android, explains that she was programmed that way, Ripley asks incredulously, "You're programmed to be an asshole? You're the new asshole model they're putting out?" Call is, ironically, the most humane character in the film, and her concern for others is incomprehensible to Ripley.

Like the male action-adventure or science fiction hero, the contemporary Byronic heroine must define her own moral code, often resorting to violence to accomplish her aims. Catherine could only ask for a whip as a child; by the time she reaches adulthood, she gets her way with her violent temper by virtue of her ill health, as she is not permitted physical aggression. Eustacia's only physical outlet, and a restricted one at that, is her role as the Turkish Knight. Contemporary heroines, however, have access to weapons. Just as the contemporary Byronic hero is an outlaw, using violence to enforce his own form of justice, the contemporary Byronic heroine uses violence to rebel against institutionalized oppression, appropriating guns, the traditional symbol of male dominance and power. The Byronic heroine does not define any constructive solution to male oppression of women; she does, however, allow the audience a vicarious experience of empowerment, a fantasy whereby the possession of a gun gives one absolute control over even the most hostile environment.

Terminator 2 and the *Alien* films make a particularly ironic use of female violence, since in both cases, the primary motivation of both Sarah Connor and Ellen Ripley is to preserve as many human lives as possible. Sarah is trying to avert a future nuclear war, followed by an endless war against the machines; Ripley is trying to prevent the loss of life that will necessarily result from any attempt by the Company to bring back one of the aliens. In both cases, however, despite their concern for human life, both women resort to spectacular violence to accomplish their aims, and in ways very satisfying for a female audience. The heroines enact their viewers' own frustration with patriarchal, institutional power. In the real world, the pace of change is slow; and for many women, genuine improvement in their condition may seem unreachable. As a fantasy, Ripley and Sarah's take-no-prisoners approach has a clear appeal. The image of empowerment is evident in our first view of Sarah Connor. She has transformed herself from the ditzy waitress of the first *Terminator* movie into an athletic, well-muscled woman who will do anything to escape from the institution to save her son; Rushing and Frentz accurately describe her "mechanical determination and tunnel vision that befits both Terminators" (188). Her transformation begins in the first film when she manages to crush the Terminator with industrial machinery, dispatching him with a satisfying "You're terminated, fucker!" As J. P. Telotte suggests, in transforming her body and acquiring military skills, Sarah has also "subjugated her emotions"; she has thus "technologized herself, shaped herself into the best *human* cyborg possible." In effect, "she has become much like what she struggles against" with "an almost impenetrably hard, unfeeling surface that denies depth by disallowing displays of emotion or caring" (31). During her escape attempt, she holds Silberman hostage with a hypodermic needle filled with liquid rooter *after* breaking his arm, threatening "There are 215 bones in the human body. That's one." Still adhering to feminine stereotypes, Silberman refuses to believe that she will kill him, but Sarah's knowledge of impending nuclear devastation allows her to be casual about individual lives: "You're already dead, Silberman. Everybody dies. You know I believe it, so don't *fuck* with me."

Sarah's most questionable use of violence is her plan to assassinate Miles Dyson (Joe Morton), the future designer of the Skynet computer, to prevent it from being built and thereby avert the war. She wounds Dyson in the attempt but fails to kill him, eventually collapsing in tears.

As Telotte remarks, "Seeing *herself as Terminator,* she stays her hand" (31). The implication is that Sarah's wholesale adoption of violence as a solution to complex problems is unnatural, that as a woman she cannot reconcile herself to killing. Just as Eustacia must be decorous in her role as the Turkish Knight, Sarah Connor cannot adapt readily to violence, in spite of her surface toughness. Blowing up Dyson's home computer and the Cyberdyne lab is a much more acceptable solution for Sarah. Like Hardy and Brontë, contemporary filmmakers try to have it both ways; they allow their heroines brief episodes of empowerment but also show them as unable to handle violence emotionally. After Catherine pinches Nelly and Edgar threatens to leave, she cries; and after their marriage, she resorts to illness to justify her violent temper. The films discussed herein frequently have the women burst into tears as a response to rage and frustration as well, as if to suggest that a woman can imitate a Byronic hero but cannot become one altogether. For all their presumed feminism in portraying female heroes, gender stereotypes remain. Except for the ten-year-old boy John Connor (Edward Furlong), we never see the male characters in *Terminator 2* or the *Alien* series cry while engaging in violence.

In her series of battles against the aliens, we see Ripley armed with a variety of weapons, particularly flamethrowers. Like Sarah Connor, Ripley is resourceful and handles weapons with ease. When she asks the marine, Hicks (Michael Biehn), to teach her how to use a sophisticated rifle, she insists, "Show me everything. I can handle myself." He replies, "Yeah, I noticed." Ripley has no compunction about destroying hundreds of alien eggs with a flamethrower and finally has to engage in direct combat with the queen alien, using the loader, which transforms her into a superhuman robot. Paula Graham remarks

> Ripley's "missing" phallus is more than generously supplied—she wins out through firepower and phallic hardware rather than cautious, "feminine" reflection and self-control as in *Alien.* There is sheer phallic pleasure in wielding all that wham-bam megavolt hardware and blasting all those ugly critters to smithereens. (205)

Cameron, in directing *Aliens,* engages in a wholesale violation of traditional gender roles; the toughest marine on the ship is a woman, the butch Vasquez (Jeanette Goldstein), who can't wait to get out and start shooting. Testifying to the traditional expectations women must contend with in Cameron's vision of the future, one of the male marines asks, "Hey,

Vasquez, have you ever been mistaken for a man?" to which she replies, "No, have you?" In *Alien³*, ironically, Ripley again takes on the leadership role, proving herself "tougher" than a prison full of excessively violent convicts; it is Ripley at the end who finally kills the attacking alien by dumping a load of hot lead on it.

By the fourth film, Ripley has become the monster she is fighting. After she kills one of the aliens, Call is shocked that Ripley would kill one of her "own kind." Ripley merely responds, "It was in my way." And in fact, Ripley is behaving precisely like the aliens, who kill one of their own in the lab to use its blood to burn through the floor. Ripley pulls the tongue out of the alien she killed, presenting it to a repulsed Call as "a nice souvenir." Ripley's most violent and unnatural act is the killing of her own "granddaughter," the half-human offspring of the queen alien, a creature that apparently bonded to Ripley rather than to its own mother. When the creature threatens Call, Ripley uses her own blood to burn a hole in a port, and the creature is sucked slowly into space, disintegrating into a gory spray of blood and clumps of flesh. The red blood of the creature testifies to its relation to Ripley (the other aliens have yellowish blood). Ripley must shut down her own emotional attachment to her "granddaughter" and harden herself to kill it. Like Sarah Connor, she cries, torn between her emotions and her goals, which are in inevitable conflict.

Eustacia's cross-dressing and Catherine's hot temper both constitute a type of role-playing, a trying-on of a stereotypically masculine role in an attempt to feel empowered, however briefly. The films in question similarly show the heroines engaged in role-playing, ritualistically taking on the identity of a male action-adventure hero, trying it on to see whether it fits. In *Terminator 2* and *Aliens,* Sarah and Ripley engage in a type of cross-dressing, ritualistically transforming themselves into soldiers, as if they have to don the right apparel to steel themselves to kill. Before her attempted assassination of Miles Dyson, Sarah attires herself in black combat gear, complete with weapons and belts bursting with ammunition; puts on the obligatory sunglasses; and pulls her hair back into a tight ponytail. Ripley similarly transforms herself into a soldier in *Aliens,* ritualistically donning more and more weapons as she slowly rides down an elevator in her rescue of the little girl, Newt.[4] This warrior persona, too, does not remain. Both *Alien* and *Aliens* conclude with Ripley in very revealing underwear, about to go into "hypersleep." The third film in the series also stresses the significance of cross-dressing; here Ripley's ship crashes with her wearing only underwear; on the planet, she has her head shaved to avoid lice and must wear a male prisoner's uniform, the only clothes available. Just as Eustacia's mumming of the Turkish Knight is just a role she is playacting, the filmmakers suggest that their heroines' adoption of male appearance and male violence is only temporary, an attempt to secure masculine power and privilege, but one they must renounce to regain their "natural" femininity.

Catherine and Eustacia rebel against traditional female roles not only through their violent tempers and their "unfeminine" desire to triumph over others but also through their isolation and alienation from their society. Within her own and her husband's family, Catherine is an outsider; she never feels she belongs in either household and ultimately must ratify her isolation by becoming a ghost, perpetually wandering the moors until Heathcliff can join her. Eustacia is also isolated. The villagers look on her as an eccentric and even a witch, and Eustacia's attitude of conscious superiority only reinforces the distance between herself and her neighbors. The contemporary Byronic heroine, like Manfred and Victor Frankenstein, is also isolated from her fellow beings. James Cameron gives Sarah Connor a particularly metaphysical isolation. Just as Manfred and Victor Frankenstein are isolated by the extent of their forbidden and superior knowledge, Sarah is isolated by her knowledge of certain future nuclear devastation. Naturally enough, everyone believes that Sarah is insane and rejects her; even her own son categorizes her as "a real loser." The knowledge that millions of people are doomed to die on a certain date in 1997 lends Sarah the aura of an unheard prophet, a Cassandra in a mental hospital. She has Prometheus's knowledge of the future, but no one wants to hear it. When she embarks on her mission to kill Dyson, she leaves alone, knowing her son John and the Terminator will try to stop her. Ironically, as Sarah is transforming herself into a killing machine, the Terminator is becoming more human. It is only when the three join together with Dyson to destroy the Cyberdyne lab that they can have a positive impact on the future.

Like her fellow heroine, Ripley is also repeatedly isolated. As Inness notes, "Ripley adheres to a higher code of morality than her fellows, and she is able to make the difficult decisions that no one else will. . . . She speaks the truth, even when no one wishes to hear it" (106). At the end of the first movie, the only film in which she enjoys a real camaraderie with the crew, Ripley is the sole survivor (besides the cat). *Aliens* opens with Ripley having been in hypersleep for decades and thus having lost everyone she knew. On the mission with the marines, she is isolated, like Sarah Connor, by her knowledge of the aliens. As before, most of the supporting characters are killed by the alien. The film concludes with Hicks, the little girl Newt, and the android Bishop having survived in addition to Ripley. However, *Alien³* opens with Ripley as the miraculous sole survivor of the crash of her capsule. She has to fight back her maternal emotions to insist upon and witness an autopsy of Newt, in order to ensure her own survival. She thus loses Newt, her "adopted" child, and is further isolated by being the only woman on the planet where she crashes. Again, Ripley has to overcome the skepticism and distrust of others to assemble a team to combat the alien. It is only when she can enlist the cooperation of the surviving prisoners that she can destroy the creature. Even so, the film emphasizes Ripley's "alienation" (pun intended) by revealing that she has been infected with and is essentially gestating a Queen Alien, an egg layer. When Ripley discovers the alien's presence inside her, she is further isolated from the remaining human survivors. Ripley knows and understands that her own death must occur; she is aware of the devastating consequences of allowing the Queen to hatch. In her complete isolation from other human beings, Ripley is becoming one with the alien, and she knows the only way to destroy it is to destroy herself. Of course, *Alien Resurrection* increases Ripley's isolation with her liminal status between human and alien, in addition to the two-hundred-year gap since her physical death. Returning to Earth with the android Call, Ripley answers her question "What happens now?" with "I don't know. I'm a stranger here myself." The burden of knowledge they carry gives Sarah Connor and Ripley a particularly Byronic sense of superiority; they have a knowledge forbidden from or inaccessible to the rest of humankind, and this knowledge prevents them from attaining any real companionship.

As in the action-adventure and science fiction movies with male heroes, the institutionalized forces of society (police, mental hospitals, the Company) in films with female heroes are shown to be either inept or corrupt, or both; thus the heroine must act on her own and take a leadership role to defeat a mortal danger of vastly superior ability and strength. These films' popular success lies in their enlisting audience sympathy on the side of the female outlaw, who must defy authority and take matters into her own hands. However, these films are not gender-neutral in their evocation of heroic action; Sarah Connor and Ellen Ripley not only share the isolation and alienation of the male outlaw but are further isolated in their rebellion against traditional female roles. Because she cannot or will not conform to such traditional modes of female behavior, the Byronic heroine does not perceive any options other than emulating the Byronic male, the Romantic outlaw, in his anger, violence, and isolation. She has no satisfactory role models to follow, and neither Brontë nor Hardy, nor the creators of the *Terminator* and *Alien* films, can conceive of another alternative, an image of female competence that does not imitate the stereotypical, excessive masculinity of the Byronic hero. By contrast, the film *Tank Girl* (1995) reveals a heroine (Lori Petty) who is courageous, competent, and successful, and who survives and thrives at the end of the film. Unlike Ripley and Sarah, who are grimly serious, Rebecca has an irreverent, wisecracking, exuberant, and defiant sense of humor that surfaces even in the most dire circumstances. Yet *Tank Girl* made hardly a ripple at the box office, and its heroine is far less well known than Ripley and Sarah. Even in 1995, it seems mainstream viewers were not prepared for a successful, well-adjusted female action hero.

Given their inability to conform to the rigid gender expectations of Victorian England, it is not surprising that both Catherine and Eustacia exhibit a Byronic restlessness and ambition, romantically aspiring to transcend the conditions that have been imposed upon them. Catherine and Eustacia can only frame their ambition in gender-appropriate terms, that is, the desire for a marriage that will elevate their social position. Their dissatisfaction with their lot as women reveals itself in the extent of their aspiration toward a higher state, just as the Byronic hero rejects his own mortality and aspires to a transcendent condition.

Upon being exposed to the Lintons' comfortable and luxurious way of living, Catherine can no longer return to the simplicity of her romps with Heathcliff on the moors. She has become aware of the economic realities of her society and realizes that the only way she can attain any degree of power and material comfort is to marry into a wealthy family. At Wuthering Heights she is misunderstood and misused, and if she were married to Heathcliff she would starve. Edgar, on the other hand, "will be rich, and I shall like to be the greatest woman of the neighborhood, and I shall be proud of having such a husband" (70). No one forces Catherine to marry Edgar; she makes the decision herself. Given the situation of women in her society and her own particular circumstances, she feels she has no choice.[5] Catherine marries Edgar, but her attitude toward him is plainly exploitive; she marries him only for the concrete benefits he can provide for her. Unlike Heathcliff, who can improve his social standing through his own exertions, as he does during his three-year absence, Catherine can only realize her ambitions through marriage.

In the striking "Queen of Night" chapter, Hardy portrays Eustacia as a woman whose aspirations outreach her grasp. He repeatedly evokes pagan images in his characterization: "Eustacia Vye was the raw material of a divinity. On Olympus she would have done well with little preparation. She had the passions and instincts which make a model goddess, that is, those which make not quite a model woman" (71). At the same time, as Judith Mitchell remarks, "Hardy's females are . . . exposed to the shared gaze of an overtly male narrator and a projected male reader" (175). Kristin Brady asserts that

> the feminist dimension in Hardy's novels—manifest in his characterizations and his plots—makes these works all the more hysterical by provoking in the male narrator acute anxiety and a resulting impulse for disavowal: the unconventional aspects of the women he constructs threaten his own imaginary sense of masculinity, triggering his fear of castration. (90)

The Romantic impulse to idealize and deify the female is a form of disempowering and containment; a flesh and blood female is much more threatening to the Byronic male than a bodiless abstraction. Thus Hardy's narrator remarks, "In a dim light, and with a slight rearrangement of her hair, her general figure might have stood for that of either of the higher female deities" (72).

Hardy's characterization of Eustacia here both idealizes her as an object of desire and gives her the superhuman quality of a Romantic hero. Just as the Byronic hero's dilated self-image makes him unfit to associate with his fellow humans, Eustacia's "divine" qualities render her unfit for the traditional female role. In Hardy's description, Eustacia appears to be altogether another order of being from the inhabitants of Egdon Heath:

> But celestial imperiousness, love, wrath, and fervour had proved to be somewhat thrown away on netherward Egdon. . . . Her appearance accorded well with this smouldering rebelliousness, and the

shady splendour of her beauty was the real surface of the sad and stifled warmth within her. (73)

Her "imperiousness, love, wrath, and fervour," as well as her "rebelliousness" place her directly within the Romantic heroic tradition. Unable to efface herself to conform with society's expectations (unlike Thomasin, who marries a man she no longer respects, ironically to retain her respectability), Eustacia adopts the excessive self-assertion of the Byronic hero, elevating herself to the status of a queen to emphasize her separation from the inhabitants of Egdon. As Hardy wryly observes, "The only way to look queenly without realms or hearts to queen it over is to look as if you had lost them; and Eustacia did that to a triumph" (74). Unlike Brontë, who provides her heroine with a supernatural postmortem existence, potentially allowing her the scope to exercise her superhuman energies, Hardy cannot allow Eustacia's Promethean posturing to be taken too seriously; ultimately it becomes merely the fantasy of a frustrated young woman. As Brady suggests

> While challenging courtship rituals that privilege virginity and deny women's sexual responses, Hardy's narrators persist in constructing and interpreting female characters according to standard notions about woman's weakness, inconstancy, and tendency to hysteria. (89)

Hardy creates an assertive, ambitious heroine, yet he must contain the threat she poses. As Eggenschwiler observes, this Promethean state of perpetual aspiration can end for Eustacia, as it does for the Byronic hero, only in death:

> Death consummates the romantic quest for an experience that transmutes what Eustacia considers the banality of her life. . . . Eustacia, as well as the narrator, seems to realize at times that her longings cannot be satisfied in life, not even by Budmouth or Paris. (452)

While such Byronic heroes as Manfred and Victor Frankenstein aspire beyond their human limitations by attaining supernatural or divine powers, the Byronic heroine has enough to do with aspiring beyond the restrictions placed on her as a woman. The same is true of contemporary film heroes and heroines. The male action-adventure or science fiction hero, as we have seen, often has superhuman abilities. The female action-adventure hero aspires to transcend the normal condition of women, to have the same powers and capacity for action as men. When she *does* attain a superhuman condition, as Ripley does in *Alien Resurrection*, she is presented as a freakish monster. As Gediman (Brad Dourif) asks, Ripley is "something of a predator, isn't she?" While the nineteenth-century Byronic heroine can fulfill her ambitions for a better life only through marriage, the contemporary heroine has more opportunities to fulfill herself; what hasn't changed, however, is that both nineteenth-century and contemporary heroines are frequently punished for their presumption.

For Sarah Connor and Ellen Ripley, Byronic self-assertion and aspiration take the form of asserting the rights of individuals in the face of a repressive, increasingly institutionalized society. While most of the action of *Terminator 2* takes place in the present, Cameron's vision is of an impersonal society dominated by large institutions, in which a killing machine in a police uniform has unlimited power and access, uniformed mental hospital attendants exploit the patients in their care, and the U.S. government is on the verge of turning over major strategic defense decisions to a computer. Sarah Connor's ambition is merely to save the human race from its reliance on technology and bureaucratic decision making, and therefore she is locked up in a mental hospital. Her ultimate goal is particularly ambitious; it is to change the future and rewrite history, her slogan "No fate but what we make." Initially, she defined her role as subordinate to her son's; her goal was to prepare him to be "a great military leader," as John sarcastically puts it. Not satisfied with that role, however, Sarah undergoes a transformation; she wishes ultimately to make John's leadership of the human resistance unnecessary by changing the future single-handedly. Ellen Ripley is also ambitious in her refusal to conform blindly to the corporate guidelines of the Company; in her valuing of human life over corporate profit, she is an anomaly in the future envisioned in the *Alien* series. The extent to which Ripley has diverged from her traditional role is revealed in *Alien³* when Dillon lambastes the men as "pussies" for being afraid to battle the alien. The implication, of course, is that if men are cowardly, they are acting like women, and if a woman is willing to lead the attempt, the term *pussies* is all the more humiliating. Ripley is convinced that bringing an alien back to the Company's labs will result in unparalleled loss of life; like Sarah Connor, she wishes to save the human race from its own mistakes. Cut off from any lasting personal relationships, Ripley has only one "object to live for," the extermination of the aliens. Both Sarah and Ripley's goals partake of the single-minded, apocalyptic obsessiveness of the Byronic hero, like Victor Frankenstein, who subordinates family, relationships, and all other concerns in the pursuit of a single aim. Both women aspire to a godlike power, to rewrite history on Sarah's part, to determine the extinction of an entire species on Ripley's. Not bound by the limitations that hamper Catherine and Eustacia, Sarah and Ripley come close to achieving the self-determination, self-sufficiency, and superhuman knowledge and ability of the Byronic hero; but these qualities are not without a cost.

Sarah and Ripley's creators emphasize the severe consequences of rejecting a conventional feminine role. They do this in several ways, depicting the characters' heroism as something neither to be desired nor emulated. They attain this result by painting the characters as freakish, unflatteringly unfeminine, and unnatural, while making a point of reminding the viewers of their persistent feminine vulnerability. Unable to find or keep love, Sarah and Ripley narcissistically exploit men as a means to accomplish their own ambitions while strenuously avoiding intimacy. For the strong heroines of films made in the late twentieth century, romantic relationships apparently still entail a loss of independence and autonomy. Just as the Byronic hero defines himself by separation, eliminating his loved one when he feels his self-sufficiency to be threatened, the Byronic heroine in contemporary films selects and discards men according to their usefulness in achieving her own ends. These women find men useful, but they nevertheless fear that a lover or husband will ultimately impede their progress in attaining their aspirations. The relationships they have are meant to fulfill a particular purpose of theirs at the time. Just as Catherine Earnshaw marries Edgar to improve her social position, and Eustacia pursues Clym as a ticket to Paris, Sarah Connor uses men in her quest to remake herself as a soldier and the trainer of her son, while mourning her short-lived love and the father of her son, Kyle Reese (Michael Biehn), but refusing to acknowledge her feelings for him. John remarks, "She still loves him, I guess. I see her crying sometimes. She totally denies it, of course, like she got something stuck in her eye." In one scene, John recounts his mother's sex life to the Terminator: "She'd shack up with anybody she could learn from so I could become this great military leader." Sarah uses her sexuality as a tool; she is so consumed in a larger purpose that her only interest in men is in what concrete benefit they can contribute to that larger purpose. The unstated subtext of John's narration here is that Sarah Connor, despite her superior knowledge and ability, still has to resort to prostituting herself to achieve her goals; even the tough heroine must rely on the conventional feminine means of using sex as a tool to get what she needs. Because these men with their military skills are the image of what she needs to become, Sarah uses her body as a commodity to get the training she desires.

Ironically, given her interest in preserving life, it is the Terminator who is Sarah's true mirror and soul mate. Significantly, in her dreams of nuclear destruction, Sarah envisions her younger self (as she appeared in the original movie) being blown up with her infant son on the playground during the war, although this is chronologically impossible. It is that earlier, vulnerable self that Sarah needs to shed; ironically it is the Terminator from the first movie that becomes her role model in her quest to remake herself as an invulnerable soldier during the ten-year interim between the action of the first film and its sequel. Again we see the Byronic heroine imitating the most macho of masculine figures in her rebellion against traditional female roles. While the Terminator becomes more human during the sequel, Sarah attempts to transform herself into a cold-blooded killing machine in order to assassinate Miles Dyson. When Sarah muses on the Terminator's surprising appropriateness as a father for John, what is unstated is his appropriateness as her companion and kindred spirit: "It would always be there, and it would die to protect him. Of all the would-be fathers who came and went over the years, this thing, this machine, was the only one who measured up." Since he is a machine, she does not need to engage him in a sexual relationship to get him to do what she wants; she simply has to command him to fulfill the programming she indirectly engendered. He is both literally and figuratively her narcissistic self-projection, the ultimate partner in her intention to change the future: literally, because he has been reprogrammed, essentially recreated, by her own son in the future; figuratively, because he is the embodiment of what she feels she has to become. (In preparing for the role, Linda Hamilton trained extensively to attain a female version of Arnold Schwarzenegger's physique.) When Sarah Connor changes into black military gear, complete with sunglasses and weapons, she begins to resemble the Terminator even more (figs. 5, 6). Toward the end of *Terminator 2,* her goal almost accomplished, like the Byronic hero, she must eliminate her mirror, her counterpart, this "soul out of her soul." It is Sarah who presses the button lowering the Terminator into the molten steel. He cannot "self-terminate" because he is a part of Sarah that she must destroy; he is not really a separate being to her. Just as Manfred destroys Astarte, the human and tender side of himself, Sarah Connor must destroy the Terminator, the inhuman and violent side of herself, to be reintegrated back into the world, into the less violent future she has orchestrated.

Ripley simultaneously avoids intimacy while using men to help her attain the knowledge she requires. Although she risks her life to rescue her cat (in *Alien*) and can briefly accommodate motherhood (in *Aliens*), Ripley is far too absorbed in her quest to exterminate the creatures to contemplate romantic relationships. In *Aliens,* she flirts with Hicks, but they both know that they have higher priorities than romance. When Hicks provides Ripley with a locator, a kind of homing beacon, he quips, "It doesn't mean we're engaged or anything." Ripley, giving Newt a higher priority, gives the locator to her, deciding that it is more important that she be able to rescue the child, than Hicks be able to rescue her. Hicks is primarily valuable for his knowledge and military ability, and Ripley both learns from him how to use a pulse rifle and makes a pact with him to kill her should she be impregnated by an alien: "Hicks, I'm not going to end up like those others. You'll take care of that, won't you?" They seem to get a sexual charge from the training session with the rifle, but both Hicks and Ripley know that their environment is too dangerous for romantic interludes. In *Alien³,* Ripley makes a pass at Clemens (Charles Dance), the only passably attractive man in the prison colony. Again, she is looking not for intimacy but rather some temporary gratification. He is surprised by her "masculine" aggressiveness, remarking "You're very direct." When Clemens is killed by the alien, Ripley does not waste time in grief she probably minimally feels; true intimacy with a man is impossible given her all-consuming obsession with the aliens. Ultimately she feels she has to "seduce" the male alien into killing her; she sees this as the only way to eliminate the egg-laying alien inside her body. In a scene of grotesque intimacy, the male alien puts its face right up to Ripley but does not attack. With Ripley's bald head and the alien's smooth skull, they mirror each other dramatically, a shot frequently used in publicity for the film. One review, in fact, captions the photograph "Sigourney Weaver and alter ego" (Strick 47). As she later puts it, she's "part of the family," implying that the alien won't kill her. At this point in the film series, Ripley and the alien have formed a self-sufficient universe where nothing else exists; in a nightmarish parody of the romantic self-sufficiency of new lovers, Ripley says to the alien, "You've been in my life so long. I can't remember anything else." Joking about the connection between her character Ripley and the alien, Weaver says, "I don't know how to put this . . . but I've developed a warm spot for that alien. There's something really, I don't know, *sensuous* about him. He's kinda sexy" (Hochman 21). It is only in killing the alien and subsequently herself that Ripley can regain her autonomy and break the bond that the alien forced on her by "impregnating" her. In a gruesome abortion parable, Ripley can restore the integrity of her own body only by killing herself.[6]

The Byronic heroine, then, rejects the traditionally feminine passive role in sexual relationships. Instead of defining herself in terms of a relationship, she wishes to maintain a large degree of autonomy and control. Thus she often takes the traditionally masculine role of initiating a relationship, and she reserves the right to end such a relationship when it poses a potential threat to her autonomy. Her lover often serves as a mirror of her aspirations or a vehicle to help her attain those aspirations, or both. Once he has served that function and is no longer useful, she discards him, avoiding intimacy and retaining her Byronic self-sufficiency.

Sarah and Ripley are also unable to combine mothering with the aggressive, Byronic parts of themselves. James Cameron explores this disjunction between the nurturing and aggressive sides of the Byronic heroine fully in *Terminator 2* and *Aliens. Terminator 2* explicitly contrasts the militaristic Sarah Connor with the earlier, ditzier version of herself in the first film. As discussed above, in her nightmares of nuclear holocaust, Sarah imagines her younger self (performed by Hamilton's twin sister, Leslie Hamilton Gearren) playing with John as a toddler in a playground. To Sarah, this younger self represents a vulnerability to institutional forces that the present Sarah cannot accept. After one of these nightmares, she makes the decision to murder Miles Dyson, replacing her perceived vulnerability with an aggressive active attempt to control her future. Cameron indicates that in rejecting traditional femininity altogether, Sarah has somehow lost her humanity as well; ironically, the Terminator proves to be a better parent than she is. Sarah callously berates John for helping her escape, exclaiming, "John, it was *stupid* of you to go there. God damn it! You have to be smarter than that; you almost got yourself killed. What were you thinking? You cannot risk yourself even for me."

When John insists that he had to rescue her, she reduces him to tears by snapping, "I didn't need your help. I can take care of myself." The Terminator, on the other hand, listens to John uncritically and inquires about his feelings. While Sarah is too occupied with her military preparations to enjoy John's presence, the Terminator willingly participates in a game of high fives with John. In her adoption of a traditionally masculine aggression, Sarah is unable to integrate that side of herself with her maternal role. She will go to any lengths to preserve John's life, because she sees him as a future savior; but she has failed to bond with him to the extent that he tells his friend toward the beginning of the film that his mother is a "psycho" and a "real loser." Rushing and Frentz suggest that "John has become to her, not so much a son, as the means to an end" (188). As he tells the Terminator about his childhood, it is very clear that Sarah has been much more interested in training John to be "this great military leader" (a phrase John states with a voice dripping with sarcasm) than in forging a loving relationship with him.[7]

Ellen Ripley is given a chance at motherhood in the second film of the *Alien* series. As with Sarah Connor, Ripley's nurturing and aggressive sides are so unintegrated that she seems two separate people. The end of the first film suggests that a woman's emotional side makes her vulnerable. In this film, she goes back to find her cat, thereby risking her life in another encounter with the alien. In *Aliens,* when the little girl, Newt (Carrie Henn), is discovered, Ripley automatically takes on the nurturing role, in effect adopting the orphaned child. The original script had made the relationship between Ripley and Newt more poignant by revealing that Ripley's own daughter had grown up and died during Ripley's fifty-seven years in hypersleep (Gross 48–49). I would argue that the filmmakers' decision to give Ripley a maternal role is part of the process of refeminizing the Byronic heroine, a way of making her sympathetic to the audience. Graham draws a similar conclusion:

> Through her relationships with the child Newt and with Hicks, Ripley is narratively returned to the heterosexual family structure. . . . Motherhood is a central theme of *Aliens* and functions as an "excuse" for female transgressive behaviour, as disavowal of lesbianism, and as *locus standi* of all female aggression. (206)

Thus, in the first and third films, Ripley focuses on exterminating the alien species, whereas in *Aliens,* her principal motivation is to protect Newt from the worst possible fate, becoming a human incubator for the aliens. Yet the film raises disconcerting questions, as Lynda Zwinger reveals:

> So the Bad Mother (the Bug) is both a Good Mother (from an alien-ated point of view), and a baaaad Mutha (in the Marine tongue). And Ripley looks disconcertingly like Sylvester Stallone as Rambo as often as she looks like Claire Huxtable. Does this mean that Mother *is* a bitch? That the rescuing, nurturing, protective mom is indistinguishable from the aggressive, raging, fierce, scary Mother? And if the lethal virgin and mother are both in actuality aggressive, bloody, bossy, enraged, enraging, fierce, murderous, how are we going to get out alive?
>
> The narrative has an answer that will work, well, "most of the time." (83)

Zwinger suggests that the answer is that when Ripley uses the "phallic weaponry of the marines, she does so by permission" (instructed by Hicks), and "her subsequent Rambo masquerade is performed *for the sake of her child*." Thus, "it is only in order to preserve her position as new, nuclear, sentimentalized mom that Ripley appropriates military, masculine attributes" (84). Nevertheless, Ripley's character fluctuates wildly between her two sides, and her maternal instinct doesn't quite recuperate her Rambo-esque masculinity, as will be detailed below. One moment she is tenderly tucking Newt into bed; the next she is slamming Burke into the wall. On her mission to rescue Newt, who has been captured by the alien, Ripley, without any compunction, destroys hundreds of alien eggs with a flamethrower:

> the asexual virgin mother Ripley appropriates the big phalli of the Colonial Marine Corps and becomes a monstrous killing machine in order to fight an even more monstrous mother (supplied with multiple *organic* phalli) and thereby defeats the monster/mother in herself as well. (Zwinger 82)

In the final battle over possession of Newt, Ripley tries to divert the queen alien toward herself, yelling, "Get away from her, you bitch!" Of course, the "bitch" is merely trying to ensure the survival of her own offspring, but Ripley is completely unable to identify with her.

Despite her urgent desire to protect Newt, Ripley repeatedly endangers her in the process of battling the alien. Ultimately, Ripley cannot function as mother and warrior simultaneously. When she is engaged in hand-to-hand combat with the alien, operating the loader (which transforms her into a type of robot), she almost destroys Newt when she opens the air lock to eject the alien. Newt is nearly sucked out into space as well, but she is saved by the android Bishop. While the film ends "happily," with Ripley tucking Newt into a presumably safe "hypersleep" capsule, *Alien³* opens with the revelation that Newt has been killed by the failure of the seals of her capsule in the crash. In this film, Ripley has to stifle her maternal feelings to order a grotesque autopsy of Newt. The suggestion is that to pursue her goal of exterminating the aliens, Ripley must suspend all traditionally female emotions. Just as she endangered herself in *Alien* by returning for the cat, she allowed the alien to deposit eggs into her ship during the delay caused by her rescue of Newt. *Aliens* develops a mutually beneficial, loving relationship between Newt and Ripley, leaving both viewer and Ripley devastated at the opening of the third film with the revelation of Newt's death. Yet even if we look at *Aliens* outside the context of the other films, we see that Ripley must become two incompatible people—a nurturing mother and a violent warrior—and that whenever she allows her maternal side to take over, she puts her own life in danger. When Ripley curls up to sleep with Newt under the bed in the lab, she allows Burke the opportunity to trap both of them with an alien larva (by locking the lab door), and when she goes back to rescue Newt, she endangers herself and the two surviving members of the crew. James Cameron, in both *Terminator 2* and *Aliens,* suggests that a woman cannot integrate a nurturing ethic of care with the violence and emotional detachment required for heroic action. By providing Sarah Connor and Ripley with children, Cameron emphasizes even more pointedly the extent to which they have transformed themselves in the image of the male action-adventure and science fiction hero. Sarah and Ripley's inability to integrate their maternal roles with their Byronic or hypermasculine traits highlights the extent to which the Byronic heroine must isolate and desensitize herself to attain her goals.

Ripley is even more violently torn in *Alien Resurrection.* Ironically, it is her human side that is deadly, while her identification with the aliens brings out nurturing qualities. Before she kills her alien "granddaughter," Ripley caresses and hugs it. As it is slowly and gruesomely sucked into space, we see tears in her eyes. Again, Ripley is given a child to nurture, only to lose it horribly, as her human desire to protect Call overrides her "alien" maternal instinct. When Call initially encounters Ripley and demands where the queen is, Ripley replies sardonically, "You mean my baby?" Ripley is a warrior, and the film series suggests that, as such, she must fail as a mother.

Catherine Earnshaw and Eustacia Vye, in rejecting those traditional female roles prescribed by their patriarchal society, emulate the Byronic male in an attempt to define a self, an identity, but they never escape being bound and defined by their gender. Sarah and Ripley are allowed partially to transcend the limits of their gender roles, but in doing so, they are depicted as monstrous and unnatural. And this transcendence is only partial; they remain defined by gender no matter how hard they try to escape it, and in the *Alien* films femaleness itself becomes something monstrous and grotesque.

For Catherine the question of identity remains central throughout her short life. Although she rejects conventional female behavior, she cannot envision an existence independent of a man, an existence in which she is not deprived of her own identity. Thus Lockwood discovers her writing scratched on the paint of her room: "*Catherine Earnshaw,* here and there varied to *Catherine Heathcliff,* and then again to *Catherine Linton*" (25). Catherine Earnshaw must yield either to Catherine Heathcliff or Catherine Linton, thereby becoming another person. Andrew Elfenbein insists that the novel suggests

> that the only way for a female character not to submit to a male one is to be split between two men at the same time. Catherine's relation to contemporary literary modes appears as a choice between two equally problematic men. Heathcliff, romance, and Byronism are set against Edgar, realism, and anti-Byronism. (158)

He notes further, "She succumbs to neither, but the struggle kills her" (164). Thus, when she is ill after quarreling with Edgar, she is horrified at her reflection in the mirror, afraid that the room is "haunted" and devastated to learn that it is herself she sees: "It's true then; that's dreadful!" (105–06). Catherine's reaction to her own reflection is significant, for she feels convinced that it must be another person haunting her. Her conviction testifies to the alteration she has undergone in her marriage, to the loss of identity that has occurred. When she recounts her recurring dream to Nelly about returning to her childhood, she comments,

"Most strangely, the whole last seven years of my life grew a blank! I did not recall that they had been at all" (107). In her delirious state, she has abolished from memory her whole life from her first visit to the Lintons. She explains the significance of her despair in terms of her sense of an utter loss of identity:

> But, supposing at twelve years old, I had been wrenched from the Heights, and every early association, and my all in all, as Heathcliff was at that time, and been converted at a stroke into Mrs. Linton, the lady of Thrushcross Grange, and the wife of a stranger; an exile, and outcast, thenceforth, from what had been my world. You may fancy a glimpse of the abyss where I grovelled! (107)

Thrushcross Grange is indeed another world to Catherine and one in which she must assume another identity, one defined in terms of gendered expectations of behavior. Ultimately this loss of identity cannot be resolved. Catherine can rebel against her marriage in Byronic fashion, she can emulate the bad temper and imperious rage of the Byronic male, but she cannot escape the actual circumstances of her marriage. The only way for Catherine to reclaim any sense of selfhood is to cease to be altogether.

Like Catherine, Eustacia is embroiled in questions of identity. Her very name is suspect to the inhabitants of Egdon, for her father, a musician whose "pockets were as light as his occupation" (73), had adopted his wife's name instead of the other way around. Wishing to reclaim some sense of herself after her marriage, she attends the village festival without her husband and dances with Wildeve. At one point she bitterly asks him, "What do you think of me as a furze-cutter's wife?" and Wildeve replies, "I think the same as ever of you, Eustacia. Nothing of that sort can degrade you: you ennoble the occupation of your husband" (267). Wildeve, in his renewed state of infatuation, perceives Eustacia as the same person she was before marriage, but in her despondency at being trapped in a hopeless situation, she can only see *herself* as "a furze-cutter's wife," not as her own person. As Morgan points out, "Apart from her status as Clym's wife, she is totally without identity" (81). The role of Wildeve's illicit mistress does not appeal to her either, and like Catherine Earnshaw Linton, she can only assert her sense of herself as a separate person through death. Ironically, Hardy does not allow her solitude even then; in death she is joined with Wildeve.

For Sarah Connor and Ellen Ripley, the question of gender identity is more subtle and more complex; however competent and aggressive they become, their gender is always an issue. We are continually reminded that they are women and therefore cannot escape the social construction of their gender identities. Both of them have been transformed by an apocalyptic knowledge; both of them have to adjust to the burden of knowledge of a force that can destroy the human race, while at the same time facing the skepticism of those who don't believe them. The Sarah Connor of *The Terminator* is a kind of ditzy waitress, with no larger concerns than being stood up for a date, although she does demonstrate a feisty self-sufficiency. When Reese tells her about her future, she exclaims, "Come on! Do I look like the mother of the *future*? Am I tough? Organized? I can't even balance my checkbook!" However, in the ten fictional years intervening between that movie and the sequel, she has radically transformed herself into a new person, both physically and psychologically. In the sequel, Sarah Connor is infinitely resourceful, as seen in her escape from the mental institution. She unlocks her restraints and the door to her room with a stolen paper clip, overpowers the attendant with a broken-off mop handle, and secures the necessary keys by holding the director hostage with a syringe full of liquid rooter. She also obviously has extensive training in using a variety of weapons. In trying to cope with her knowledge of impending nuclear destruction and the knowledge that her son is the future savior of the human race, Sarah emulates her culture's icon of heroic behavior: the violent male outlaw of countless westerns, action, and science fiction movies. It does not occur to her to adopt a creed of nonviolence; as above, in recreating her own identity, she takes on the machinelike, ruthless, and efficient violence of her antagonist in the original film, the first Terminator.

She remains bound, however, by feminine stereotypes. Sarah Connor characterizes her violence as a reaction to the destruction wrought by *men* in the diatribe she launches at Dyson, who protests that he had no way of knowing his inventions would lead to three billion deaths. Sarah snaps:

> Yeah right, how were you supposed to know? Fucking men like you built the hydrogen bomb; men like you thought it up. You think you're so creative. You don't know what it's like to really create something, to create a life, to feel it growing inside you. All you know how to create is death.

As Rushing and Frentz note, "Sarah is valuable first and foremost as a breeder," "the mother of the future" (176). Sarah sees technology as an inevitably destructive force, an unnatural appropriation, on the part of men, of women's creative power, a power she conceives of in the most simplistic and reductionist biologically deterministic terms. The context of this scene undermines Sarah's speech, however. She delivers it right after having attempted murder with an entire arsenal of advanced weapons, and her histrionics prevent a discussion of the real work to be done in preventing the Skynet computer from ever being built. Thus John, again portrayed as wiser than his mother, interrupts, "Can we be just a little more constructive here?" Cameron essentially has it both ways; his heroine does deliver a feminist message, but she does so in such hyperbolic terms that she actually ends up fulfilling the stereotype of the hysterical female.

Similarly, Ellen Ripley becomes more and more like the violent members of the Marine Corps unit in *Aliens* and the violent prisoners in *Alien³* in her single-minded goal of exterminating the alien species. However, she is forcibly reminded throughout the series that she is a woman who has overstepped her bounds. As Graham notes, with respect to the final scene in *Alien,* which shows Ripley in her underwear, "Without her masculine clothing, Ripley appears feminized as a vulnerable sex object" (201). And Inness argues, "Ripley has become resexualized as a woman. The message is that it is fine for a woman to act tough and take control in outer space, but she had better be a lady when she returns to society." Thus "Ripley is and will always be a sexy, feminine woman, which at least for our society, suggests that she is a potential victim for men." Inness concludes that *Alien* "seems uncomfortable leaving viewers with an image of Ripley that is *too* tough" (107). Thomas B. Byers puts it more bluntly: "Sexual violence can bring uppity Ripley down from her achieved position," and he notes specifically that this is a warning to female viewers: "It is also to put back in her traditional (non)place the female spectator who may mistakenly have begun to think that she could be the subject of the viewing experience." Thus, this scene reasserts "a male dominance that will weaken and stabilize the female and make her safe for patriarchy" (86–87).[8] Like the films discussed in chapter 2, the *Alien* series does not want to encourage spectators to emulate the actions and attitude of the Byronic hero(ine). *Alien³* places Ripley in an environment particularly threatening for a woman, a prison described as a "Double Y

Chromosome Work Correctional Facility," with a population of inmates who have all committed violent crimes, including rape, and who haven't seen a woman in years. The charismatic Rev. Dillon has converted the men to a cult of celibacy, predicated on an extreme misogyny. It is not that these men have rigid preconceptions of female behavior (although one prisoner does ask Ripley why she doesn't get married and have children); instead, they have concluded that they must eliminate the presence of women altogether. Predictably enough, Ripley's presence disturbs the order Dillon has imposed, and she becomes the intended victim of an attempted gang rape and has to be rescued with Dillon's intervention. Undaunted, she punches out one of the intended rapists, then returns to her investigation of the aliens, but the point has been made. She is vulnerable because she is a woman.[9] Thus the only way Ripley can function in this environment, where, at least initially, the threat from the inmates is as great as the threat posed by the aliens, is to emulate their hypermasculinity. When they are reluctant to help her pursue the alien, she mocks them as cowards, directly attacking their manhood, just as Dillon later does when he calls them "pussies." To earn the prisoners' respect, Ripley has to become one of them. In this environment, there is no midway point between the passive feminine victim and the violent masculine aggressor. Although oppressed by male expectations and exploitation of women, the Byronic heroine can see no other possibility than to construct her identity in supermasculine terms. In the fourth film, Ripley is, again, the product of her gender—both a vessel to incubate the alien queen and a desired object of the male gaze. In a scene in *Alien Resurrection,* Ripley is shooting baskets when the macho Johner (Ron Perlman) makes a crude pass at her. She out-machoes him with her superhuman skills (she can dunk and keep the ball away from him), then beats him up, outdoing Johner's own hypermasculinity. As will be seen below, she ultimately identifies with and becomes one with the aliens herself in a grotesque redefining of her own identity. Although Ripley's character in the first film was originally conceived as male, all of the films self-consciously call attention to her gender.

Like Victorian novelists, filmmakers often continue to promulgate the angel-monster dichotomy in their depictions of women.[10] The female action-adventure heroine ultimately cannot be considered a feminist heroine, for in her rebellion against traditional female roles, she emulates the violence and callousness of the most stereotypical extremes of masculinity, even surpassing them, effectively becoming a monster herself: the heroine "must become what she fights, a technologized hunter possessed by an egoic perfectionism that fuels an almost demonic drive to destroy her nemesis, even if that obsession means the ruin of herself and those around her" (Rushing and Frentz 214). In *Terminator 2,* Sarah Connor is introduced to the audience as a mental patient, and her appearance gives her a monstrous quality: her hair is sweaty and matted, and her teeth are clenched in an expression of pure rage as the director, Silberman, displays her to the visiting students. Another scene shows Sarah on video-tape, screaming profanities and lunging across the table in an attempted attack on Silberman. The videotape (which Silberman and Sarah are view-ing) is then frozen on a frame that shows Sarah's face distorted with rage, making her look less than human. Given the near-impossibility of achiev-ing her goals, Sarah cannot envision any means other than violence. Her decision to assassinate Miles Dyson reveals her at her most monstrous and most Terminator-like. Sarah shatters the window of Dyson's subur-ban home with automatic weapons fire, and after entering the house, she is about to kill him in front of his wife and child when she finally becomes aware of the inhumanity of her intentions. At that moment, her son ar-rives to intervene. To compensate for her powerlessness in an impersonal society that is soon to turn over its defense decisions to a machine, Sa-rah believes she must become a killing machine herself. She does not just reject traditional femininity; she represses her humanity altogether, re-making herself in the image of the Terminator.

The *Alien* series also explores the way in which the heroine must make herself into a monster to combat a much more powerful enemy. As the series progresses, Ripley becomes more violent, more impervious to emotion, and more and more like an alien herself, a process that is liter-alized in *Alien Resurrection,* when she is cloned as a human-alien hybrid. As Judith Halberstam notes, "All of the *Alien* films have been moving toward the theme that this installment embraces: the similarities between Ripley and the alien" (12). We see the beginnings of Ripley's transforma-tion in *Aliens* when she uses a flamethrower to destroy the alien's eggs. Despite her own maternal feelings toward Newt, Ripley cannot empa-thize with the alien's maternal desire to protect her own young. The film makes the alien's methods of incubating its offspring so horrific that Ripley's violence is justified. At that point, the alien is entirely "other" to her, and she does not perceive her own behavior as potentially monstrous.

Ripley in the third film becomes increasingly monstrous but cannot avoid being used as a human incubator for the aliens. Inness accurately notes that this film "is structured around confining the threat posed by her toughness" (112). Thus, in *Alien³*, Ripley's identification with the aliens becomes more pronounced and is explored much more explicitly.[11] At the prison colony, Ripley's femininity is definitely a liability; by shaving her head and donning prison gear, she effectively displays the androgyny her character suggested throughout the series. In this film, however, it is not enough for Ripley to transform herself into a pseudomale; she must dehumanize herself utterly, as Sarah Connor does, to combat an inhuman enemy.

What makes *Alien³* particularly interesting is Ripley's consciousness that she is indeed becoming "one of them." She has suspected all along that she is incubating one inside her, and when its presence is confirmed with a type of futuristic X-ray, she realizes that her own destruction will be the only way to ensure the destruction of the alien. At this point, she and the alien are inextricably linked. Her "alienness" is further confirmed by her realization that the male alien will not kill her as it has the other humans; she is, as she bitterly remarks to the alien, "part of the family." The quest to destroy the Alien species has so consumed and transformed her that it is the only part of her life that has any significance: "You've been in my life so long I can't remember anything else." In the final frames of the movie, when Ripley dives backward into the molten lead, just as the alien is exploding out of her body, the viewer sees her hands (initially stretched out in a Christlike pose) move to her chest. The impression is, of course, that she is trying to contain the alien inside her, so it cannot escape their mutual destruction. Yet a close look at the film in slow motion reveals Ripley's hands apparently caressing the creature as it emerges from her chest. She has become one with the alien and in giving birth to her counterpart, she acknowledges that identification with the alien with a caress before both plunge to their deaths.

Alien Resurrection emphasizes Ripley's "alienness" throughout. From the first time that we see the scientists referring to her as "the host" and as "Number 8" (in a series of clones), she has been completely stripped of her humanity. As a result, like the Terminator or Eric Draven, she has superhuman strength and coordination. Her blood has the acidic quality of the aliens'—she can use it to burn through bulkheads and ports. During her initial encounter with Call, she drives a knife through her own hand without injury. Call informs her that she is not Ellen Ripley, who "died two hundred years ago." She says, "You're a thing, a construct. They grew you in a fucking lab." Although the queen has been removed from her body, Ripley says, "Not all the way out. I can feel it behind my eyes. I can hear it moving." She has a brutal arrogance and confidence and an ironic detachment about her own previous death (when someone says, "Hey, I thought you were dead," she answers, "Yeah, I get that a lot"), until she finds the room full of clones numbered 1–7, their alien and human body parts distorted and disproportionate and mingled into grotesque forms. The most recent version, number 7, is still alive, although horribly malformed and in constant pain, and begs Ripley to kill her. Ripley torches the entire lab with a flame thrower, as one glass tank after another explodes, while Ripley absorbs the full implications of her unnatural creation. When Ripley is later pulled into an alien nest, being caressed by what appear to be slimy tentacles and limbs, she looks right at home with her "own kind." Her half-human/half-alien "granddaughter" destroys its own mother, bonding with Ripley instead. Ripley has a double consciousness, aware that her own callousness and detachment are not particularly human: "I'm finding a lot of things funny lately, but I don't think they are." Ripley, the "monster's mother," has literally become the enemy, a product of dehumanizing technology and alien physiology, in what may be a cautionary tale of the results of female empowerment.

Alien Resurrection ultimately suggests that female anatomy and reproduction are monstrous in and of themselves, with the principal women presented as unnatural and freakish. The film does offer a veiled and subtextually coded possibility of a relationship and a kinship between Ripley and Call. Call is a member of a line of advanced androids who rebelled against their creators. Beset with self-loathing, she describes herself as "disgusting," and drawing a parallel between herself and the equally unnatural Ripley, she asks, "How can you stand being what you are?" Ripley and Call may be mirrors and soul mates, but it is by virtue of the film's misogynistic revulsion at the female body that this likeness exists. Call is disgusted by the milky fluid that serves as android "blood" and by the tubes and wires that protrude from her body when she is shot, and Ripley (tattooed with a number "8") is repelled by a roomful of failed and grotesquely malformed earlier clones of herself, floating in womblike tanks. Ripley and Call are both freaks, nightmare visions of female anatomy, surpassed only by the queen alien, who now gives birth in human fashion instead of laying eggs. The female reproductive process is presented in the most grotesque terms possible, with the queen's hugely distended abdomen seeping thick yellowish blood before her (also female) half-human offspring is born, a new monstrosity with a mostly human body and an alien head, graced by human teeth and eyes, like Keats's Lamia. Of course, this theme was anticipated in *Aliens*. Bundtzen argues,

> The Alien Other, I believe, quite literally embodies woman's reproductive powers. She arouses primal anxieties about woman's sexual organs and in her combination of multiple tentacles and oozing jaws is the phallic mother of nightmare. (14)

The film's revulsion at female anatomy and its portrayal of such as grotesque and unnatural is its most disturbingly misogynistic element, suggesting that if Ripley and Call are indeed kindred spirits, it is because no one else will have them. They are mirrors in their shared freakishness and unnatural origins, in as vicious a parody of the idea of soul mates as Ripley's bond with the male alien was in *Alien³*. The end of the film, with a return to Earth, seems to leave open the possibility of a fifth installment in the series, and one can only wonder what sort of metamorphosis Ripley will next undergo.

For both nineteenth-century writers and late-twentieth-century filmmakers, despite their sympathy with their heroines, the strong, competent female who strikes a middle ground between "feminine" compassion and "masculine" assertiveness does not exist. In rebelling against traditional female roles, these women ultimately become monsters. For Brontë and Hardy, the Byronic heroine must adopt a callous indifference to the needs and feelings of others in order to pursue her own goals. Catherine's violent temper and Eustacia's gloating triumphs over lovers and rivals alike render them ultimately unsympathetic to a large proportion of readers, as the studies cited toward the opening of this chapter suggest. My own students, for all their understanding of the heroines' situations, have a hard time sympathizing with these two characters. While Brontë and Hardy go out of their way to explore the reasons why their heroines behave as they do, it cannot be accidental that they render their heroines so negatively as to alienate the reader's tendency to identify with the protagonist. Similarly, the filmmakers under consideration in this chapter take their heroines to an unsympathetic extreme. Sarah and Ripley ultimately become the monsters they are fighting against. In both the novels and all the films in question, the message to female readers and viewers is clear: Don't try this at home! The female viewer may vicariously identify with the heroines' experiences of self-empowerment, but she must reject the almost inevitable monstrousness that results. The Byronic heroine, like the Byronic hero, is not a role model but rather someone who performs heroic deeds and suffers the consequences of her presumption.

The Byronic hero's aspiration toward immortality is ultimately a death wish; the only way he can transcend his human condition is to die. For Catherine and Eustacia, their Byronic stance masks their actual desire, which is not to transcend humankind but rather simply to be fully human. They wish to be able to define their own position in the world, not be the shadow of another. Yet in Victorian society, this desire leads to death as well, because it makes these women feel that their condition is intolerable and they lack any viable means to improve upon it. The only option these Victorian women can exercise is that of self-destruction. If Heathcliff and Edgar will not concede to her demands during her lifetime, Catherine hopes that, by dying, she will ensure a lifetime of suffering and guilt for both of them while securing her own freedom from their demands. Her creator refeminizes Catherine by putting her in the condition of a helpless and frail invalid, a traditional image of delicate and ethereal femininity. In death, she becomes a suitable object for the audience's sympathy, for she is now more beautiful than any "angel in heaven" (137).

Eustacia similarly uses death as the only power she can exercise and as an escape from an utterly untenable situation.[12] Her marriage is unacceptable, and escape is impossible; and on a night where "never was harmony more perfect than that between the chaos of her mind and the chaos of the world without" (355), she drowns herself. After her body is recovered, Hardy describes the expression frozen on her face as "in a momentary transition between fervour and resignation" (377)—fervour because she realizes that she finally has the opportunity to make a choice and resignation because the only choice she is allowed to exercise is that of her own death. Like Catherine, Eustacia is more beautiful in death, for she "eclipsed all her living phases" (377). Hardy again dwells on the details of her physical appearance; as a romanticized aesthetic object, the dead Eustacia regains the sympathy of her readers. Hardy writes that her "stateliness of look . . . had at last found an artistically happy background," suggesting that her "stateliness" can only be appropriate in death (377). What particularly links Brontë's and Hardy's destruction of their heroines is their need to nullify the threat such independent women pose to their societies (and presumably to their readers). Even Emily Brontë, a rebel herself, cannot allow her fictional female rebel to succeed in her aims and thrive. Both Eustacia and Catherine receive the death penalty from their creators for their presumption and warn us that the Byronic heroine, in spite of the moments of empowerment she achieves, cannot be a role model for us.

Like her nineteenth-century sisters, the contemporary Byronic heroine faces a similar lack of options. Although she may provide an escapist fantasy of empowerment for her audiences, the contemporary Byronic heroine is not allowed to retain her self-assertion and autonomy. If she is not killed off like Catherine and Eustacia, then she is tamed and "refeminized" so that she can be reintegrated into what is still a male-dominated society that does not tolerate unconventional women. Film-makers will give their audiences strong, aggressive heroines, but what they give with one hand they frequently take away with the other. Sarah Connor survives, but with much of her Byronic stance stripped away from her. She also undergoes a process of what I call "refeminization" during the course of *Terminator 2*, subordinating herself to her ten-year-old son's authority. When John arrives at Dyson's home to prevent his mother from committing murder, Sarah immediately crumples. Her previously tough demeanor dissolves, and she sobs in John's arms. He becomes the authority figure, snapping at Sarah when she launches into her feminist tirade against men. Cameron repudiates the notion of the Byronic heroine as a viable option for women. As we have seen, Sarah essentially becomes a Terminator herself in her use of violence, ironically disregarding the value of Dyson's life in her quest to save the human species from nuclear destruction. Having learned her lesson, Sarah does not embark on any more solitary, independent missions but works coop-eratively with her son, the Terminator, and Dyson to destroy the Cyberdyne lab and prevent the Skynet computer from being developed. In their escape from the Cyberdyne building, the trio is once again pursued by the T-1000, and Sarah receives a gunshot wound in the leg. Rendered help-less, barely able to walk, she is forced to surrender the parent role again to John, as she is now physically dependent on him. By having Sarah be the one who is wounded and then revealing her weakness before the T-1000 (who impales her in the shoulder), Cameron is continuing the process of "refeminizing" his heroine as a victim. She can defy the T-1000 with passive resistance (refusing to betray John's location) and she can muster an obligatory "Fuck you," but she must depend on the Terminator to come through at the last minute to save her life: "His ability points out her inability, reducing the threat that tough women like Sarah pose to society's codes of femininity" (Inness 131). A battle between the two machines ensues. While the Terminator is temporarily out of commission, Sarah fires repeatedly at the T-1000, running out of ammunition, of course. It shakes a finger at her mockingly and is again on the verge of killing her when, once again, the Terminator recovers in time to save her by firing at his adversary and blowing him into a pool of molten steel. At the beginning of the film, Sarah was effective in using violence to further her own ends, but by the final scenes of the film, her attempts at violence are shown to be misguided (in the attack on Dyson) or ineffective (in the final battle with the T-1000). Although she survives, she must destroy her soul mate, her violent double, the Terminator. In pressing the button that lowers him into the steel, she eradicates her own violent side, her Byronic stance, so that she and John can rejoin society. Presumably, she has erased her "masculine" tendencies toward violence, so she can return to her "feminine" role as John's mother. Inness suggests that "audience members learn that her tough image and attitude are too severe, too masculine, and too emotionless, and thus must be softened in order for society to tolerate her" (126).

In her own adoption of the violence of the male action-adventure hero and the monstrous ruthlessness of the aliens, Ellen Ripley has transgressed beyond the point where she can be reintegrated into society. She gets killed off in the third film only to be resurrected as a vampirish half-alien creature. Her Byronic isolation is more profound than Sarah Connor's, for she loses her "daughter" instead of regaining a son and ultimately loses her humanity as well in the grotesque isolation the scientists of United Systems Military perpetrate upon her. Ripley has no family, no significant others, and no possibility for returning to a normal life. She is wholly isolated and wholly obsessed; once she discovers her "infection" by the alien in the third film, she is cut adrift from human society and human contact. She could now be the source of contagion rather than the eradicator of it. Her own death becomes her first priority, and she tries to taunt first Dillon and then the alien to prove themselves by killing her. She asks the alien, "Now do something for me. It's easy. Just do what you do." Neither potential murderer is up to the task, and ultimately Ripley must regain control of her invaded body the only way she can, by killing herself. It is an interesting comparison to note that Catherine Earnshaw Linton shows no interest in her own pregnancy and, by starving herself, she does her best to end it, just as Ripley does with her own process of "gestation." To Catherine, a baby would be an alien being, one who would restrict her already limited freedom even further. It must seem altogether too much for Catherine to have two men battling over her soul and then to have her future child taking over her body. Like Catherine's, Ripley's "pregnancy" makes her physically ill; as the film progresses, she begins to cough more and more and experience moments of weakness. Nevertheless, she is able to destroy the male alien and, unwilling to allow her body to be used by the female alien or by the Company, she dives backward into the molten lead, arms outstretched in a Christlike pose, just as the alien starts to emerge from her chest. She knows if she allows the egg-laying queen inside her to emerge, thousands more of the creatures will be created, and she knows that she will die anyway when the alien bursts out.

Like the other heroines under consideration, Ripley has run out of options; despite her violence, her exceptional leadership, her proficiency with weapons, and her successful one-on-one battles with the aliens, Ripley's body has been invaded and taken over. By the end of *Alien³*, in spite of all of her capabilities, she is utterly powerless, caught between the Company without and an invader within. As Inness contends, "Her death serves as a warning to women who, like Ripley, might rebel against gender constraints and adopt tough personas" (113). Ripley's Christlike pose suggests that she is sacrificing herself for the benefit of the human race; yet her ultimate clutching of the alien emerging out of her renders the terms of the struggle entirely intimate and personal, as she fights to contain its emergence yet caresses the creature at the same time. Ripley can only preserve the semblance of her self as an autonomous being by simultaneously killing herself and the alien, but as has been argued, the danger posed by the aliens has so overwhelmed and taken over her life, and Ripley has had to sacrifice so much of her human feelings, that by the end of the third film, Ripley and the alien have become one being. Sailing through the air, Ripley and alien inhabit their own universe; they merge into "one life, one death, / One Heaven, one Hell, one Immortality, / And one annihilation" in a grotesquely intimate union of birth and death (P. B. Shelley, *Epipsychidion* 585–87). While Ripley's character is immensely appealing to both male and female viewers, she, like the Byronic hero, must be rehumanized, must be shown to be vulnerable and mortal, in order to gain the ultimate allegiance of her audience. She has been transformed by her experiences and by her violence so radically as to be unable to be reintegrated into any type of society. Sarah Connor has both her son and hope for the future to give her a new life; Ripley is utterly isolated from other people, and despite her defeat of the aliens, the Company is still in power. Her death is simultaneously her only possible means of redemption and rehumanization, as well as her most daring act of Byronic self-assertion. Again Ripley serves the purpose of escapist fantasy for her audience: she is a lone warrior almost single-handedly defeating an overwhelmingly powerful enemy and thwarting the goals of a monstrously inhuman bureaucracy at the same time. Despite her almost superhuman abilities and strengths, Ripley, like the other heroines discussed in this chapter, is not given an option of triumphing over her adversaries *and* surviving with her Byronic self-assertiveness intact. Reduced to functioning as an incubator for an alien species, she knows the only way she can restore her humanity is suicide. Once again, choosing the means of her own death becomes one of the very few options remaining for a female hero.

The fourth film, however, takes even her death away from her, as she is forced to become the "Eve" of the species she devoted her life to eradicating. The film refeminizes Ripley by making her entirely the product of her own biology, a biology manipulated by scientists in a lab, while revealing a male revulsion against female reproduction, what Gediman describes as "Ripley's gift" to the queen. Although the deranged Gediman sees the queen as "perfect" now, the birth scene is a nightmarish phantasmagoria of oozing slime and a huge, distended, gaping abdomen that seems to embody every nightmare of the "devouring mother." In *Alien Resurrection,* the female body is a site of revulsion and self-hatred. The triumph of Ripley's suicide in *Alien³* is stripped from her, as the scientists violate her bodily integrity altogether, depriving her even of the option of suicide or, for that matter, the right to choose an abortion, another issue the film raises. When Call asks Ripley why she goes on living, and Ripley answers, "Not much choice," it is literally true. She has no choice about whether to submit to being an incubator for the aliens. If she can be cloned from a drop of blood, then she is left entirely without autonomy or self-determination.

Characterizing societies in which a woman is not allowed to assert herself, Brontë and Hardy invest their heroines with the stance of the Byronic hero, a stance that offers merely the *illusion* of autonomy, self-sufficiency, and self-definition. Women in the nineteenth century had very few options; both Catherine and Eustacia find their choices narrowed down to an unbearable existence or death. Sarah Connor and Ellen Ripley show us that imitating the worst traits of stereotypical masculinity is not a desirable option for the women of their time either. Like Catherine and Eustacia, they experience fleeting moments of exhilaration and power, but they too arrive at the conviction that conforming to society's expectations or self-destructing are the only options remaining to them. As fictional characters, Catherine and Eustacia represent a time when women had to choose between extremes—survival in the self-abnegating role of the Victorian angel or a self-assertion that ends in an early death. Our film heroines similarly feel that they must adopt the violence and aggressiveness of the male outlaw to survive. While such heroines provide their audiences with a vicarious fantasy of empowerment, the filmmakers ultimately repudiate the heroines' Byronic stance and deny its effectiveness as a means to attain their goals. In both nineteenth-century and late-twentieth-century contexts, the heroine's Byronism fails her in the end; and she must resort to dependence on men or self-destruction, or both, in a final bid to define her identity and her status as a human being, unless even those options are taken away from her.

The Byronic heroine has clearly evolved since the production of the *Alien* and the *Terminator* movies. A particularly representative example is Sara "Pez" Pezzini (Yancy Butler), the hero of the television series *Witchblade* (first aired June 2001). The series combines a *noir*-ish, gritty realism with a Gothic, supernatural concept. Pez is a tough, no-nonsense, brusque New York City homicide detective who encounters a supernatural object, the Witchblade, a bracelet that gives her extrasensory visions and also transforms into a spiked gauntlet and sword during battle. The series has made clear that Pez is somehow destined to wield the Witchblade, and that she is in some way descended from a long line of women warriors (including Joan of Arc) who also wielded the powerful Witchblade.

Sara Pezzini is quintessentially Byronic. She is a loner who prefers to solve crimes her own way, not according to the strictures imposed by her superiors. She repeatedly manages to evade and abandon her newly assigned partner, so that she can work on her own, and she defies anyone who tries to control her. She is isolated both by her mysterious connection with the Witchblade and by a series of deaths of people close to her. Pez has the hallmarks of an outlaw, and she is often portrayed riding a black motorcycle at impressive speeds, wearing a black leather jacket and an opaque black helmet. She defies her corrupt superiors in the police department, following her own firmly founded moral code. She also has the mysterious past of the Byronic hero, having been raised by adoptive parents, while the identities of her birth parents are only hinted at. Yet it is this biological ancestry that links Pez to the Witchblade.

Unlike Ellen Ripley and Sarah Connor, Pez is not a female "Terminator" clone. She is tough, ultracompetent, and frequently violent, but she integrates those qualities with compassion and the capacity to form deep attachments with friends and lovers. While Ripley and Sarah could not integrate their "masculine" aggressiveness with their attempts at traditionally feminine roles, Pez does not suffer from the same internal conflicts. An iconic and repeated image of Pez shows her pulling off her motorcycle helmet and shaking out a long mane of hair, relaxed and comfortable with who she is. She seems to be neither hampered by her gender nor rejecting it. She emanates the charisma and confidence of the Byronic hero, and despite the myriad injuries inflicted on her and those close to her, she determinedly pursues her enemies and strives to uncover the mysteries of the Witchblade. Like Manfred, she wields a supernatural power, and she does not submit to the oppressive forces that try to destroy her. The series lacks the misogynistic undercurrent of the *Alien* and *Terminator* films. Unlike Sarah Connor and Ellen Ripley, Pez is not turned into a monster by her creators. Although the series lasted only two seasons, it was the object of a vigorous fan campaign to restore it. At the same time, new Byronic heroines are emerging on film, on television, in comic books, and in video games. The increasing popularity of female action heroes suggests that in the twenty-first century, the Byronic heroine may be able to fight her battles without being hampered by nineteenth- and twentieth-century biases about and stereotypes of assertive, strong, competent, and powerful women.

Conclusion
The Vampire with the Face of an Angel

As the twenty-first century begins, Byronic heroes are still hot popular culture commodities. One quintessentially Byronic hero existing concurrent with the writing of this book is the vampire Angel of the eponymous television series. Angel (David Boreanaz) first appeared as a character on *Buffy the Vampire Slayer,* and his popularity was such that Buffy's creators granted him his own series, which first aired in fall 1999. Angel has the Byronic look and demeanor par excellence (fig. 7). He has dark hair, heavy eyebrows, and an almost perpetually grim expression on his face. He wears a long black duster, suggestive of a cape. He is beset by melancholy, guilt, and what the other characters tend to refer to as "brooding." Angel has not only superhuman abilities to fight injustice (including oppressive institutional power) but also the angst and long-suffering of Rice's vampires Louis and Lestat, as well as Gaiman's Dream. He also has the Byronic isolation of being an anomaly, a vampire with a soul, unable to fit into the human or vampire worlds. The restoration of his soul occurred as a result of a gypsy curse, which left him doomed to feel guilt and anguish and remorse over the crimes he committed as a vampire. He works toward his own redemption by fighting evil, but at the same time he has to combat his own dark side, which lies precariously close to the surface.

Typical of any "decent" Byronic hero, Angel has the Romantic dilemma of having an unavailable and inaccessible soul mate, Buffy. The two fell in love during Angel's tenure on the original series, but after making love, they learn a principal clause of the gypsy curse: A moment of "perfect happiness" will strip Angel of his soul, making him, once again, a source of evil and destruction. His soul is eventually restored, and he returns to the forces of good, but the price is his separation from Buffy. In a cross-over episode ("Sanctuary") that includes characters from both series, Buffy (Sarah Michelle Gellar) tells Angel about her new boyfriend, Riley, and Angel angrily characterizes his own forced isolation: "You moved on. I can't. You found someone new. I'm not allowed to, remember? I see you again, it cuts me up inside, and the person I share that with is *me*."

Angel cannot allow himself release from his suffering because he believes he can never fully atone for the crimes of his past. Several episodes of both *Buffy the Vampire Slayer* and *Angel* provide flashbacks to Angel's past, when he was known as the master vampire Angelus, "the scourge of Europe." We learn that he slaughtered his own family soon after becoming a vampire, and we see him callously and smilingly engage in acts of murder and destruction. In fact, Angelus is presented as not merely violent but sadistic. He slowly drove one of his victims, Drusilla (Juliet Landau), insane by systematically murdering members of her family while she watched and then turning her into a vampire so that her insanity would torment her forever. While Angel perpetually seeks redemption for such acts, he also suggests that complete redemption may be impossible, no matter how much good he does in his current ensouled incarnation. In the episode "In the Dark," Angel comes by a magical ring that will allow him to be outside by daylight without being burned to death. Despite his feeling of awe and wonder at seeing the sun, he announces to his friend and colleague Doyle (Glenn Quinn), "I'm not going to wear the ring." Shocked, Doyle complains, "You got a real addiction to the brooding part of life." Angel explains, however, that he has to continue to bear the burden of his guilt:

> ANGEL. I've thought of it from every angle. What I figure is I did a
>   lot of damage in my day—more than you can imagine.
> DOYLE. What? You don't get the ring because your period of self-

flagellation isn't over yet? Think of all the daytime people you
could help between nine and five.

ANGEL. They have help. The whole world is designed for them. So
much that they have no idea what goes on around them after
dark. They don't see the weak ones, lost in the night or the things
that prey on them. And if I join them, maybe I'd stop seeing too.
. . . I was brought back for a reason, Doyle. As much as I'd like to
kid myself, I don't think it was for eighteen holes at Rancho.

He insists that his role is not to enjoy himself, but to continue to work
for redemption—at night and in the dark.

Like the typical outlaw-hero, Angel will use any means necessary to
combat evil. He usually tries, however, to avoid killing humans, killing
only demons and vampires. There are times, however, when he practices
a kind of vigilante justice, reminiscent of Eric in *The Crow*. Angel's principal nemesis is the law firm Wolfram and Hart, which is wholly corrupt
and embroiled in supernatural dealings that are very much on the dark
side. Because of his fight against evil, the law firm has tried to kill Angel
on several occasions. But in the episode "Reunion," he has an opportunity to strike back, and he conveniently disregards his usual rule about
not killing humans. He allows the top executives of the law firm to be
slaughtered by two female vampires, and, ignoring the lawyers' pleas for
help, he locks the door, leaving the vampires to their depredations. This
act temporarily alienates Angel from his few friends (the staff members
of his detective firm), who all refuse to work for him any longer. That he
consistently operates outside the law is particularly revealed in his dealings
with police detective Kate Lockley (Elisabeth Rohm). Although Angel has
helped her on several occasions, she remains suspicious of him and of
his methods. In fact, she becomes obsessed with trying to prove that
Angel has committed misdeeds.

Both series provide opportunity after opportunity to inflict Angel with
guilt and suffering. The restoration of his soul has given him a perpetual
feeling of remorse over the humans he brutally killed as a soulless vampire. He also feels guilt for abandoning his vampire family, his sire Darla
(Julie Benz), his childe Drusilla, and his grand-childe Spike (James
Marsters). He feels guilty over his relationship with Buffy, and he feels guilty
over his separation from Buffy. While his soul is temporarily taken from
him on *Buffy*, he tortures her Watcher (a kind of guide and mentor) Giles

(Anthony Stewart Head) and kills Jenny Calendar (Robia LaMorte), who is a teacher at Buffy's high school, Giles's lover, and a helper to Buffy and her friends. And his treatment of Buffy and Spike is particularly sadistic and vicious, as he singles them out as victims for his cruelty. His punishment is particularly severe, because immediately after his soul is restored to him, he is cast into Hell to suffer for five hundred years (time apparently moving differently there). On his own series, he repeatedly makes mistakes or takes actions that earn him the disapprobation of his friends and colleagues and add to his burden of guilt and angst. Like the other Byronic heroes discussed here, Angel is rehumanized throughout the series. The return of his soul makes him far more human than other vampires, and in flashbacks to his evil past, we see how radically he has been transformed. Yet the series also hints that Angel's complete redemption may allow him to become fully human someday, as the episode "To Shanshu in L.A." reveals.

Angel's creators have something in common with Byron and with Gaiman in that they do not allow their audience to take Angel's self-imposed martyr complex entirely seriously. They undermine his Byronic pose in a coyly self-referential fashion as much as they exploit it. In the episode "The Yoko Factor," Buffy's new boyfriend Riley (Marc Blucas) worries that she isn't over her attraction to Angel and comments on his appeal to women: "Even when he's good, he's all Mr.-Billowy-Coat-King-of-Pain, and girls really . . . ." Here he is interrupted by Buffy, but he is clearly about to say something along the lines of "and girls really dig that type." Riley's jealousy is provoked by the romantic and sexual appeal of such dark heroes as Heathcliff, Lestat, and Angel, and in his protest, the series' creators self-referentially comment on Angel's perpetual angst and on the fans who find that angst irresistibly attractive. Angel's creators also undermine his heroic and self-sacrificing stance. "In the Dark" opens with Angel being mocked by his nemesis, Spike. Angel has just rescued a young woman from being killed by a drunken boyfriend, and Spike, watching from a rooftop, provides a sarcastic voiceover, presenting his own version of the dialogue. He has the rescued woman ask, in the mode of a stereotypical damsel in distress, "How can I thank you, you mysterious black-clad hunk of a knight-thing?" and then has Angel reply in an exaggerated John-Wayne-like western hero's vocal inflection: "No need, little lady. Your tears of gratitude are enough for me. You see, I was once a bad-ass vampire, but love, and a pesky curse, defanged me, and now

I'm just a big fluffy puppy with bad teeth." Spike, like Gaiman's Mervyn, dismisses Angel's Byronic theatrics as a mere pose, a product of fashion, the affectation of "a great pouf," who uses "nancy-boy hair gel."

Like Byron, some contemporary creators of Byronic heroes realize that there is something comical as well as tragic about the brooding, self-absorbed loner. Discussions about contemporary Byronic heroes in class allow students to explore the longstanding and pervasive appeal of Byron's creations. Like popular culture scholar Henry Jenkins, my students and I can be fans of popular culture at the same time that we examine it from an academic perspective, and this seeming dichotomy can only enrich the experience of the texts under consideration.[1] The Byronic hero is a figure of autonomy, self-reliance, defiance, and power, and he is an outlaw who lives by his own moral code. The appeal of this loner to the audience is the same in Byron's times as it is in ours: Manfred and the heroes described here can successfully act on their desires to defy authority and can successfully confront obstacles in their paths. They do not have to bow to institutional power or to oppressive forces, for they have both the supernatural abilities and the attitude required to fight them. At the same time, they validate their audience's own doubts and fears and sorrows. Many fans can relate to Eric's and Dream's and Angel's grief over the unattainability of perfect love. Many fans can relate to Lestat's perpetual questioning of his purpose in life. As fans we may envy the power of Manfred and Q and Lestat and Angel, but we do not envy their boredom with their immortality and their perpetual gloom and isolation. Contemporary Byronic heroes give us, just as Manfred does, a vicarious experience of utter autonomy and power, but at the same time they suggest that in our powerlessness, we may be better off and almost surely happier than they are. In Byron's *Manfred,* when the self-pitying hero is advised to seek patience by the Chamois Hunter who has prevented his suicide, Manfred haughtily and pompously responds,

> Patience and patience! Hence—that word was made
> For brutes of burthen not for birds of prey;
> Preach it to mortals of a dust like thine,—
> I am not of thine order.

> (2.2.35–38)

Expressing his own relief, as well as that of Byron's readers, the hunter exclaims "Thanks to Heaven! / I would not be of thine for the free fame / Of

William Tell" (2.2.38–40). Byron here comically undermines Manfred's pretensions to superiority. In a similar fashion, Gaiman and *Angel's* creators use the skepticism of characters like Mervyn and Spike, respectively, to strip off some of the glamour and luster of Dream's and Angel's self-satisfaction in their own long-suffering. Resonances such as these suggest that the connections between Byron's heroes and the Byronic hero in contemporary culture have an almost unlimited potential yet to be explored.[2]

Notes
Works Cited and Consulted
Index

Notes

1. "A Fire and Motion of the Soul": Nineteenth-Century Origins

1. See Peter L. Thorslev, *The Byronic Hero: Types and Prototypes,* and Walter L. Reed, *Meditations on the Hero: A Study of the Romantic Hero in Nineteenth-Century Fiction.*

2. "Not Such a Dork": The Rehumanization of the Byronic Hero

1. Gallafent also makes this assumption: "It emerges slowly for us that he is in some occult sense Duncan, returned to revenge himself on the killers and on the town" (113). And Knapp says, "Because the Stranger dreams of Duncan's death, it can be argued that the Stranger is Duncan's spirit, haunting Lago until it can be released from limbo" (61).

2. See Harvey, 34–37, for a detailed discussion of the portrayal of the police and other institutional authorities in the film.

3. Harvey's description of this scene is particularly and drily evocative:

Having had his moment, the Terminator, as Dadlike as Homer Simpson, mutters, "I need a vacation." At the height of his endearing, individuated, paternal role, when he has begun to seem the good ol' Terminator, a bit of a clunker but reliable in a pinch, he reminds Sarah and John that if they really want to save the world, they must melt him down too. His lowering into the steel, marked by John's agony and Sarah's wary respect, presents the wrenching and fascinating spectacle of the father's body slowly eradicated, his vision winking out like a switched-off television. The poor Terminator has got his vacation. (40)

4. Introducing students to this type in the classroom allows them to understand both the context of Byron's times and the ways in which a character type transcends its own time and place. Such a contemporary context illuminates

Byron's poetry, as well as helping students develop a critical perspective on the popular culture they "consume." Such class discussions can also fire their enthusiasm to engage in similar analyses. My students have analyzed as Byronic heroes such characters as Batman of the *Dark Knight* comics and Luke Skywalker and Darth Vader of the *Star Wars* films. The pervasiveness of Byronic types in contemporary popular culture can also be seen in the readiness with which my students write parodies or updated versions of Byron's *Manfred* (in verse) by plugging in a fictional or actual figure from popular culture. A student of mine wrote a version of *Manfred* with Darth Vader reflecting on his transformation from Anakin Skywalker and feeling guilt over his crimes. Other students have written versions of *Manfred* from the perspective of Robert Smith of the band the Cure, the late Kurt Cobain of Nirvana, and Trent Reznor of Nine Inch Nails. The students whose papers I've cited are, respectively, Erik Benson, Corinna Evett, Andrea Yoshida, Erin Murphy, Jennifer Meglemre, and Oscar Fuentes.

3. "I Just Want Something I Can Never Have": Angst, Egoism, and Immortality

1. I learned about this phenomenon from "An Interview with Vampires," an unpublished paper by Victoria Sanchez (1997).

2. The Smiths' androgynous and sensitive Morrissey (what Louis would have been if he became a rock star) was a cult favorite, and the Cure's also androgynous Robert Smith, with his jet-black hair, exaggerated makeup, and the darkly romantic themes of his songs had a similarly popular appeal in the 1980s and 1990s. Rice's novels have in fact been inspiration for rock songs, including Concrete Blonde's "Bloodletting: The Vampire Song" (Concrete Blonde, *Bloodletting,* International Record Syndicate, 1990).

3. It is not surprising that there are groups of people who dress as vampires and even have custom-made fangs fitted by a dentist. In the parking lot nearest my office, I've regularly seen two cars with vampire-related license plates.

4. *Star Trek*'s Q: A Byronic Hero for *The Next Generation*

1. A much shorter version of this chapter was delivered at the Romanticism session of the Philological Association of the Pacific Coast annual meeting on November 4, 1994. Three books I have consulted to confirm plot details, spelling of proper nouns, and so forth are Michael Okuda, Denise Okuda, and Debbie Mirek, *The Star Trek Encyclopedia: A Reference Guide to the Future;* Larry Nemecek, *The Star Trek The Next Generation Companion;* and Phil Farrand, *The Nitpicker's Guide for Next Generation Trekkers.* The date 2369 for the first season of *Star Trek: Deep Space Nine* comes from *The Star Trek Encyclopedia.*

2. Q has appeared on eight episodes of *Star Trek: TNG,* which I will list for convenience here: "Encounter at Farpoint," "Hide and Q," "Q Who," "Deja Q," "Qpid," "True Q," "Tapestry," and "All Good Things . . . ." He also appeared on one episode of *Star Trek: Deep Space Nine* ("Q-Less") and three episodes of *Star Trek: Voyager* ("Death Wish," "The Q and the Grey," and "Q2").

3. I discuss the relationship between Q and Picard in detail in "Minding One's P's and Q's: Homoeroticism in *Star Trek: The Next Generation*," *Genders* 27 (1998), <http://www.genders.org/g27/g27_st.html>.

4. In his role as satanic tempter, Q particularly reminds me of another nineteenth-century Byronic hero–Gothic villain, Maturin's Melmoth the Wanderer. In Q's case, he does not have to find people in desperate situations to tempt; he can simply *create* desperate situations to put them in, then gloat when they require his help.

5. In his comments, de Lancie indicated that he wanted to portray Q as more dangerous than he was written in "Qpid" and "True Q." For instance, in "True Q," when Q tells Amanda, "I really do enjoy you, you know," de Lancie delivers the line with such menace that one is convinced he *is* going to kill her. In that episode, de Lancie actually wanted Q to be an assassin and go through with killing Amanda. The show's creators, of course, could not allow that to happen. At that point in his development (*Star Trek: TNG*'s sixth season), Q was clearly supposed to be heroic, not murderous. For him to kill Amanda would actually be more "politically correct" in that it would reveal him as a ruthless tyrant, who should be resisted and disobeyed. Instead, however, he appears as a merciful judge. Presumably Amanda should be grateful to him for sparing her life.

6. In "Shifting Paradigms for Leadership in *Star Trek* and *Star Trek: The Next Generation*," *Popular Culture Review* 5 (1994), Monica Johnstone cogently argues that Picard represents a more open style of leadership than Captain Kirk of the original series. I agree that this conclusion is mostly accurate, but I find interesting the extent to which Picard is forced to defer to Q's extremely tyrannical and capricious mode of leadership. Picard also has a tendency to slip occasionally into a more autocratic style, characterized by a stiff and formal demeanor, rather than Q's flamboyance.

7. Moore also noted that the personal relationship between Q and Picard was central to Q's appearances on the series and a key to his popularity.

8. Given how touchy a subject homosexuality was on television during *TNG*'s run, the series' creators must have concluded that the relationship between Q and Picard had to be rendered *relatively* explicit, particularly in two bedroom scenes between Q and Picard. The bedroom scene in "Tapestry" originally had the actors sitting on the bed, and they came up with the idea of performing it *in* bed instead. In another scene, which was cut, de Lancie kissed Stewart on the forehead, but this act was apparently considered *too* explicit. In "Qpid," when Q confesses his own desire to discover a "vulnerability" in Picard, the scene takes place in Picard's quarters, with the Captain clad in skimpy and sexy black pajamas. In "Tapestry," as the scene referenced in the text opens, the camera pans over Picard's clothes strewn across the floor. He is clearly supposed to be naked when Q materializes next to him in bed. His initial reaction to Q's presence is to yank the covers up to his chin, but as the scene continues, the two converse rather naturally and intimately in bed, and Picard at one point impulsively pulls down the covers

to his waist, no doubt for the benefit of those of Patrick Stewart's fans who see him as a sex object. De Lancie, in fact, describes Q as not merely bisexual but as "bispecial." Presumably, Q's species has evolved beyond the point where gender or species would limit an individual's choice of romantic partners.

5. "She Moves in Mysterious Ways": The Byronic Heroine

1. While Osborn's essay briefly details parallels between Catherine Earnshaw and Byron's Childe Harold and examines the way Catherine's "awareness of the role deemed to her by society and her desire to acquiesce to the extent possible forces her to reject Heathcliff and marry Edgar" (48), her essay does not analyze Catherine's Byronism in detail, nor does it account for the ways in which, as I shall argue, Catherine is rebelling against *Heathcliff's* demands on her, as well as society's.

2. See, for example, Rushing, who compares Ellen Ripley of the *Alien* series to the western hero.

3. For an overview of the reviews of *Alien* and the reviewers' assessment of the heroine, see Bell-Metereau 209–12.

4. Judith Newton argues that "Ripley's character . . . appropriates qualities traditionally associated with male, but not masculinist, heroes" (294). This may be the case in the first film, but in the sequels, Ripley clearly emulates the "masculinist" violence of the stereotypical action-adventure or science fiction hero. What is significant is that this appropriation of masculine qualities is temporary and alternates with traditional feminine behavior in a mutually exclusive fashion.

5. Gilbert and Gubar insist on this point:

Catherine has no meaningful choices. Driven from Wuthering Heights to Thrushcross Grange by her brother's marriage, seized by Thrushcross Grange and held fast in the jaws of reason, education, decorum, she cannot do otherwise than as she does, must marry Edgar because there is no one else for her to marry and a lady must marry. (277)

6. The entire series, of course, rests on representations of rape, forced pregnancy, caesarean birth, and abortion. For studies addressing this issue, see, for example, Greenberg; Cobbs; and Eaton.

7. Inness also comments in detail about "the schism between [Sarah's] adopted persona and her 'natural' one" (128).

8. Newton similarly characterizes *Alien* as embodying both "wish-fulfillment and repression" in its depiction of Ripley as a feminist hero. Thus Ripley is the target of male hostility (particularly in the attack by Ash), and as Newton remarks, in its final moments, "The film subtly reinvests Ripley with traditionally feminine qualities," thus making her more acceptable to a "white, middle-class, male" audience" (296). Like Byers, Greenberg particularly characterizes

Ripley's vulnerability to rape in that scene: The alien "extends a ramrod tongue, tipped with hinged teeth from which drips luminescent slime (KY jelly!), and hisses voluptuously. The very air is charged with the palpable threat of rape—and worse" (97).

9. Inness also comments at length about the way *Alien3* emphasizes Ripley's vulnerability and femininity (112–13).

10. In her discussion of Stephen King's *Carrie*, Clover characterizes what she calls "the female victim-hero" who becomes monstrous "insofar as she has herself become excessive, demonic" (4). Clover's description applies equally effectively to the action-adventure heroine. Thus she categorizes the character of Ripley as combining "the functions of suffering victim and avenging hero," a combined role made possible by the women's movement, which allowed for "the image of an angry woman—a woman so angry that she can be imagined as a credible perpetrator . . . of the kind of violence on which, in the low-mythic universe, the status of full protagonist rests" (17).

11. Rushing's archetypal analysis of the female monster as the "Devouring Mother" (14), the underworld counterpart to the "Good Mother" Ripley (17), seems to anticipate the union of the two that takes place in the third film. It is suggestive that both Sarah Connor and Ellen Ripley have a violent, monstrous counterpart or alter ego, which becomes a part of themselves that they must eventually eliminate. Rushing's article helps us see the patriarchal bias of the entire series, for the union of both parts of the goddess is seen as a shatteringly destructive event in *Alien3*, so destructive that Ripley can redeem herself only through self-destruction.

12. Giordano; Deen (208); and Mickelson (73) are among the critics who argue that Eustacia's death is definitely a suicide, and I agree with them. Martin offers an argument that Hardy evenly balances the evidence that her death is suicidal and that it is accidental, suggesting that what is significant is "why Hardy fails to tell us" (622). He argues that Hardy casts Eustacia aside "once she had served what seemed the more important concerns of the novel" (625), that is, the character of Clym Yeobright. I contend, however, that Eustacia is at least as important a character for Hardy's concerns as Clym is and that her suicide is a conscious choice.

Conclusion: The Vampire with the Face of an Angel

1. See, in particular, Henry Jenkins, *Textual Poachers: Television Fans and Participatory Culture* (New York: Routledge, 1992); Henry Jenkins and John Tulloch, *Science Fiction Audiences: Watching Dr. Who and Star Trek* (New York: Routledge, 1995).

2. I discuss similar themes in Stein, "Immortals and Vampires and Ghosts, Oh My!: Byronic Heroes in Popular Culture."

Works Cited and Consulted

Alien. Dir. Ridley Scott. Perf. Sigourney Weaver. Twentieth Century Fox, 1979.

Alien Resurrection. Dir. Jean-Pierre Jeunet. Perf. Sigourney Weaver and Winona Ryder. Twentieth Century Fox, 1997.

Aliens. Dir. James Cameron. Perf. Sigourney Weaver. Twentieth Century Fox, 1986.

Alien³. Dir. David Fincher. Perf. Sigourney Weaver. Twentieth Century Fox, 1992.

"All Good Things . . . ." *Star Trek: The Next Generation.* Writ. Brannon Braga and Ronald D. Moore. Dir. Rick Kolbe. Paramount Pictures. First aired 1994.

Auerbach, Nina. *Our Vampires, Ourselves.* Chicago: U of Chicago P, 1995.

Beahm, George. "The Quotable Anne Rice." Beahm, *Unauthorized* 135–38.

——, ed. *The Unauthorized Anne Rice Companion.* Kansas City: Andrews, 1996.

Bell-Metereau, Rebecca. *Hollywood Androgyny.* New York: Columbia UP, 1985.

Bender, Hy. *The Sandman Companion.* New York: Vertigo–DC Comics, 1999.

Benvenuto, Richard. "Another Look at the Other Eustacia." *Novel* 4 (1970): 77–79.

Berman, Jeffrey. *Narcissism and the Novel.* New York: New York UP, 1990.

Bingham, Dennis. *Acting Male: Masculinities in the Films of James Stewart, Jack Nicholson, and Clint Eastwood.* New Brunswick, NJ: Rutgers UP, 1994.

Boumelha, Penny. *Thomas Hardy and Women: Sexual Ideology and Narrative Form.* Madison: U of Wisconsin P, 1982.

Brady, Kristin. "Textual Hysteria: Hardy's Narrator on Women." Higonnet 87–106.

Brewer, William D. *The Shelley-Byron Conversation.* Gainesville: UP of Florida, 1994.

Brontë, Emily. *Wuthering Heights.* Ed. William M. Sale. 2nd ed. New York: Norton, 1972.

Bundtzen, Lynda K. "Monstrous Mothers: Medusa, Grendel, and now Alien." *Film Quarterly* 40 (1987): 11–17.

Byers, Thomas B. "Kissing Becky: Masculine Fears and Misogynist Moments in Science Fiction Films." *Arizona Quarterly* 45 (1989): 77–95.

Byron, George Gordon, Lord. *Cain.* Byron, *Complete.* 6.227–95.

———. *Childe Harold.* Byron, *Complete.* 2.1–186.

———. *The Complete Poetical Works.* Ed. Jerome J. McGann. 7 vols. Oxford: Clarendon, 1981.

———. *The Corsair.* Byron, *Complete.* 3.148–214.

———. *Don Juan.* Byron, *Complete.* 5.1–662.

———. *Lara.* Byron, *Complete.* 3.214–56.

———. *Manfred.* Byron, *Complete.* 4.51–102.

———. "Ode to Napoleon Buonaparte." Byron, *Complete.* 3.259–65.

Carlyle, Thomas. *On Heroes, Hero-Worship, and the Heroic in History.* Ed. Michael K. Goldberg, Joel J. Brattin, and Mark Engel. Berkeley: U of California P, 1993.

Carter, Margaret L. "The Vampire as Alien in Contemporary Fiction." *Blood Read: The Vampire as Metaphor in Contemporary Culture.* Ed. Joan Gordon and Veronica Hollinger. Philadelphia: U of Pennsylvania P, 1997. 27–44.

Cawelti, John G. *Adventure, Mystery, and Romance: Formula Stories as Art and Popular Culture.* Chicago: U of Chicago P, 1976.

Chitham, Edward. *A Life of Emily Brontë.* Oxford: Basil Blackwell, 1987.

Chodorow, Nancy. *The Reproduction of Mothering: Psychoanalysis and the Sociology of Gender.* Berkeley: U of California P, 1978.

Clover, Carol J. *Men, Women, and Chainsaws: Gender in the Modern Horror Film.* Princeton, NJ: Princeton UP, 1992.

Cobbs, John L. "*Alien* as an Abortion Parable." *Literature/Film Quarterly* 18 (1990): 198–201.

Combs, Richard. "Shadowing the Hero." *Sight and Sound* 2.6 (1992): 12–16.

Conger, Syndy McMillen. "The Reconstruction of the Gothic Feminine Ideal in Emily Brontë's *Wuthering Heights.*" *The Female Gothic.* Ed. Juliann E. Fleenor. Montreal: Eden, 1983. 91–106.

Constant, Benjamin. *Political Writings.* Cambridge: Cambridge UP, 1988.

Craik, W. A. *The Brontë Novels.* London: Methuen, 1968.

The Crow. Dir. Alex Proyas. Perf. Brandon Lee, Rochelle Davis, Ernie Hudson, and Michael Wincott. Miramax/Dimension Films, 1994.

The Crow: City of Angels. Dir. Tim Pope. Perf. Vincent Perez, Mia Kirshner, and Richard Brooks. Miramax/Dimension Films, 1996.

"Death Wish." *Star Trek: Voyager.* Writ. Shawn Piller and Michael Piller. Dir. James L. Conway. Paramount Pictures. First aired 1995.

Deen, Leonard W. "Heroism and Pathos in Hardy's *Return of the Native.*" *Nineteenth-Century Fiction* 15 (1960): 207–19.

"Deja Q." *Star Trek: The Next Generation.* Writ. Richard Danus. Dir. Les Landau. Paramount Pictures. First aired 1990.

Doane, Janice, and Devon Hodges. "Undoing Feminism: From the Preoedipal to Postfeminism in Anne Rice's Vampire Chronicles." *American Literary History* 2 (1990): 422–42.

Downing, David, and Gary Herman. *Clint Eastwood: All-American Anti-Hero.* London: Omnibus, 1977.

Eaton, Michael. "Born Again." *Sight and Sound* 7 (Dec. 1997): 6–9.

Eggenschwiler, David. "Eustacia Vye, Queen of Night and Courtly Pretender." *Nineteenth-Century Fiction* 25 (1971): 444–54.

Eisler, Benita. *Byron: Child of Passion, Fool of Fame.* New York: Vintage, 2000.

Elfenbein, Andrew. *Byron and the Victorians.* Cambridge: Cambridge UP, 1995.

"Encounter at Farpoint." *Star Trek: The Next Generation.* Writ. D. C. Fontana and Gene Roddenberry. Dir. Corey Allen. Paramount Pictures. First aired 1987.

Engel, Len. "Rewriting Western Myths in Clint Eastwood's New 'Old Western.'" *Western American Literature* 29 (1994): 261–69.

Erickson, Steve. "Dreamland." *Los Angeles Times Magazine* 3 Sept. 1995. 14.

Evans, Robert. "The Other Eustacia." *Novel* 1 (1968): 251–59.

Farrand, Phil. *The Nitpicker's Guide for* Next Generation *Trekkers.* New York: Dell, 1993.

Fontana, Biancamaria. "Introduction." *Political Writings.* By Benjamin Constant. Cambridge: Cambridge UP, 1988. 1–42.

Frayling, Christopher. Rev. of *Unforgiven,* dir. Clint Eastwood. *Sight and Sound* 2.6 (1992): 58.

Gaiman, Neil (writ.), Chris Bachalo, Mark Buckingham, and Dave McKean (illus.). *Death: The High Cost of Living.* New York: DC Comics, 1994.

Gaiman, Neil (writ.), Sam Kieth, and Mike Dringenberg (illus.). "Dream a Little Dream of Me." *The Sandman: Preludes and Nocturnes.* New York: DC Comics, 1995. 1–24.

Gaiman, Neil (writ.), Sam Kieth, and Mike Dringenberg (illus.). "A Hope in Hell." *The Sandman: Preludes and Nocturnes.* New York: DC Comics, 1995. 107–30.

Gaiman, Neil (writ.), Sam Kieth, and Mike Dringenberg (illus.). "Imperfect Hosts." *The Sandman: Preludes and Nocturnes.* New York: DC Comics, 1995. 55–78.

Gaiman, Neil (writ.), Mike Dringenberg, and Malcolm Jones III (illus.). "Lost Hearts." *The Sandman: The Doll's House.* New York: DC Comics, 1990. Part 7, n. pag.

Gaiman, Neil (writ.), Michael Zulli, and Steve Parkhouse (illus.). "Men of Good Fortune." *The Sandman: The Doll's House.* New York: DC Comics, 1990. Part 4, n. pag.

Gaiman, Neil (writ.), and Charles Vess (illus.). "A Midsummer Night's Dream." *The Sandman: Dream Country.* New York: DC Comics, 1991. 1–24.

Gaiman, Neil. "Original Script of 'Calliope.'" *The Sandman: Dream Country.* New York: DC Comics, 1991. 1–39.

Gaiman, Neil (writ.), Chris Bachalo, and Malcolm Jones (illus.). "Playing House." *The Sandman: The Doll's House.* New York: DC Comics, 1990. Part 3, n. pag.

Gaiman, Neil (writ.), Kelley Jones, Mike Dringenberg, and Malcolm Jones III (illus.). "Prologue." *The Sandman: Season of Mists.* New York: DC Comics, 1992. Episode 0, 1–24.

Gaiman, Neil (writ.), Jill Thompson, and Vince Locke (illus.). *The Sandman: Brief Lives.* New York: DC Comics, 1994.

Gaiman, Neil (writ.), Michael Zulli, Steve Parkhouse, Mike Dringenberg, Chris Bachalo, and Malcolm Jones III (illus.). *The Sandman: The Doll's House.* New York: DC Comics, 1990.

Gaiman, Neil (writ.), and Charles Vess (illus.). *The Sandman: Dream Country.* New York: DC Comics, 1991.

Gaiman, Neil (writ.), Bryan Talbot, and Mark Buckingham (illus.). *The Sandman: Fables and Reflections.* New York: DC Comics, 1993.

Gaiman, Neil (writ.), and Shawn McManus (illus.). *The Sandman: A Game of You.* New York: DC Comics, 1993.

Gaiman, Neil (writ.), and Marc Hempel (illus.). *The Sandman: The Kindly Ones.* New York: DC Comics, 1996.

Gaiman, Neil (writ.), Sam Kieth, Mike Dringenberg, and Malcolm Jones III (illus.). *The Sandman: Preludes and Nocturnes.* New York: DC Comics, 1995.

Gaiman, Neil (writ.), Kelley Jones, Mike Dringenberg, and Malcolm Jones III (illus.). *The Sandman: Season of Mists.* New York: DC Comics, 1992.

Gaiman, Neil (writ.), Michael Zulli, Jon J. Muth, and Charles Vess (illus.). *The Sandman: The Wake.* New York: DC Comics, 1996.

Gaiman, Neil (writ.), Sam Kieth, and Mike Dringenberg (illus.). "Sleep of the Just." *The Sandman: Preludes and Nocturnes.* New York: DC Comics, 1995. 1–40.

Gaiman, Neil (writ.), Bryan Talbot, and Mark Buckingham (illus.). "The Song of Orpheus." *The Sandman: Fables and Reflections.* New York: DC Comics, 1993. 149–98.

Gaiman, Neil (writ.), Mike Dringenberg, and Malcolm Jones III (illus.). "The Sound of Her Wings." *The Sandman: Preludes and Nocturnes.* New York: DC Comics, 1995. N. pag.

Gaiman, Neil (writ.), Mike Dringenberg, and Malcolm Jones III (illus.). "Tales in the Sand." *The Sandman: The Doll's House.* New York: DC Comics, 1990. N. pag.

Gallafent, Edward. *Clint Eastwood: Filmmaker and Star.* New York: Continuum, 1994.

Garber, Frederick. "Self, Society, Value, and the Romantic Hero." *Comparative Literature* 19 (1967): 321–33.

Gelder, Ken. *Reading the Vampire.* London: Routledge, 1994.

Gilbert, Sandra M., and Susan Gubar. *The Madwoman in the Attic: The Woman*

Writer and the Nineteenth-Century Literary Imagination. New Haven: Yale UP, 1979.

Gilligan, Carol. *In a Different Voice: Psychological Theory and Women's Development.* Cambridge: Harvard UP, 1982.

Gilmore, Mikal. "Introduction." *The Sandman: The Wake.* By Neil Gaiman. New York: DC Comics, 1996. 8–12.

Giordano, Frank R., Jr. "Eustacia Vye's Suicide." *Texas Studies in Literature and Language* 22 (1980): 504–21.

Goetz, William R. "Genealogy and Incest in *Wuthering Heights.*" *Studies in the Novel* 14 (1982): 359–76.

Goldberg, Jonathan. "Recalling Totalities: The Mirrored Stages of Arnold Schwarzenegger." *Differences: A Journal of Feminist Cultural Studies* 4 (1992): 172–204.

Gose, Elliott B., Jr. *Imagination Indulged: The Irrational in the Nineteenth-Century Novel.* Montreal: McGill-Queen's UP, 1972.

Graham, Paula. "Looking Lesbian: Amazons and Aliens in Science Fiction Cinema." *The Good, the Bad and the Gorgeous: Popular Culture's Romance with Lesbianism.* Ed. Diane Hamer and Belinda Budge. San Francisco: Pandora, 1994: 196–217.

Greenberg, Harvey. "Reimagining the Gargoyle: Psychoanalytic Notes on *Alien.*" *Camera Obscura* 15 (1986): 87–108.

Gross, Edward. "Lights . . . Cameron . . . Action." *Cinescape Insider* 3.9 (1997): 47–55.

Guérif, François. *Clint Eastwood.* Trans. Lisa Nesselson. New York: St. Martin's, 1986.

Hafley, James. "The Villain in *Wuthering Heights.*" *Nineteenth-Century Fiction* 13 (1958): 199–215.

Halberstam, Judith. Rev. of *Alien Resurrection. Girlfriends* Mar. 1998: 12.

Hall, Jean. "The Evolution of the Surface Self: Byron's Poetic Career." *Keats-Shelley Journal* 36 (1987): 134–57.

Hardy, Thomas. *The Return of the Native.* New York: Harper, 1966.

Harvey, Anne-Marie. "Terminating the Father: Technology, Paternity, and Patriarchy in *Terminator 2.*" *Masculinities* 3.2 (1995): 25–42.

"Hide and Q." *Star Trek: The Next Generation.* Writ. C. J. Holland and Gene Roddenberry. Dir. Cliff Bole. Paramount Pictures. First aired 1987.

High Plains Drifter. Dir. Clint Eastwood. Perf. Clint Eastwood. Universal Pictures, 1973.

Higonnet, Margaret R., ed. *The Sense of Sex: Feminist Perspectives on Hardy.* Urbana: U of Illinois P, 1993.

Hochman, David. "Beauties and the Beast." *Entertainment Weekly* Dec. 5, 1997: 18–26.

Holland, Tom. *Lord of the Dead.* New York: Pocket, 1995.

———. "Undead Byron." Wilson, *Byromania* 154–65.

Hoppenstand, Gary, and Ray B. Browne, eds. *The Gothic World of Anne Rice.* Bowling Green, OH: Bowling Green State U Popular P, 1996.

Hyman, Virginia R. *Ethical Perspective in the Novels of Thomas Hardy.* Port Washington, NY: Kennikat, 1975.

"In the Dark." *Angel.* Writ. Douglas Petrie. Dir. Bruce Seth Green. The WB. First aired Oct. 19, 1999.

Inness, Sherrie A. *Tough Girls: Women Warriors and Wonder Women in Popular Culture.* Philadelphia: U of Pennsylvania P, 1999.

Interview with the Vampire: The Vampire Chronicles. Dir. Neil Jordan. Perf. Tom Cruise and Brad Pitt. Geffen Pictures, 1994.

Jeffords, Susan. "'The Battle of the Big Mamas': Feminism and the Alienation of Women." *Journal of American Culture* 10.3 (1987): 73–83.

Johnstone, Monica. "Shifting Paradigms for Leadership in *Star Trek* and *Star Trek: The Next Generation.*" *Popular Culture Review* 5 (1994): 57–66.

Joyce, James. *A Portrait of the Artist as a Young Man.* New York: Viking, 1964.

Kavanaugh, James H. *Emily Brontë.* Oxford: Basil Blackwell, 1985.

Keats, John. *Lamia. Selected.* 212–28.

———. "Ode to a Nightingale." *Selected.* 205–7.

———. *Selected Poems and Letters by John Keats.* Ed. Douglas Bush. Boston: Houghton Mifflin, 1959.

Knapp, Laurence F. *Directed by Clint Eastwood: Eighteen Films Analyzed.* Jefferson, NC: McFarland, 1996.

Knapp, Shoshana. "Napoleon as Hero." *Perspectives on Nineteenth-Century Heroism.* Ed. Sara M. Putzell and David C. Leonard. Madrid: Studia Humanitatis, 1982. 75–83.

Lamb, Caroline. *Glenarvon.* Ed. Frances Wilson. London: Everyman, 1995.

Larson, Doran. "Machine as Messiah: Cyborgs, Morphs, and the American Body Politic." *Cinema Journal* 36.4 (1997): 57–75.

Leavis, Q. D. "A Fresh Approach to 'Wuthering Heights.'" *Lectures in America.* F. R. and Q. D. Leavis. London: Chatto and Windus, 1969. 83–152.

Lee, Brandon. Interview. *The Crow.* Dir. Alex Proyas. Miramax–Dimension Films–Buena Vista Home Video, 1994.

Livermore, Ann Lapraik. "Byron and Emily Brontë." *Quarterly Review* 300 (1962): 337–44.

Lockridge, Laurence S. *The Ethics of Romanticism.* Cambridge: Cambridge UP, 1989.

Manning, Peter. *Byron and His Fictions.* Detroit: Wayne State UP, 1978.

———. *Reading Romantics: Texts and Contexts.* New York: Oxford UP, 1990.

Martin, Philip W. *Byron, a Poet Before His Public.* Cambridge: Cambridge UP, 1982.

Maturin, Charles Robert. *Melmoth the Wanderer.* Oxford: Oxford UP, 1989.

McConnell, Frank. "Introduction." *The Sandman: The Kindly Ones.* By Neil Gaiman. New York: DC Comics, 1996. N. pag.

McDayter, Ghislaine. "Conjuring Byron: Byromania, Literary Commodification and the Birth of Celebrity." Wilson, *Byromania* 43–62.

McGann, Jerome. *Byron and Wordsworth.* Nottingham, Eng.: U of Nottingham School of English Studies, 1999.

———. *Fiery Dust: Byron's Poetic Development.* Chicago: U of Chicago P, 1968.

———. *The Romantic Ideology: A Critical Investigation.* Chicago: U of Chicago P, 1983.

McGinley, Kathryn. "Development of the Byronic Vampire: Byron, Stoker, Rice." Hoppenstand and Browne 71–90.

Mellor, Anne K. *Romanticism and Gender.* New York: Routledge, 1993.

Mengham, Rod. *Emily Brontë: Wuthering Heights.* London: Penguin, 1989.

Mickelson, Anne Z. *Thomas Hardy's Women and Men: The Defeat of Nature.* Metuchen, NJ: Scarecrow, 1976.

Mill, John Stuart. *On Liberty, with The Subjection of Women and Chapters on Socialism.* Ed. Stefan Collini. Cambridge: Cambridge UP, 1989.

Mitchell, Judith. "Hardy's Female Reader." Higonnet 172–87.

Morgan, Rosemarie. *Women and Sexuality in the Novels of Thomas Hardy.* London: Routledge, 1988.

Nemecek, Larry. *The* Star Trek The Next Generation *Companion.* New York: Pocket, 1992.

Newton, Judith. "Feminism and Anxiety in *Alien.*" "Symposium on *Alien.*" Ed. Charles Elkins. *Science Fiction Studies* 7 (1980): 293–97.

O'Barr, J. *The Crow.* Northampton, MA: Kitchen Sink, 1994.

Okuda, Michael, Denise Okuda, and Debbie Mirek. *The* Star Trek *Encyclopedia: A Reference Guide to the Future.* New York: Pocket, 1994.

Osborn, Judi. "The Byronic Heroine: Is She Different?" *Pleiades* 10 (1990): 45–51.

Pale Rider. Dir. Clint Eastwood. Perf. Clint Eastwood, Michael Moriarty, Richard Dysart, Sydney Penny, Carrie Snodgrass, and John Russell. Warner Brothers, 1985.

Parks, Rita. *The Western Hero in Film and Television: Mass Media Mythology.* Ann Arbor, MI: UMI Research, 1982.

Peyer, Tom. "A Brief History of Death." *The High Cost of Living.* By Neil Gaiman. New York: DC Comics, 1994. 102–3.

Polhemus, Robert M. *Erotic Faith: Being in Love from Jane Austen to D. H. Lawrence.* Chicago: U of Chicago P, 1990.

Prentis, Barbara. *The Brontë Sisters and George Eliot: A Unity of Difference.* London: Macmillan, 1988.

"The Q and the Grey." *Star Trek: Voyager.* Writ. Kenneth Biller and Shawn Piller. Dir. Cliff Bole. Paramount Pictures. First aired 1996.

"Q-Less." *Star Trek: Deep Space Nine.* Writ. Robert Hewitt Wolfe and Hannah Louise Shearer. Dir. Paul Lynch. Paramount Pictures. First aired 1993.

"Qpid." *Star Trek: The Next Generation.* Writ. Ira Steven Behr and Randee Russell. Dir. Cliff Bole. Paramount Pictures. First aired 1991.

"Q Who." *Star Trek: The Next Generation*. Writ. Maurice Hurley. Dir. Rob Bowman. Paramount Pictures. First aired 1989.

Rapping, Elayne. "Feminism Gets the Hollywood Treatment." *Cineaste* 18.4 (1991): 30–32.

Rayns, Tony. Rev. of *Terminator 2: Judgment Day,* dir. James Cameron. *Sight and Sound* 1.5 (1991): 50–51.

Reed, Walter L. *Meditations on the Hero: A Study of the Romantic Hero in Nineteenth-Century Fiction.* New Haven: Yale UP, 1974.

Reep, Diana C., Joseph F. Ceccio, and William A. Francis. "Anne Rice's *Interview with the Vampire:* Novel Versus Film." Hoppenstand and Browne 123–47.

"Reunion." *Angel*. Writ. Tim Minear and Shawn Ryan. Dir. James A. Contner. The WB. First aired Dec. 19, 2000.

Rice, Anne. Interview with Digby Diehl. *Playboy* Mar. 1993. Rpt. in Beahm, *Unauthorized* 38–58.

———. *Interview with the Vampire.* New York: Ballantine, 1976.

———. *The Vampire Lestat.* New York: Ballantine, 1985.

Richards, Thomas. *The Meaning of* Star Trek: *An Excursion into the Myth and Marvel of the* Star Trek *Universe.* New York: Doubleday, 1997.

Riley, Michael. *Conversations with Anne Rice.* New York: Ballantine, 1996.

Roberts, Bette B. *Anne Rice.* New York: Twayne, 1994.

Roberts, Robin. "Adoptive Versus Biological Parenting in *Aliens*." *Extrapolation* 30 (1989): 353–63.

Rollin, Roger R. "The Lone Ranger and Lenny Skutnik: The Hero as Popular Culture." *The Hero in Transition*. Ed. Ray B. Brown and Marshall W. Fishwick. Bowling Green, OH: Bowling Green U Popular P, 1983: 14–45.

Ross, Marlon B. *The Contours of Masculine Desire: Romanticism and the Rise of Women's Poetry.* New York: Oxford UP, 1989.

Rushing, Janice Hocker. "Evolution of 'The New Frontier' in *Alien* and *Aliens:* Patriarchal Co-optation of the Feminine Archetype." *Quarterly Journal of Speech* 75 (1989): 1–24.

Rushing, Janice Hocker, and Thomas S. Frentz. *Projecting the Shadow: The Cyborg Hero in American Film.* Chicago: U of Chicago P, 1995.

Sanchez, Victoria. "An Interview with Vampires." Unpublished essay, 1997.

"Sanctuary." *Angel*. Writ. Tim Minear and Joss Whedon. Dir. Michael Lange. The WB. First aired May 2, 2000.

Schock, Peter A. "The 'Satanism' of *Cain* in Context: Byron's Lucifer and the War Against Blasphemy." *Keats-Shelley Journal* 44 (1995): 182–215.

Sheehan, Henry. "Scraps of Hope: Clint Eastwood and the Western." *Film Comment* 28.5 (1992): 17–27.

Shelley, Mary Wollstonecraft. *Frankenstein, or The Modern Prometheus.* Peterborough, ON, Can.: Broadview, 1994.

Shelley, Percy Bysshe. *Alastor*. P. B. Shelley, *Shelley's* 69–87.

———. "A Defence of Poetry." P. B. Shelley, *Shelley's* 480–508.

————. *Epipsychidion*. P. B. Shelley, *Poetical* 297–306.

————. *The Poetical Works of Shelley*. Ed. Newell F. Ford. Boston: Houghton Mifflin, 1974.

————. Preface to *Alastor*. P. B. Shelley, *Shelley's* 69–70.

————. *Shelley's Poetry and Prose*. Ed. Donald H. Reiman and Sharon B. Powers. New York: Norton, 1977.

————. "To a Skylark." P. B. Shelley, *Poetical* 391–92.

Smith, Jennifer. *Anne Rice: A Critical Companion*. Westport, CT: Greenwood, 1996.

Smith, Paul. "Action Movie Hysteria, or Eastwood Bound." *Differences* 1 (1989): 88–107.

Solomon, Eric. "The Incest Theme in *Wuthering Heights*." *Nineteenth-Century Fiction* 14 (1959): 80–83.

Spacks, Patricia Meyer. *The Female Imagination*. New York: Knopf, 1975.

Stein, Atara. "*Epipsychidion, Achtung Baby*, and the Teaching of Romanticism." *Popular Culture Review* 6 (1995): 29–44.

————. "Immortals and Vampires and Ghosts, Oh My!: Byronic Heroes in Popular Culture." Ed. Laura Mandell and Michael Eberle-Sinatra. *Romantic Circles–Praxis* (2002) 12 pars. <http://www.rc.umd.edu/praxis/contemporary/stein/stein.html>.

————. "Minding One's P's and Q's: Homoeroticism in *Star Trek: The Next Generation*." *Genders* 27 (1998) <http://www.genders.org/g27/g27_st.html>.

Straub, Peter. "On Mortality and Change." Afterword. *The Sandman: Brief Lives*. By Neil Gaiman. New York: DC Comics, 1994. N. pag.

Strick, Philip. Rev. of *Alien³*. *Sight and Sound* 2.4 (Aug. 1992): 47.

Tank Girl. Dir. Rachel Talalay. Perf. Lori Petty, Naomi Watts, Malcolm McDowell, and Ice-T. Trilogy Entertainment Group, 1995.

"Tapestry." *Star Trek: The Next Generation*. Writ. Ronald D. Moore. Dir. Les Landau. Paramount Pictures. First aired 1993.

Telotte, J. P. "*The Terminator, Terminator 2*, and the Exposed Body." *Journal of Popular Film and Television* 20.2 (1992): 26–34.

The Terminator. Dir. James Cameron. Perf. Arnold Schwarzenegger, Linda Hamilton, Michael Biehn. Cinema '84, 1984.

Terminator 2: Judgment Day. Dir. James Cameron. Perf. Arnold Schwarzenegger, Linda Hamilton, Edward Furlong, and Robert Patrick. Carolco Pictures, 1991.

Thorslev, Peter L. *The Byronic Hero: Types and Prototypes*. Minneapolis: U of Minnesota P, 1962.

Tibbetts, John C. "Clint Eastwood and the Machinery of Violence." *Literature/ Film Quarterly* 21 (1993): 11–17.

Tompkins, Jane. *West of Everything: The Inner Life of Westerns*. New York: Oxford UP, 1992.

"To Shanshu in L.A." *Angel*. Writ. and dir. David Greenwalt. The WB. First aired May 23, 2000.

Travers, Peter. Rev. of *The Crow,* dir. Alex Proyas. *Rolling Stone* 19 May 1996: 105–6.

"True Q." *Star Trek: The Next Generation.* Writ. René Echevarria. Dir. Robert Scheerer. Paramount Pictures. First aired 1992.

Unforgiven. Dir. Clint Eastwood. Perf. Clint Eastwood, Gene Hackman, and Morgan Freeman. Warner Brothers, 1992.

Waxman, Barbara Frey. "Postexistentialisms in the Neo-Gothic Mode: Anne Rice's *Interview with the Vampire.*" *Mosaic* 25 (1992): 79–97.

Wilson, Frances, ed. *Byromania: Portraits of the Artist in Nineteenth- and Twentieth-Century Culture.* New York: St. Martin's, 1999.

———. "Introduction: Byron, Byronism and Byromaniacs." Wilson, *Byromania* 1–23.

Witchblade. Turner Network Television. First aired June 2001.

Wordsworth, William. Preface to *Lyrical Ballads. The Prose Works of William Wordsworth.* Ed. W. J. B. Owen and Jane Worthington Smyser. Oxford: Clarendon, 1974.

———. *The Prelude* (1850). *The Prelude: 1799, 1805, 1850.* Ed. Jonathan Wordsworth, M. H. Abrams, and Stephen Gill. New York: Norton, 1929.

"The Yoko Factor." *Buffy the Vampire Slayer.* Writ. Douglas Petrie. Dir. David Grossman. The WB. First aired May 9, 2000.

Zwinger, Lynda. "Blood Relations: Feminist Theory Meets the Uncanny Alien Bug Mother." *Hypatia* 7 (1992): 74–90.

Index

Index

Atara Stein is a professor of English at California State University, Fullerton, where she teaches Romanticism, the Victorian novel, the Gothic novel, science fiction, and children's literature. Her research primarily concerns the intersection of the Romantic period and popular culture.